the

Jeanne Hernandez
Theater Collection

Made Possible By
Contributions From The
Family and Friends

WILL ROGERS
AT THE ZIEGFELD FOLLIES

WILL ROGERS
AT THE ZIEGFELD FOLLIES

EDITED BY ARTHUR FRANK WERTHEIM

FOREWORD BY JOSEPH H. CARTER

UNIVERSITY OF OKLAHOMA PRESS : NORMAN AND LONDON

In Memory of My Parents
Albert and Ruth Wertheim
and My Cousin
Barbara Wertheim Tuchman

By Arthur Frank Wertheim

The New York Little Renaissance: Iconoclasm, Modernism, and Nationalism in American Culture, 1908–1917 (New York, 1976)
Radio Comedy (New York, 1979)
American Popular Culture: A Historical Bibliography (ed.) (Santa Barbara, Calif., 1984)

Library of Congress Cataloging-in-Publication Data

Rogers, Will, 1879–1935.
    Will Rogers at the Ziegfeld Follies / Will Rogers : edited by Arthur Frank Wertheim : foreword by Joseph H. Carter.
        p.   cm.
    Includes bibliographical references and index.
    ISBN 0-8061-2357-5
    1. Rogers, Will, 1879–1935—Quotations.   2. American wit and humor.   I. Wertheim, Arthur Frank, 1935– . II. Title.
PN6161.R664425   1992
792.7'028'092—dc20   92-54137
                                                             CIP

The paper in this book meets the guidelines for permanence and durability of the Committee on Production Guidelines for Book Longevity of the Council on Library Resources, Inc. ∞

PLAYBILL

LIST OF ILLUSTRATIONS

FOREWORD

By Joseph H. Carter

THE trail that Will Rogers rode to stardom in the *Ziegfeld Follies* was long and hard. It began on November 4, 1879, when he was born on his father's ranch in Indian Territory near the present town of Oologah, Oklahoma.

Built on a home atmosphere of respectable learning and culture despite the rugged frontier setting, Will Rogers' formal education spanned about ten years of classwork. But his real education stemmed from rambling years of mostly unstructured learning during the first half of his life. It included observation, experience, and extensive travel before airplanes and automobiles. Horse, train, and steamboat were the modes, but he was quick to adapt to all new technology.

Evidence shows Will Rogers driven by inner desires for achievement. His curiosity was insatiable and his concentration on perfecting tasks was intense. He practiced long hours to excel in roping.

The archives of the Will Rogers Memorial in Claremore, Oklahoma, house his preparatory notes for his routines. They reveal that he worked hard to be spontaneous—and to appear off-the-cuff—but in reality he was well prepared. Will Rogers did his homework.

He knew the sweat and energy it took to get to the top in show business. He spent ten long years on the vaudeville trail travelling around the country and across Europe. The date book he kept in 1905 shows him in Buffalo one week and Toledo the next and then on to Detroit. It was a rigorous life travelling the circuit with his show pony, Teddy.

Along the tedious trail, Will Rogers' humor kept emerging. Insight built on both cowboy and Cherokee Indian heritage spiced his thinking with perceptions, ideas, and a philosophy that influenced generations.

By age thirty-seven, the lariat expert from Indian Territory had climbed into popular view on Broadway. His extraordinary trick roping was being overshadowed by his down-home wit and comments which appeared spontaneously during his performances. Soon, the rope gave way to his humor and canny views on current affairs. Thus Will Rogers became a star in the fabulous *Ziegfeld Follies*.

On the *Follies* stage Will Rogers had his finger on the pulse of the nation during its difficult and fun times. During World War I he kept America laughing in its dark hours. In her ridiculous times, he kept America aware of its absurdities.

Will Rogers' stage appeal was recognized as ripe for the print media: newspapers, magazines, and books. V. V. McNitt of the McNaught Syndicate saw the possibility. Publisher Adolph Ochs of the *New York Times* sensed the value. Early each morning, Americans started their days with a chuckle reading Will Rogers' syndicated weekly articles and daily telegrams.

Editors wrestled with Will Rogers' spelling, syntax, and punctuation. He admonished them to "run 'er the way she lands" even if it meant getting the linotype operator drunk.

Will Rogers' typing, a friend said, "sounded like a brewery horse with a loose shoe running away across a covered bridge." Spelling and grammar fell through the cracks. Feigned backwardness took the sting from his more abrasive thoughts and telling social criticisms.

Will Rogers and Florenz Ziegfeld are two magic names in show business. The Oklahoman starred in six editions of the *Ziegfeld Follies* from 1916 to 1925. *Will Rogers at the Ziegfeld Follies* compiles Rogers' writing during this fascinating time. Through selected correspondence and remembrances, it brings to life the marvelous relationship between the humorist and the showman.

The book also gives a taste of Rogers' writing during the Roaring Twenties. The era was one of relative prosperity, political scandals, jazz, gangsters, and prohibition. Henry Ford's Model Ts, airplanes, silent pictures, radios, and Will Rogers' shy grin and quick wit were chic. The Republicans Harding and Coolidge ruled the White House and Will Rogers needled them with his pinpoint barbs. The *Ziegfeld Follies* was then the most glamorous and greatest show on earth.

Time has passed and technology has exploded, but conditions in the 1990s are in many ways comparable to the 1920s—political corruption, economic wheeling and dealing, and folks interested in comforting wisdom and a quiet laugh. Will Rogers' comment about Congress remains timeless: "Every time they make a joke it's a law. And every time they make a law it's a joke." Truth lives forever.

That a single human's influence remains strong for such a long time is significant. Will Rogers used all media—stage, screen, radio, lecture tour, daily and weekly newspaper columns, magazines, and books—to enlighten and entertain. He pioneered radio network broadcasts, set trends for the modern cinema, and brought new credence to satirical humor.

This is intended to be a popular edition of Rogers' writing during the time he worked with Florenz Ziegfeld. As the only book dealing with Will Rogers on the stage, it fills an important gap in the life story of the humorist. *Will Rogers at the Ziegfeld Follies* invites readers to savor this great American humorist's wit and wisdom and to relive his fabulous years on Broadway.

A NOTE ON THE TEXT AND ACKNOWLEDGMENTS

WILL ROGERS AT THE ZIEGFELD FOLLIES comprises the rich variety of Rogers' writing and humor during the period from 1915 to 1925 when he performed in the *Follies*. The book also includes impressions of Rogers by contemporary observers and friends. Through correspondence and remembrances, it highlights Rogers' relationship with Ziegfeld and two of his other stars, W. C. Fields and Eddie Cantor.

In assembling the collection, the editor has attempted to select material that was published during the time when Rogers was appearing in the *Follies*. The texts of the two Rogers books reprinted in this volume, *The Cowboy Philosopher on the Peace Conference* and *The Cowboy Philosopher on Prohibition*, are those of the first editions published in 1919 by Harper and Brothers. Rogers' weekly articles are for the most part derived from the versions published in the *New York Times*. Most of the previously unpublished material comes from the Will Rogers Memorial in Claremore, Oklahoma, the museum archive that contains the majority of Rogers' papers.

The overall editorial goal of the book is to present Rogers' writing as authentically as possible. To that end I have kept editorial intrusions to the minimum and retained Rogers' idiosyncratic spelling, punctuation, and grammar. Only in rare cases, when the writing was indecipherable or contained factual errors, was it necessary to make interpolations for purposes of clarification.

To keep the text uncluttered, I have elected not to use footnote annotations. The reader is urged to consult the alphabetized biographical glossary at the end of the book for information pertaining to the many individuals mentioned in the text.

I wish to thank Patricia Ziegfeld Stephenson for granting me permission to publish documents pertaining to her mother, Billie Burke, and father, Florenz Ziegfeld. Ronald J. Fields also allowed me to print material about his grandfather, W. C. Fields, from his book, *W. C. Fields by Himself*. Richard Ziegfeld also shared important information about the *Follies* with me, as did Miles Kreuger of the Institute of the American Musical in Los Angeles.

I would also like to thank the staff of the Will Rogers Memorial in Claremore for their assistance in preparing the book: Joseph H. Carter, director; Gregory Malak, curator; Patricia Lowe, librarian/archivist; Marjorie Williams, fiscal coordinator; Melanie Landers, administrative assistant; and Dorothy Bruffett. Without their help and support this book would not have been completed. *Will Rogers at the Ziegfeld Follies* belongs to the legacy they are creating for America's most-beloved humorist.

ARTHUR FRANK WERTHEIM

Los Angeles, California

HIGHLIGHTS OF WILL ROGERS' CAREER

1879   November 4, William Penn Adair Rogers is born on his father's ranch near Oologah, Indian Territory.

1899   July 4, wins first prize in steer-roping contest in Claremore. In October, participates in a roping and riding contest organized by Zach Mulhall at St. Louis annual fair. Later, joins Mulhall tour of state fairs as a steer roper.

1900   July 4, enters a roping contest in Oklahoma City at a reunion of Theodore Roosevelt's Rough Riders; meets Roosevelt.

1901   May–June, helps organize riding and roping contest at Confederate Veterans' Reunion in Memphis. In September, participates in steer-roping contest at Elks Convention, Springfield, Missouri. In October, enters steer-roping contest at San Antonio Interntional Exposition.

1902   In December, joins Texas Jack's American Circus and Wild West Show in South Africa as a bronco rider and lasso thrower. Billed as the "Cherokee Kid."

1903–   Performs a rough-riding and lassoing act with Wirth
1904   Brothers' Circus in Australia and New Zealand. Returns home April 1904.

1904   Joins Colonel Zach Mulhall's Wild West Show as a fancy roper at the World's Fair in St. Louis. Performs at St.

Louis's Standard Theatre. In October, plays in a vaudeville bill at the Cleveland Theatre in Chicago.

1905   April, with the Mulhall Show at the Horse Fair in New
York City's Madison Square Garden. Receives considerable publicity for helping to rope a runaway bull that
had run into the stands.

June 11, 1905, first New York vaudeville appearance at
B. F. Keith's Union Square Theatre. Performs a roping
act on stage with his pony Teddy. On June 19 moves to
Hammerstein's Paradise Roof Garden. Buck McKee becomes his partner, riding Will's horse on stage.

1906   Spring, European tour with his roping-horse act. Ap-
pears at Berlin's Wintergarten and London's Palace
Theatre. Invited to perform at London's Ranelagh
Club; King Edward VII is in the audience.

1907   April–May, forms his own Wild West act and travels to
England, but the show is a flop. Plays in *The Girl
Rangers* with Reine Davies, September–October.

1908   Vaudeville tour around the U.S. doing his horse-roping
act with Buck McKee. Marries Betty Blake on November 25.

1909   Tours on the Orpheum Circuit. Forms a trick riding
and roping troupe. By year's end he decides to perform
alone without a horse and begins to use more humorous patter on stage.

1912   Spring, appears in the Broadway musical *The Wall
Street Girl*, starring Blanche Ring.

1914   Performs in the musical *The Merry-Go-Round*, featuring Nora Bayes, at London's Empire Theater.

1915   January 5, Ziegfeld's *Midnight Frolic* cabaret opens on
the roof of the New Amsterdam Theatre.

February, Rogers performs his lariat stunts at New York's famous Palace Theatre.

July, performs in the Shubert musical *Hands Up* at the Forty-fourth Street Theatre. By mistake, the lights go out during his act, and the audience demands his return to the stage.

August 23, Rogers' first appearance in the *Midnight Frolic*, as part of the revue *Just Girls*.

September–November, performs in Ned Wayburn's revue, *Town Topics*, at the Century Theatre.

1916   May, Rogers performs before Woodrow Wilson in a Friars Club revue at Baltimore, and the good reviews inspire him to continue his topical humor.

July, joins Ziegfeld's *Follies of 1916*, which had opened on June 12. Fanny Brice, Bert Williams, W. C. Fields, Ann Pennington, Ina Claire, Marion Davies, and Justine Johnstone are in the cast.

Rogers continues to perform at the *Midnight Frolic* intermittently between 1916 and 1919.

1917   June 12, opening night of the *Follies of 1917*, starring Rogers, Eddie Cantor, W. C. Fields, Bert Williams, Fanny Brice, Lilyan Tashman, Dolores, Allyn King, and Peggy Hopkins.

1918   June 18, opening night of the *Follies of 1918*, featuring Rogers, W. C. Fields, Eddie Cantor, Marilyn Miller, Lillian Lorraine, Kay Laurell, Dolores, Allyn King, Ann Pennington, and Harry Kelly.

1919   Publishes *The Cowboy Philosopher on the Peace Conference* and *The Cowboy Philosopher on Prohibition*. He leaves the *Follies* in June to star in silent films produced by Samuel Goldwyn.

1921   November, returns to star in the *Midnight Frolic*.

1922   Tours with the *Ziegfeld Frolic* stage show. In February, Will's skit *The Disagreement Conference* lampoons President Harding.

June 5, opening night of the *Follies of 1922* starring Rogers, Gilda Gray, Gallagher and Shean, Andrew Tombes, and the Tiller Girls.

In December, Will begins writing weekly newspaper articles for the McNaught Syndicate.

1923   Leaves the *Follies* in the summer to do silent film comedies for Hal Roach.

1924   Returns to the *Follies*, and on June 24 the *Follies of 1924* opens, featuring Rogers, Evelyn Law, Lupino Lane, Vivienne Segal, and Ann Pennington. Publishes *The Illiterate Digest*, a collection of his writings.

1925   Appears in the *Follies of 1925* with W. C. Fields, Ray Dooley, Peggy Fears, and the Tiller Girls. Leaves the *Follies* permanently and begins a nationwide lecture tour in October.

1926   July, plays in the *Cochran Revue of 1926* in London. Refuses to be paid by the producer, Charles Cochran, for the performances, which he calls fun.

1928   December, replaces the injured Fred Stone in the musical comedy *Three Cheers* with Dorothy Stone.

1929–   Rogers stars in twenty-one films for the Fox Film
1935   Corporation.

1930   Spring, does a series of radio broadcasts for E. R. Squibb and Sons.

1933– Rogers' famous talks on the Gulf Oil radio broadcasts
1935   reach millions of listeners.

1934   Spring, performs in Eugene O'Neill's *Ah, Wilderness!*
       in California.

1935   August 15, Will Rogers is killed with his friend Wiley
       Post in an airplane crash near Point Barrow, Alaska.

WILL ROGERS
AT THE ZIEGFELD FOLLIES

SOURCE NOTE SYMBOLS USED IN THE VOLUME

TYPES OF DOCUMENTS

ALS	Autograph Letter Signed
AMs	Autograph Manuscript
TD	Typewritten Document
TG	Telegram
TMs	Typewritten Manuscript
TL	Typewritten Letter
TLS	Typewritten Letter Signed

REPOSITORIES

CPpR	Will Rogers State Historic Park, Pacific Palisades, California
OkClaW	Will Rogers Memorial, Claremore, Oklahoma

PROLOGUE

"ZIGGY gave me my start," Will Rogers once said. "If there is anything I can do to repay him, nothing could be too much."[1] Florenz Ziegfeld, Jr., the famous Broadway producer, played a pivotal role in Rogers' career. In 1915 he began performing in Ziegfeld's *Midnight Frolic*, a popular New York cabaret–stage show. Joining the *Frolic* started a long, profitable relationship with the flamboyant showman—an association that led to Rogers' debut in the *Ziegfeld Follies* and eventually to national fame for the Oklahoman.

Gene Buck, the producer's right-hand man, actually discovered Will for the Ziegfeld productions. Once characterized as having "the soul of a Sister of Charity and the efficiency of a [Charles] Schwab," the talented Buck worked diligently behind the scenes to make Ziegfeld's shows the most spectacular on Broadway.[2] He wrote the book and lyrics for many *Follies* productions. The songwriter helped create the *Midnight Frolic*, considered the first modern cabaret revue, which opened on 5 January 1915. Possessing a talent for spotting funny comedians, Buck had earlier signed Ed Wynn and W. C. Fields for the

1. Michel Mok, "The Cowboy Ambassador: A Life Story of Will Rogers," newspaper clipping, n.d., in scrapbook entitled "Will Rogers: Humorist, Philosopher, Humanitarian, 1879–1935," Will Rogers State Historical Park, Pacific Palisades, California (CPpR).

2. "Gene Buck," *Current Biography 1941* (New York: H. W. Wilson Co., 1941), 116. Information on Buck also stems from "Profiles: Czar of Song," *New Yorker*, 17 December 1932, 22–25 and 24 December 1932, 19–22; Marjorie Farnsworth, *The Ziegfeld Follies* (New York: G. P. Putnam's Sons, 1956), 148–150. For the importance of the *Midnight Frolic* see Lewis A. Erenberg, *Steppin' Out: New York Nightlife and the Transformation of American Culture, 1890–1930* (Westport, Conn.: Greenwood Press, 1981), 206–230. Charles Schwab (1862–1939), owner of Bethlehem Steel, was a well-known industrialist known for his efficient business skills. Later as president of the American Society of Composers, Authors, and Publishers (ASCAP), Buck played an instrumental role in getting song writers royalties when their music was played over the radio.

Follies. One night he saw Rogers perform his comic routine on the stage, probably in the musical *Hands Up* at Broadway's Forty-fourth Street Theatre. He felt instinctively that Will would be a hit at the *Frolic*.[3]

Rogers was then a successful vaudeville entertainer known for his dexterity with the lariat and his wry patter. Although not a headliner, or the main attraction on the bill, he had played in big-time vaudeville houses on various circuits around the country since 1905, first doing a unique horse act with Buck McGee, his partner, and then doing a solo specialty. He performed many fancy tricks, including twirling two lariats simultaneously and the "Big Crinoline," a huge sixty-foot circle of rope spun around his body. As he whirled his lariat, Rogers joked about his roping, made wisecracks about other acts, and sometimes performed imitations. But he had not yet begun to make humorous comments about the day's news.

As he watched Will perform, Buck recognized that Rogers was a unique humorist different from slapstick, blackface, and other ethnic comedians (the Irish, Jewish, and "Dutch" or German-speaking pranksters) who dominated vaudeville. The ethnic comics appealed to the immigrant masses in large cities where vaudeville excelled as an extremely popular form of entertainment.[4] By contrast, Rogers' roots were in the heartland of America.

Born in Indian Territory in 1879, the son of a prosperous cattle rancher, Rogers learned to rope at an early age. He travelled around the Southwest entering steer-roping contests at fairs and exhibitions from 1899 to 1901. Between 1902 and 1905 he performed a trick riding and roping act with rodeos and Wild West shows. The latter were colorful spectacles derived from

3. In the musical revue *Hands Up*, Rogers had created a sensation on opening night when the lights were accidentally turned off during his act. Embarrassed by the incident, Rogers refused to return to the stage, but the audience demanded his return. He continued his routine and received a standing ovation. See Donald Day, *Will Rogers: A Biography* (New York: David McKay Co., 1962), 75; Homer Croy, *Our Will Rogers* (New York: Duell, Sloan and Pearce, 1953), 135; and Betty Rogers, *Will Rogers: His Wife's Story* (1941; Norman: University of Oklahoma Press, 1989), 126–127.

4. Robert C. Toll, *On with the Show: The First Century of Show Business in America* (New York: Oxford University Press, 1976), 289–293; and Douglas Gilbert, *American Vaudeville: Its Life and Times* (New York: Whittlesey House, 1940; Dover Publications, 1963), 61–85, 269–292.

William F. ("Buffalo Bill") Cody's popular Wild West (1883). They became a national mania at the turn of the century, featuring cowboys, Indians, mock stagecoach attacks, riding exhibitions, animal acts, parades, and bands. According to the historian Russel Nye, they "embedded in the popular cultural tradition, as nothing else did, the great, romantic legend of the American West."[5]

The romanticization of the West and the cowboy continued to flourish in other forms of mass culture during the first two decades of the twentieth century. Popular at the time Will joined the *Follies* in 1916 were the silent films of Gilbert Anderson, featuring Bronco Billy, considered the first cinematic cowboy hero. Equally appealing to the public were the movies of William S. Hart, featuring western badmen reformed by virtuous heroines, and the two-reelers of Tom Mix, whom Rogers had met earlier on the rodeo and Wild West show circuits.[6]

Rogers' stage persona evoked the rustic cowboy. On his vaudeville tours Rogers billed himself under various names, including the Oklahoma Cowboy, the Great Lasso Expert, and the Lasso King. Show publicity routinely described the entertainer as a western plainsman and a Cherokee cowpuncher from Indian Territory. Asked once by a reporter how long he had being roping, Rogers replied: "Well, I can remember when I was two years old, of chasing and roping my mother's turkeys out on the ranch and I could catch 'em too."[7] Through his cowboy outfit (leather chaps, flannel shirt, boots, spurs, and soft hat), stage mannerisms (grin and head scratching) and southwestern drawl,

5. Russel Nye, *The Unembarrassed Muse: The Popular Arts in America* (New York: Dial Press, 1970), 193. See also Don B. Wilmeth, *Variety Entertainment and Outdoor Amusements: A Reference Guide* (Westport, Conn.: Greenwood Press, 1982), 80–81; Don Russell, *The Wild West: A History of the Wild West Show* (Fort Worth, Texas: Amon Carter Museum of Western Art, 1970).

6. Robert C. Toll, *The Entertainment Machine: American Show Business in the Twentieth Century* (New York: Oxford University Press, 1982), 77–80. For Rogers' friendship with Mix, see Croy, *Our Will Rogers*, 92, 95.

7. "Throws Two Lariats at the Same Time," clipping [25 October 1905], in scrapbook A-1, Will Rogers Memorial, Claremore, Oklahoma (OkClaW). The various vaudeville names Rogers used can also be found in scrapbook A-2 (1900–1909), OkClaW. On the subject of Rogers' cowboy persona see William W. Savage, Jr., *The Cowboy Hero: His Image in American History and Culture* (Norman: University of Oklahoma Press, 1979), 19–22; and William W. Savage, Jr., "Top Hand: Will Rogers and the Cowboy Image in America," *Chronicles of Oklahoma* 57 (Fall 1979): 376–384.

he personified the Old West on stage—a frontier of open ranges and the rugged life that had largely vanished through population growth and the coming of the railroad.

In one story Rogers was described as a "westerner with cherokee blood, slim legs in careless chaparrals, and a fetching drawl, [who] seems to fit that femininely adored type of [Owen] Wister's Virginian." Instrumental in accelerating the cowboy-hero fad was Wister's best-selling novel *The Virginian* (1902), which depicted the West as "the true America" and the cowboy as "the last of the freedom-loving Americans."[8]

The West was especially idealized by wealthy urban Easterners such as Wister and his friend Theodore Roosevelt. A rancher in the Dakota Badlands in the 1880s, Roosevelt lauded the cowboy in his books *Ranch Life and the Hunting Trail* (1888) and *The Rough Riders* (1899). As a counterpoint to the congestion of New York and other East Coast cities, the social elite yearned for the wide open landscape of the West and discovered the outdoors in big-game hunting clubs, hiking, and camping.[9]

According to one account, Gene Buck also admired the American cowboy and particularly liked Frederic Remington's western paintings depicting bronco busters, cowpunchers, and heroic cavalrymen.[10] Wealthy and fashionable New Yorkers largely patronized the *Midnight Frolic*, Ziegfeld's swank Manhattan nightclub. Buck felt that Rogers' lasso act might appeal to these affluent business men and members of café society.

Buck engaged Will for the second edition of the *Midnight Frolic*, entitled *Just Girls*, which premiered on 23 August 1915. The chic cabaret was located on the roof of the elegant New Amsterdam Theatre where the *Ziegfeld Follies* played in the main auditorium downstairs. When the *Follies* finished, many theatergoers would take the elevator to see the midnight

8. "Will Rogers, Cow-Puncher, Has a Heart-Armor Piercing Manner," clipping, n.d., in scrapbook A-2 (1900–1902), OkClaW; and Nye, *The Unembarrassed Muse*, 290.

9. Roderick Nash, *Wilderness and the American Mind*, rev. ed. (New Haven: Yale University Press, 1973), 141–160; and G. Edward White, *The Eastern Establishment and the Western Experience: The West of Frederic Remington, Theodore Roosevelt, and Owen Wister* (New Haven: Yale University Press, 1968).

10. "Profiles: Czar of Song—I," *New Yorker*, 17 December 1932, 23. Remington was also a friend of Theodore Roosevelt, and both shared a love of the Old West. Remington illustrated TR's articles on ranching in the *Century* magazine in 1888 (White, *The Eastern Establishment and the Western Experience*, 102).

show at Ziegfeld's "Aerial Gardens." The *Frolic* served as an experimental theater where Ziegfeld tested new talent, skits, songs, and scene designs on a stage similar to the main one downstairs.

Considered New York's most lavish and popular cabaret show, the *Frolic* showcased boisterous entertainment focused on uninhibited fun and fast-paced action. The cabaret featured glamorous show girls, variety acts, delicious food, and dancing to a live orchestra. The *Frolic* offered its clientele the chance to temporarily enjoy a world of frivolity and fantasy. The speed and timing of the acts were organized to create a sense of stimulation and excitement—the "vision of the city as a land of pleasure and the fast life."[11] The noisy patrons applauded the acts by banging on tables with small wooden hammers and tooting noisemakers. The popular cabaret inspired other late-night Manhattan revues and was fashionable until 1921 when Prohibition forced its closing.

Ziegfeld spent considerable money in making the *Frolic* New York's most expensive nightclub show. The talented Austrian scene designer Joseph Urban was hired to transform the roof into an exotic environment. Urban installed a moveable stage and glass see-through runway which enabled the audience to watch the show girls descend to the stage. His spectacular set designs in an array of colors created a dazzling backdrop to the chorus girls, who were the major focus of the revue.

The chorines made many costume changes, appearing in stunning gowns, scanty tights, and zany outfits. Dressed as clocks, zeppelins, and switchboards, the show girls were encouraged to mingle with the audience. Telephone girls circulated around the room, and customers could call them from their tables. Rogers' first engagement at the *Frolic* was highlighted by the Balloon Girls, who dressed with balloons attached to theirs skirts and headdresses. As they moved among the tables, the men popped the balloons with their lighted cigars and cigarettes.

In this ambience of revelry, Rogers played the role of the cowboy humorist to the hilt. He joked, spun his lariat, and often roped the chorines and the guests. Will's rustic charm and

11. Erenberg, *Steppin' Out*, 210.

manner offered the perfect contrast to the sophisticated milieu of the nightclub, and his act appeared as a humorous anachronism in the stylish environment. The image he portrayed reminded his urbane audience nostalgically of the vanishing West.

The *Frolic* patrons delighted in his performance and loudly applauded his routine, and the reviews suggested he was a hit. Rogers "provides the only comic note" wrote a reporter the day after the opening. Another critic caught the nuances of his act: "He plays with a rope, hat on the back of his head, a bit of gum between his teeth to keep him company—a shy Westerner venturing out alone in this mass of wild New Yorkers—and the rope comes to life, writhing flickering life. . . . And all the while he talks—eyes on the floor, stepping by your table on his way around the floor, cracking delicious jokes in a soft drawl."[12]

Despite the favorable reactions of the critics and the audience, Ziegfeld was unimpressed. He felt that the gum-chewing cowboy did not fit in with the café's cosmopolitan atmosphere. "That damn cowboy has to go," he told Buck. "I am leaving for a couple of weeks and when I return I don't want him around here."[13] Buck, nonetheless, believed Rogers was popular with the audience, and he let Will continue while Ziegfeld was out of town.

To keep the clientele amused, Rogers needed new material every night for his performance. Many *Frolic* customers were "repeaters," who attended the show regularly. "There are lots of folks that come to the *Frolic* every night," said Rogers. "And I should say that 50 per cent, or more of the audience is there two or three times a week."[14] He thought about using topical jokes about the day's news and personalities in the headlines. "My wife says I ought to talk about what I read in the papers," he told Buck. "She says I'm always readin' the papers, so why not pass along what I read?"[15]

Will bought every edition of the New York press and spent hours searching for material. "So I started to reading about

12. "Midnight Frolic Again," *New York Times*, 24 August 1915, p. 11; clipping from "Rogers' Tenure with the Ziegfeld Follies and the Midnight Frolic (1916–1917)," n.d., in scrapbook #559–1–5787, CPpR.

13. Day, *Will Rogers*, 77.

14. "If He Could Warble One Song," clipping, n.d., scrapbook #20, OkClaW.

15. Croy, *Our Will Rogers*, 137.

Congress," Will recalled, "and, believe me, I found they are funnier three hundred and sixty-five days a year than anything I ever heard of."[16] Armed with numerous topical gags, Rogers commented about the day's headlines and lampooned celebrities from politicians and sports heroes to show-business stars and royalty. Rogers possessed an innate talent for getting to the heart of an issue, and he preferred jokes that had an element of truth. He said, "I like one where, if you are with a friend, and hear it, it makes you think, and you nudge your friend and say; 'he's right about that.'"[17]

Each night he came out with fresh jokes, delivering a snappy, short monologue that roamed from one subject to another. In an early *Frolic* routine he jested about Henry Ford and his Peace Ship. Hoping to help end the outbreak of World War I in Europe, Ford had chartered the vessel *Oscar II*, which transported pacifists and other antiwar advocates to Europe for peace talks. Rogers felt that it should have included the Ziegfeld Girls. "If Mr. Ford had taken this bunch of girls, in this show, and let 'em wear the same costumes they wear here, and marched them down between the trenches, believe me, the boys would have been out before Christmas!"[18]

Buck told Ziegfeld about his new style when the producer returned to New York. The showman was angry that Buck had not fired him. "Why don't you come tonight and watch him?" asked Buck. "He gets the biggest laughs in the show."[19] Ziegfeld saw Rogers perform again and was still not convinced. But he knew Rogers was well liked by his customers. He kept Will on as a regular with the *Frolic*, and his popularity as a witty commentator on the news continued to grow.

Rogers' next big break occurred the following year when Ziegfeld was rehearsing the *Follies of 1916*. The production suffered from an excessive amount of musical numbers and lacked comedy. Ziegfeld was now convinced that Rogers was a rare talent, and he asked Will to help save the show. At first he declined

16. Donald Day, ed., *The Autobiography of Will Rogers* (Boston: Houghton Mifflin Co., 1949), 38.
17. Ibid., 39.
18. Ibid., 38.
19. Croy, *Our Will Rogers*, 138.

the offer, agreeing with his wife, Betty, that the salary was too low and he would have to spend too much time away from his family when the show toured.[20]

Rogers soon began to regret the decision. On June 12 he and Betty attended the opening night of the 1916 *Follies* and found the show dull. During the performance Will whispered to his wife: "See, Blake, what did I tell you. This was my one big chance. Boy, I wish I could have got my crack at it."[21]

Legend has it that Rogers was standing in the lobby of the New Amsterdam Theatre when Ziegfeld asked him again to join the *Follies*.[22] This time he was not going to refuse Ziegfeld. He quickly agreed, rushed backstage, and startled the audience by his unexpected appearance. It was "the very proudest moment of our lives," remembered Betty. "When Will went on the stage that night, the audience broke into applause. Never had he gone over so well."[23]

The critics seemed to agree. On July 23 the *New York Times* reported that "Will Rogers, has tiptoed into the cast since the opening night and intrenched himself firmly."[24] Rogers eventually got star billing in the 1916 edition and helped make it one of Ziegfeld's most successful presentations.

The *Follies* was considered the most glamorous, spectacular production on Broadway, the most successful of all the musical variety shows that flourished during the first three decades of the twentieth century. Behind its creation lay Ziegfeld himself, a daring, visionary showman, who raised the revue to new levels of artistic creation.

Many influences shaped the impresario's aspirations for the American musical theatre. Early in his life Ziegfeld had displayed the show-business and promotional skills that would make the *Follies* a national institution. The showman was born in 1867 in Chicago, where his father was the founder of the Chicago Musical College. Ziegfeld began by importing bands

20. Betty Rogers, *Will Rogers*, 131.
21. Ibid., 127.
22. "Ziegfeld Signs Will Rogers, Cowboy," clipping, n.d., in "Rogers' Tenure with the Ziegfeld Follies and the Midnight Frolic (1916–1917)," scrapbook #559–1–5787, CPpR.
23. Betty Rogers, *Will Rogers*, 132.
24. "Between Seasons," *New York Times*, 23 July 1916, sec. 2, p. 7.

and circus acts for the 1893 World's Fair and then managed the vaudeville strongman Eugene Sandow, making him a sensation through clever publicity stunts.

The genesis of the *Follies* hinged partially on a chance encounter. An inveterate traveller abroad, Ziegfeld met in London Anna Held, the Polish-French actress famous for her hour-glass figure, saucy sexuality, and well-publicized milk baths. Captivated by her charm both on and off stage, Ziegfeld produced a series of Broadway musical plays starring Held. They lived together for many years and eventually she became his common-law wife.

Ziegfeld was influenced by the vogue for revues and cabaret-theaters on the Continent. At one time Held was under contract with the Folies Bergères, and the two often saw the revue in Paris. She urged Ziegfeld to stage a similar musical show in America. Held adored elegant fashions and expensive jewelry, and she gave the impresario the sense of good taste and refinement that became known as the "Ziegfeld touch."[25] The producer was also aware of the small-scale musical revues that flourished in the early 1900s at summer theatrical roof gardens on Broadway.[26]

Ziegfeld sensed the time was right to produce a lavish variety revue, and in 1907 he opened his first *Follies* in the Jardin de Paris on the roof of the New York Theatre. Although not a box-office hit, it was popular with the public, and its blend of bosomy showgirls, bouncy music, and burlesque comics heralded greater editions to come.[27] Ziegfeld followed it with the succession of annual *Follies* that were to delight New Yorkers and out-of-towners through the 1920s.

Beginning in 1913, the *Follies* took place at the exquisite New Amsterdam Theatre on Forty-second Street, west of Broadway in the heart of Times Square. Built in 1903, the theatre was

25. Richard Ziegfeld, telephone interview by editor, 28 July 1991. Also Billie Burke, *With a Feather on My Nose* (New York: Appleton-Century-Crofts, 1949), 144–145.

26. *Dictionary of American Biography*, vol. 20, s.v. "Ziegfeld, Florence"; Charles Higham, *Ziegfeld* (Chicago: Henry Regnery Co., 1972), 50–52; Robert Baral, *Revue: The Great Broadway Period* (New York: Fleet Press Corp., 1962), 45; Gerald Boardman, *American Musical Revue: From the Passing Show to Sugar Babies* (New York: Oxford University Press, 1985), 30–31; Toll, *The Entertainment Machine*, 183; and Erenberg, *Steppin' Out*, 207.

27. Baral, *Revue*, 45–46.

designed by the architects Henry Herts and Hugh Tallant in the Art Nouveau style. Inside, theater patrons were surrounded by luxurious decorations ranging from richly hand-carved wall panels in the lobby to allegorical murals over the proscenium arch in the main auditorium, from a grand staircase made of green onyx to an ornate fireplace of Caen stone and Irish marble in the Grand Reception Room.[28]

The golden age of the *Follies* occurred between 1915 and 1922. These were the years when the elaborate productions reached their peak and became classics of the musical-comedy stage. During this period the *Follies* were called a "national institution"—the extravaganzas were the attraction every visitor to New York had to see. Ziegfeld's extremely popular presentations inspired other revues such as George White's *Scandals*, Earl Carroll's *Vanities*, and Irving Berlin's *Music Box Revue*. The *Follies* showcased many well-known singers, dancers, and comedians. During the golden age Rogers starred in four annual editions (1916, 1917, 1918, 1922) as well as the *Follies* of 1924 and 1925.[29]

Along with Rogers, the *Follies* featured an extraordinary number of talented comedians, including Bert Williams, W. C. Fields, Eddie Cantor, Ed Wynn, Leon Errol, Frank Tinney, and Fanny Brice. In the *Follies of 1917*, one of Ziegfeld's biggest hits, the audience was entertained by an unmatched lineup of comics on the same bill. Will entertained the audience with his lariat tricks and wry political comments; Fanny Brice sang and danced to a *Follies* rag; W. C. Fields did a takeoff on a tennis match; a blackface Eddie Cantor pranced and played the banjo; and the inimitable Bert Williams sang his famous droll songs and performed pantomime. After seeing this all-star production the critic Percy Hammond proclaimed the *Follies* "the greatest show on earth."[30]

The *Ziegfeld Follies* broke new ground in the American musical theater through its blending of entertaining comedy,

28. For a thorough discussion of the theatre see "The New Amsterdam Theatre," *Theatre Historical Society Annual* 5 (1978).

29. Baral, *Revue*, 44–104.

30. Percy Hammond, "Women and Song (Ziegfeld Follies, 1917)," in *The Passionate Playgoer*, ed. George Oppenheimer (New York: Viking Press, 1958), 555. See also "Follies of 1917 Is a Fine Spectacle," *New York Times*, 13 June 1917, p. 11.

innovative stage designs, precision dancing, lighting effects, dazzling costumes, and catchy songs. A typical bill comprised about twenty scenes featuring a potpourri of dancing, skits, comic routines, tableaux, and chorus numbers. To write the shows' music, Ziegfeld employed the era's most talented song writers, including Irving Berlin, Jerome Kern, and Victor Herbert. Many *Follies* tunes became Tin Pan Alley classics, ranging from "Shine on, Harvest Moon" (1908) to Berlin's "A Pretty Girl Is Like a Melody" (1919). Fanny Brice's renditions of "Second Hand Rose" and "My Man" stopped the show in the *Follies of 1921*. Productions were also highlighted by Joseph Urban's opulent pointillist set designs painted in rich, dazzling colors.

A successful *Follies* hit exuded a perfect balance of all these components. Ziegfeld gave the audience a tantalizing taste of each form in short rapid routines and production numbers. "The Ziegfeld technique is the caviare technique," wrote the critic George Jean Nathan, a *Follies* fan; he "gives them just enough to make them thirsty."[31]

Ziegfeld, who was passionately devoted to the theater, aimed for perfection in every detail of the show. He ruled over the rehearsals with military discipline, taking care that each production number was correctly staged. "When I start to do a thing I don't stop until I finish it," said Ziegfeld, who during rehearsals often worked for days without sleeping.[32] The impresario spent enormous sums of money to present his elaborate extravaganzas. His productions in the 1920s often cost over $200,000, an unheard-of sum for the time.

He spent lavishly on adorning his beautiful show girls in expensive outfits. To design the costumes, he hired Lady Lucile Duff-Gordon, a British couturier whose fashions were the rage of Manhattan's upper crust. During the show the chorines made numerous costume changes, appearing in gowns of flowing chiffon, silk, and satin and wrapped in mink and chinchilla. The Girls strutted on stage doing the Ziegfeld Walk, a slow concen-

31. George Jean Nathan, *The World in Falseface* (New York: Alfred A. Knopf, 1923), 108.

32. "Ziegfeld Rose to Fame in the Follies on Success with Sandow and Anna Held," *New York World Telegram*, 23 July 1932, clipping in Florenz Ziegfeld Collection, New York Public Library Performing Arts Research Center, Lincoln Center, New York City. See also Burke, *With a Feather on My Nose*, 152.

trated straight-back gait accenting the pelvis, the lifted shoulder, and "breasts jutting out sharply."[33] The famous White Peacock dress, made of white embroidery embellished with sequins and paillettes, was the all-time showstopper. The gown was worn in the 1919 *Midnight Frolic* by the stately Dolores, a gorgeous model with classic features, who was considered the penultimate show girl.[34]

The Girls also performed in bathing suits, short skirts and tights, and in risqué costumes with plunging necklines. A popular feature of the *Follies* was Ben Ali Haggin's dramatic tableaux, living pictures with the Girls and other cast members depicting an Old Master painting, a historical scene, or an allegorical subject. In the tableaux the chorines often posed on stage in the nude, a daring innovation for the time for a respectable Broadway show. Provocative costumes and scenes in the *Follies* before 1920 reflected a loosening of moral taboos and censorship in urban America before the Jazz Age.

The *Follies* became known for "Glorifying the American Girl," and each production featured about sixty to eighty chorines. The beautiful show girls were vital to the *Follies*' appeal, and Ziegfeld took pride in paying them more than other producers (fifty dollars a week in 1919). Many young women around the country dreamed of becoming a Ziegfeld Girl. In well-publicized "call auditions," Ziegfeld and Ned Wayburn, his director, selected the chorines according to three main criteria: an attractive slender figure, a pretty face, and youthful looks. Personality and talent were two other factors that could get a chorus girl a small part or even top billing. "It is the girl with less perfect features, but with a vivid personality and some talent which she has worked hard to develop, who walks away with the honors," Ziegfeld wrote.[35] The impresario discovered numerous beauties, among them Marion Davies, Olive Thomas, Lilyan Tashman, and Peggy Hopkins. He also developed the tal-

33. Higham, *Ziegfeld*, 108.
34. Baral, *Revue*, 54–55, 74.
35. Florenz Ziegfeld, Jr., "Picking Out Pretty Girls for the Stage," *American Magazine* 88 (December 1919): 119. See also Erenberg, *Steppin' Out*, 219; and Bernard Sobel, *Broadway Heartbeat: Memoirs of a Press Agent* (New York: Hermitage House, 1953), 109–110. Sobel was Ziegfeld's publicity agent.

ents of many stars, including Marilyn Miller, Ina Claire, Lillian Lorraine, and Ann Pennington.

Surrounded by a "garden" of stunning showgirls, Rogers portrayed the bashful cowboy on the *Follies* stage. Dressed in his cowboy attire, he often acted as a foil to the glamorous chorines and pretended to be embarrassed by their flirtations. A photograph from the 1917 *Follies* shows Rogers, lasso in hand, standing sheepishly on the stage in the middle of a group of chorus girls dressed in Chinese costumes.[36] Another photograph shows him shyly avoiding the flirtations of a Ziegfeld Girl.[37]

In his gag book Will jotted down the following: "All these beautiful girls I am the contrast. Somebody has to do something while [the] girls change clothes even if they dont have much to change."[38] Rogers was well aware that the contrast between the charming, innocent cowboy persona and the ravishing showgirls could be used repeatedly for jokes and routines.

Ziegfeld had a reputation that he lacked a sense of humor, disliked comedians, and only hired them as fillers between chorus-girl numbers. But actually the producer appreciated a funny story and sometimes played practical jokes on his friends.[39] He realized the importance of comedy stars to the commercial success of his shows. As a shrewd businessman, he knew that popular humorists like Rogers could sell tickets and consequently he gave his top comedians star billing. Rogers' name, for example, was prominently displayed in advertisements as the main attraction in the *Follies of 1924*.

The producer's second wife, the actress Billie Burke, once called Rogers "Ziegfeld's greatest star," and his salary reflected his increasing importance to the showman.[40] In the 1915 *Mid-*

36. Farnsworth, *The Ziegfeld Follies*, 71. See photograph, p. 88 below.
37. Richard M. Ketchum, *Will Rogers: His Life and Times* (New York: American Heritage Publishing Co., 1973), 146. See photograph, p. 40 below.
38. Will Rogers, "Gag Book" [1915–1916], AMs, OkClaW.
39. Patricia Ziegfeld Stephenson, interview by editor, tape recording, Los Angeles, 26 April 1991. See also Burke, *With a Feather on My Nose*, 157. For the standard interpretation that Ziegfeld did not appreciate comedy, see Ketchum, *Will Rogers*, 142, and Farnsworth, *The Ziegfeld Follies*, 76.
40. Bryan B. Sterling and Frances N. Sterling, *Will Rogers in Hollywood: An Illustrated History of the Film Career of America's Favorite Humorist* (New York: Crown Publishers, Inc., 1984), 2.

night Frolic he earned about $175 a week, by 1924 he was making over $3000 weekly as the highest paid performer in the *Follies*.[41] Rogers and Ziegfeld supposedly never signed a written contract and sealed their agreements with a handshake. "I don't like contracts," Will once told the producer. "You can trust me and I know I can trust you."[42]

Ziegfeld grew to greatly admire Rogers' humor not only because Will helped make his shows commercially successful but also because Ziegfeld enjoyed his topical jokes. "Half the great comedians I've had in my shows that I paid a lot of money to and who made my customers shriek were not only not funny to me, but I couldn't understand why they seemed funny to anybody," he said. "But this Rogers, I never miss him if I can help it. . . ."[43]

The producer also developed a very close friendship with Rogers, a special relationship that he lacked with most of his other stars. In contrast to his public life, Ziegfeld in private was basically a reserved, informal person who disliked dishonesty and insincerity.[44] Thus he appreciated Will's integrity and candidness. The two also shared a love for the outdoors and the West. An expert marksman, Ziegfeld enjoyed hunting in the wilds of Canada and staying at "Patricia," his Canadian wilderness camp named for his and Billie Burke's daughter.[45] An avid horseman, he liked to ride horses at Will's ranch in California. The two occasionally had minor differences over business matters, but basically they had a rare friendship based on mutual trust.

The producer gave Rogers' comic monologue an entire scene in the *Follies*. His specialty usually came near the end of the

41. "Salary List for Week Ending March 14th, 1925," TD, Florenz Ziegfeld Collection, New York Public Library Performing Arts Research Center, Lincoln Center, New York City.

42. Ketchum, *Will Rogers*, 149. Some newspapers reported that Rogers did sign a contract; see, for example, "Rogers Signs a Two-Year Contract," clipping, n.d., in Scrapbook A-2 (1900–1907), OkClaW.

43. Farnsworth, *The Ziegfeld Follies*, 76.

44. Richard Ziegfeld, telephone interview with editor, 28 July 1991.

45. Billie Burke, *With a Feather on My Nose*, 137, 150, 184–186. Ziegfeld liked to tell the story (never proven) that he briefly left home as a teenager to join Buffalo Bill's Wild West show, having once beaten Annie Oakley in a shooting match (see Higham, *Ziegfeld*, 8–9). For further discussion of their relationship, see the section "Will and the Boss."

first act and was called different names, ranging from "Timely Topics" to "Yankee Philosophy" and "Out West." With the house-lights lit, the humorist delivered a monologue that lasted about eight to twelve minutes. As he swung his lariat, he made wise-cracks about prominent people and events. Some jokes were one-liners; others comprised several sentences with the punch line at the end. Will possessed a masterful sense of timing. He would broach a subject, get the laughter going, pause, wait un-til the audience quieted down, and then deliver the topper.

Each night he came out with new material based on what he had read in the newspapers. The playbill on the opening night of the *Follies of 1917* described Rogers as a comedian "liable to talk about anything or anybody." Occasionally, he asked the au-dience to name a prominent person and event, and he could quickly create a joke about a subject in the news. Even when he was stumped he was ready with a gag. Once someone yelled the name of "Jake Shubert," the theatrical producer. "The act was going great until that," Will replied, shaking his head.[46]

The audience believed his jokes were spontaneous, and many were. If a particular subject was going well, he would often im-provise according to the audience's reactions. But other jokes were planned in advance. He would type out notes and drafts for his routines on a typewriter in his dressing room. These writings ranged from key words and phrases to gags several sen-tences in length. He relied on his incredible memory during a performance, and to keep his jokes fresh, he never rehearsed the material he planned to use. At the rehearsals he would joke instead about members of the cast, the *Follies*, and other incidents.[47]

The staff kept him informed about well-known people in the audience, and he would pick out prominent individuals and joke about them. Often he would throw his rope around a celebrity and pull the person to the stage. Once he lassoed Al Smith, who had just been reelected governor of New York in November 1924. As the audience cheered, Rogers brought him to the stage as the band played "The Sidewalks of New York." After introduc-

46. *Ziegfeld Follies* playbill, June 12, 1917, in the Institute of the American Musical, Inc., Los Angeles; clipping from *Variety*, n.d., in "Rogers' Tenure with the Ziegfeld Follies and the Midnight Frolic (1916–1917)," scrapbook #559–1–5787, CPpR.
47. Sobel, *Broadway Heartbeat*, 144; Croy, *Our Will Rogers*, 150.

ing him as the next Democratic president, Rogers asked, "What we would like to know is whether you would be willing to go down to Washington? You have a trucking outfit, you know, and you are the only man I know who could move from Albany to Washington cheaper than anyone else." "If you came along as my secretary I might take a chance," replied the governor.[48]

The audience loved these impromptu sessions, and one never knew who would show up at the *Follies*. The dignitaries also enjoyed the publicity and the prestige associated with participating in a Rogers routine. Celebrities and out-of-town guests would go backstage to visit Will in his dressing room and have their photograph taken with him. Sometimes Rogers would tease a VIP in the audience by glancing at the person and never calling his name. "Your big butter-and-egg man, your author, baseball player, and especially your politician—like attention," Rogers said. "They eat it up. And the folks who pay the tariffs at the box offices like to realize they are in prominent company."[49]

In addition to his monologue, Rogers played in comic skits and musical numbers. In the *Follies of 1918* he appeared on stage in blackface riding a mule dressed to resemble an automobile. Later in the show he joined Ann Pennington in a cowboy-and-cowgirl dance and then changed into a tux and top hat to sing "Any Old Time at All" with Lillian Lorraine. Although uncomfortable in the outfit, the audience loved the transformation of Will from a cowboy to a playboy. In a parody of baseball in the 1922 *Follies*, Will played the pitcher Cy Walters in a sketch, called *The Bull Pen*, by Ring Lardner. Rogers also wrote his own sketches, including *A Couple of Senators* and *Chloride Gas Room Capitol* for the 1924 *Follies*.[50]

Rogers' comedic style fit in well with the patriotic themes that highlighted *Follies* productions, especially during World War I. In the *Follies of 1917* a hugh American flag was unfurled over the heads of the audience as they sang "The Star-Spangled Banner," and the patriotic finale consisted of Victor Herbert's "Can't You Hear Your Country Calling?," a tableau portraying

48. "Will Rogers Ropes Governor Smith," *New York Times*, 6 November 1924, p. 3.
49. Day, *Will Rogers*, 85. See also Ketchum, *Will Rogers*, 148, 153.
50. Baral, *Revue*, 75; *Ziegfeld Follies* playbill, 22 September 1924, in the Institute of the American Musical, Los Angeles.

the midnight ride of Paul Revere, and scenes of George Washington at Valley Forge, and Abraham Lincoln at Gettysburg.[51] On stage Rogers might make fun of current events and political figures, but he was always viewed as an indigenous American comedian whose folk humor and cracker-barrel wit evolved from his roots in the Southwest.

By the time Rogers left the *Follies* in 1925 he was a national celebrity. Will was not only a big name in New York but also was well known across the country for his new style of topical humor. The annual national tour of the *Follies*, which played in many cities, made his name known to many Americans.

Rogers' fame in the *Follies* led to other opportunities that greatly increased his popularity. Once he had perfected his topical monologue on stage, he was constantly in demand as a banquet and convention speaker. In his talks, which lampooned many different subjects, he used the same humor that he had developed at the *Follies*. Many of his speeches have become classics of American oratory.

In 1923 he began recording some monologue routines for Victor Records, including "A New Slant on War" and "Timely Topics." These recordings, which were well advertised, gave people a chance to hear Rogers without going to the *Follies*. He also began to perform on radio, which was developing as an important entertainment form at the time Rogers was in the *Follies*. His first broadcast on radio, accompanied by the Ziegfeld Girls, occurred on Pittsburgh station KDKA around 1922.[52]

Rogers' name was also becoming well known through the print media. His gags began to be published in New York newspapers as well as other dailies around the country. In 1919 his *Follies* jokes—called "Rogers-isms"—were assembled to form his first two published books, *The Cowboy Philosopher on the Peace Conference* and *The Cowboy Philosopher on Prohibition*.

In December 1922, Rogers began writing a weekly column for the McNaught Syndicate. The owners of the company, V. V. McNitt and Charles McAdam, were avid fans of Rogers. Their offices were located across from the New Amsterdam Theatre,

51. "Follies of 1917 Is a Fine Spectacle," *New York Times*, 13 June 1917, p. 11.
52. Arthur Frank Wertheim, *Radio Comedy* (New York: Oxford University Press, 1979), 59.

and they felt Rogers should write a feature similar to his *Follies* routine.[53] His syndicated weekly column and daily telegrams, begun in 1926, were distributed to over five hundred newspapers and read by millions of Americans.

While working in the *Follies*, Will starred in his first silent movie, *Laughing Bill Hyde*, filmed in 1918 in Fort Lee, New Jersey. Critical success in the film and the opportunity for a career in the burgeoning movie industry caused Rogers to leave the *Follies* for several years. In 1918 he signed a film contract with Samuel Goldfish (Goldwyn) and moved to Hollywood the following year.

Rogers was one of many *Follies* stars who were leaving Ziegfeld for the movies. The producer was very perturbed by their loss, but there was little he could do about it. After suffering a series of financial losses producing his own silent movies, Rogers rejoined the *Midnight Frolic* in November 1921, and later he starred in the *Follies of 1922*. In 1923 he returned to California to perform in a series of two-reel comedies for Hal Roach.[54]

Rogers appeared in the *Follies* of 1924 and 1925, but left the show permanently in October 1925 when he signed a lucrative contract to go on a nationwide lecture tour. By then the heyday of the *Follies* was over. There would be several more editions, but these shows lacked the luster of earlier productions. What caused the show's demise was Ziegfeld's own financial excesses, the growing competition from the movies, and the desertion of many of the stars to Hollywood.

Ziegfeld's extravagant and glamorous productions evoked the glitter and glamour of the roaring Twenties. Once the stock market crashed in 1929 the mood of the country changed to one of bread lines and unemployment. The last production, *The Follies of 1931*, staged during the peak of the Great Depression, was clearly out of tune with the times. A year later Ziegfeld, who had lost a fortune in the Wall Street crash, died in Hollywood in dire financial straits. A loyal friend to the last, Rogers paid his hospital and funeral expenses, oversaw the arrangement of the funeral, and helped console his family.

53. Will Rogers, *The Illiterate Digest* (Stillwater: Oklahoma State University Press, 1974), preface by Charles V. McAdam, xix–xx.
54. Sterling, *Will Rogers in Hollywood*, 2–5, 46, 52.

The showman and the comedian had come together at exactly the right time. Between the years 1915 and 1925 Ziegfeld produced his most successful revues, and in those shows Rogers developed his insightful political jokes. By 1925 Will had established his reputation as America's favorite court jester. The "King of the Beautiful" and the "Man from Oklahoma" left an indelible mark on the history of American entertainment— Florenz Ziegfeld for his innovative spectacles in the American musical theatre, and Will Rogers for his poignant philosophy and timeless humor. In retrospect, their relationship was one of the great show-business alliances.

SCENE 1

THE MIDNIGHT FROLIC

Will Rogers' appearance in the *Midnight Frolic* cabaret in 1915 was the big break in his career. Many of the clientele were regulars who came repeatedly to the nightclub located on the roof of the New Amsterdam Theatre. Rogers' success in the *Frolic* led to his engagement in the 1916 *Follies*, but he continued to play in the café upstairs that year and intermittently through 1919. Will would deliver his *Follies* monologue and then later do an entirely different routine at the midnight *Frolic* show. Rogers returned to the nightclub in November 1921, and the following year he toured with a stage production of the best acts, called the *Ziegfeld Frolic*.

As many reviews suggest, Rogers topical humor was an immediate hit with the guests. Surrounded by a bevy of ravishing show girls, Rogers delighted the classy audience with his surefire jokes about politicians and the day's news and always drew roars of laughter from the noisy crowd.

WILL RECALLS THE FROLIC

IN 1915 I went up on Mr. Ziegfeld's roof in the Midnight Frolic show. I got two-fifty a week, and got my first car, an Overland, and drove it out on Long Island every night about two thirty. It got to knocking so much that one night the cop arrested me. "Hey, you can go down the road at night, Rogers, but you got to leave that thing. You're like an alarm clock at three A.M."

Ever know how the Midnight Shows started? Well I can tell you for I was in the first one.

The Midnight Frolic was the start of all this Midnight and late style of entertainment. That has since degenerated into a drunken orgy of off-colored songs, and close-formation dancing. It was the first midnight show. It started right on the stroke of twelve, it could have 50 or 75 people in the cast, bigger than all the modern day shows given at regular hours. It had the most beautiful girls of any show Ziegfeld ever put on, for the beautiful ones wouldent work at a matinee for they never got up that early.

Donald Day, ed., *The Autobiography of Will Rogers* (Boston: Houghton Mifflin Co., 1949), 37–38.

Midnight Frolic program, April 27, 1915. (Will Rogers Memorial)

Lolo Lorraine   Margaret St. Clair   Nancy Wallace

(Programme continued.)

Will Rogers

Olive Thomas

PART III.

10. "I WANT SOME ONE TO MAKE A FUSS OVER ME,"
    Sybil Carmen and Balloon Girls
    Misses Morris, Leslie, Cassidy, Thomas, M. St. Clair, Harting,
    D. St. Clair and Wallace.
11. PAUL GORDON..............................Up Off the Floor
12. "A GIRL'S TROUSSEAU"..........Oscar Shaw, Paul Frawley and
    Misses Thomas, Koffe, Whitney, Beverley and Wallace
13. W. HORELIK and His Original Gypsy Troupe, including Mlle. Rachell
14. "INDIAN FOX TROT BALL".......Allyn King and Indian Maidens
15. ARNAUT BROTHERS....................French Grotesques
16. FINALE (a).............................Nurses and Boy Scouts
    (b).............................Entire Company

DABNEY'S SYNCOPATED ORCHESTRA.

Costumes executed by The Schneider-Anderson Company and Lucile, Ltd.
Scenery constructed by the Joseph Brooks Studios.
Shoes by Miller.
Stockings from Peck & Peck

Marjorie Beverley

Mabel Ferry

Gypsey Mooney

Edith Whitney

EXECUTIVE STAFF FOR MR. ZIEGFELD.

John Henry Meore..........................Manager
John Brunton..............................Technical Director
Arthur R. Evans...........................Stage Manager
George A. Nichols.........................Musical Director

—MENU—

Crab Flake Ravigote

Chicken a la King

Neapolitan Ice Cream
Cakes   Coffee

Ch. de Cavonove, 1900
Clysmic   White Rock   Appolinaris

Olga Harting

Margaret Morris

Paul Frawley

Sybil Carmen   Dolly Allwyn   May Leslie   Alberta Turner

Midnight Frolic sheet-music cover. (Will Rogers Memorial)

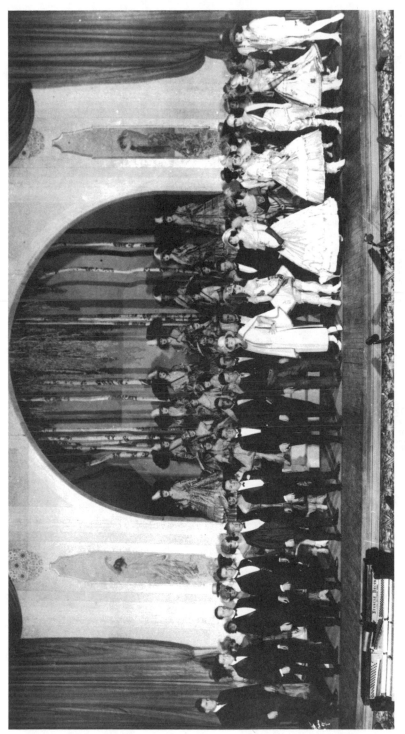

Will Rogers and cast in a *Midnight Frolic* finale. (White Studio photo, Will Rogers Memorial)

The famous *Follies* show girl Dolores dressed as the White Peacock in the *Midnight Frolic*. (Photo by Alfred Cheney Johnston, gift of Patricia Ziegfeld Stephenson, Will Rogers Memorial)

Bird Number featuring Delores in the 1919 *Midnight Frolic*. (Will Rogers Memorial)

We used to have a time getting em up for the midnight show. I dont mean I did, I dident have to go round waking any of em up but somebody did.

The same bunch of folks, that is about 50 per cent of the main ones, were up there every night.

It was for folks with lots of money. And plenty of insomnia. He would have great big musical numbers, all written especially for the show, maby 40 girls in em, led by some well known local Broadway star at that time.

We would put on a new show about every four months. Costumes and all. There has never been anything to equal it since then.

MIDNIGHT FROLIC ROUTINE

In his *Frolic* routine Rogers would joke about a wide range of subjects. In this excerpt from his "Gag Book" he cracks jokes about the Ziegfeld Girls and the balloons the chorines wore on their costumes. A favorite target of Will's ribbing in 1915 was William Jennings Bryan, then secretary of state in the Wilson administration and a flamboyant orator who lost three presidential elections.

THE reason Mr. Z[iegfeld] keeps me here is the people seem to after seeing my *act* . . . drink more. These girls certainly got on some agravating *desires*. You know I am going to stick with this fellow. I am off all the shows that go in for art. I am for Ziegfeld and dames. You know this fellow knows just how to drape em so you don't know just whether they have or have not. You keep coming back *and then* you don't know. Then I stick along and I don't get much and occasionally hand him a laugh or *two*.

"Gag Book" [1915–1916], AMs, OkClaW.

Somebody has to do something while *the girls* change clothes even if they dont have much to *change.* . . .

We have [the] Greatest Indoor Sport in the World called bursting of Toy Balloons. All you have to do is leave your Wife at home and get a front table, light a good 10 cent cigar, get a bottle . . . of Wine. Of course the More wine you have the further you will reach for a balloon. . . .

Bryan is against every public issue that comes up—about the only thing he is pleased with his *himself.* When Fords War [Peace] Ship sailed I went over to see it off (Should of been on it). I got there just in time to hear Bryan say God bless you. Thats the only thing *he says* for nothing. Well you have to give him credit he held out for more money. . . . Wilson says a Man has a right to change his mind and should but Bryan has been doing the same act for 14 years. I'm a judge of Human Nature. I heard Bryan talk years ago and said to myself that fellow will never be President.

BETTY ROGERS REMEMBERS

MANY would attend the *Follies* and then go upstairs afterward, where they could eat and drink. That demanded constant new material for Will, because he couldn't use the same jokes in both shows. The papers were full of news—the war was on, though we had not yet entered—and Will began to talk about political and national affairs. Starting with his familiar opening phrase, "Well, all I know is what I read in the papers," his remarks were as topical as the latest edition, and constantly changing. One critic described Will—and how well it fitted him—as the "columnist of the theater." Since the *Midnight Frolic* was an intimate kind of show, Will had joked with the

Betty Rogers, *Will Rogers: His Wife's Story* (1941; Norman: University of Oklahoma Press, 1989), 133.

guests who came night after night to see the performance. This eventually led to his introducing prominent personalities to the audience. The idea had caught on so well, that now he started doing the same thing downstairs in the *Follies*. Out-of-town visitors would come around to Will's dressing room during intermission. They liked to chat with him and to get a close-up view of the magnificent girls, clad in dazzling silks and satins.

WILL'S SISTER SALLIE WRITES HOME ABOUT THE MIDNIGHT FROLIC

Nov. 3, 1915

YESTERDAY morning we took a long drive about 40 or 50 miles over the island, and that evening Miss Dick [Theda Blake], your Aunt Maud and I drove in to your Uncle Willie's show "Town Topics" at the Century. He does a rope dance, aside from his specialty, with an awfully cute little girl [Lois Josephine] and he is enthusiastically received.

Just before 12 o'clock we drove up to the side entrance of the New Amsterdam (roof) Theater. It's lovely up there. Just as we stepped into the elevator a fine looking, broad-shouldered man met your Uncle Willie and shook hands very cordially and when he introduced us to William Randolph Hearst I almost fell dead in my tracks.

This theatre is for the wealthy society people and as it is on the order of a cafeteria the tickets are $2.00 apiece, aside from what you eat. Suffice to say I ate nothing but occupied every minute of my time in looking. However, your Uncle Willie would order a lemonade for both your Aunt Maud and I. His act here is practically the same as at the other theatre but the little girl [Sybil Carmen] with whom he dances here wears the cutest white wooly chaps and my how she enjoys her part! The Grand Finale consists in the whole company coming in a very jolly sort of way and your Uncle Willie roped one of the chorus girls

Paula McSpadden Love, comp., *The Will Rogers Book* (Waco: Texian Press, 1972), xiii–xv; reprinted with permission.

and quickly tied her to a wire which was just above their heads. (Understand this is not on the bill.) She turned to a gentleman sitting near and asked him to untie her. He gallantly did so and was roped in his turn and forciably pulled along with the chorus. The house went wild, and it developed afterwards that he was here visiting friends—was a substitute in the International polo games and the friends who had taken him up there were crazy about your Uncle Willie. It was all splendidly done and brought a world of applause.

A few days after Rogers opened at the *Frolic*, he received the following review in *Variety*.

I AIN'T USED TO WORKING
IN A JOINT LIKE THIS

"Just Girls," as the newest Ziegfeld "Midnight Frolic" on the Amsterdam Roof has been named, is not greatly unlike its predecessor to those who grew familiar with the first aerial Ziegfeld performance. It is mostly girls, nearly 30 of them, changing their costumes seven times within the 70 minutes the actual performance runs. The girls look as only "Ziegfeld girls" always do, and their "clothes" is not the least for the purpose of aiding "appearance." In a bathing number, the suits are particularly attractive, and to contrast probably, a film of Kay Laurell in swimming is shown at the finale, and Kay has nothing on excepting the water. Melville Ellis is making his debut as a Ziegfeld attraction, giving his pianolog shortly after the opening of the revue. . . . The other newcomer is Will Rogers, the lariat thrower, and the Roof is a pipe for Bill. In his cowboy outfit he kids any and everyone, does a few tricks and is a riot. Early in the turn Rogers remarks, "I ain't used to working in a joint like this." Later he complains of the number of girls around, re-

"Cabarets," *Variety*, 3 September 1915, p. 7.

marking "They are making me dress with two of the chorus girls' chauffeurs and Melville Ellis' valet."

MIDNIGHT FROLIC WITH WILL ROGERS MAKES IT EASY TO KEEP AWAKE

IF we had Will Rogers's gift for writing the snappy editorial paragraphs we should never waste a day worrying about Florenz Ziegfeld's promise to make us a star in musical comedy, as Will seems to be doing.

No, siree. We should be saving up our money in an old tobacco box with the fixed idea of taking it back to Oklahoma with us and buying a newspaper with it. And then, with the aid of the newspaper, we should elect ourself to Congress and become internationally famous as a party wit, if not a party whip.

Rogers could probably achieve deathless glory as an Oklahoma congressman and easily double the circulation of the "Congressional Record."

He is a rare soul among comics, this lad. . . .

William, of Oklahoma, is back on the roof of the New Amsterdam Theatre as the leading frolicker of Mr. Ziegfeld's newest midnight revel. There he has resumed his pertinent observations on the news of the day, the gossip of the hour, the scandal of the moment. Given his own field to work in, and his own crowd to work for, and there is no one who can approach within yards of him as an original entertainer. Hence his return must be welcome to the regular midnight crowd.

Burns Mantle, "Midnight Frolic with Will Rogers, Makes it Easy to Keep Awake," n.d., unidentified clipping in scrapbook #20, OkClaW.

SCENE 2

WILL AND THE ZIEGFELD GIRLS

In his *Frolic* and *Follies* routines Will enjoyed making fun of the Ziegfeld Girls. The disparity between Rogers, the cowboy philosopher (who stood for down-to-earth integrity), and the ravishing chorines (described by observers as a "sea of pulchritude") was a surefire formula that sparked hilarious moments on the *Follies* stage. The Girls also provided Will with abundant material for several of his articles.

HELPING THE GIRLS WITH THEIR INCOME TAXES

WELL, I haven't had much time lately to dope out many new jokes. I have been helping the Girls in the Follies make out their Income Tax. A vital question come up, do Presents come under the heading of Salary? You know that's a mighty big item with us. When I say Us, I don't mean Me, as no one has given me anything yet, but I stick around in case a few crumbs drop.

I have been looking for a bribe from some of our prominent men to keep their name out of my act, but the only ones who even speak to me are the ones I mention. So I guess about the only way you can get a Man sore nowadays is to ignore him.

One Girl wanted to charge off Taxi Cab fares to and from the Theatre. I told her she couldn't do that. She said, "Well, how am I to get there?" I said, "Well, as far as the Government is concerned, you can come on the Subway." She said, "Oh! What is the Subway?"

Another Girl who has been with the various Follies for ten years wanted to know what She could charge off for Depreciation. And she was absolutely right because if, after being with them for that long, and you haven't married at least one Millionaire, you certainly have a legitimate claim for Depreciation.

I reminded one of the Girls that she had neglected to include two of her Alimony allowances. She said, "Do I have to put them all in?" I said, "Why, certainly you do." The Girl said, "Well, how did the Government keep track of them? I couldn't."

The Illiterate Digest (New York: Albert & Charles Boni, 1924), 69–74.

A *Follies* Girl, Lette Goudal, flirts with Will Rogers in the *Follies of 1918*.
(Gift of the Walter Reade Organization, Will Rogers Memorial)

One Girl charged off a non-providing Husband under the heading of Bad Debts. We charged off all Cigarettes smoked in Public under the heading, Advertising.

One Sweetheart who paid for a Girl's Dinner every night, went thoroughly broke in Wall Street by trying to corner Canned Tomatoes in the late Piggledy-Wiggledy uprising. We figured up what the dinners would be for the rest of the year and charged him off as a Total Loss.

And right here I want to say what an honest bunch these Girls are. They don't want to beat the Government out of a thing. One Girl who had been away for a few weeks last winter to Palm Beach left a Husband in the good hands of her Girl Chum. When she returned the Girl Chum gave her a Two Thousand Dollar Bracelet. Now she wanted to include this Item in her Tax

Will and the Girls backstage at the *Follies of 1924*. (Will Rogers Memorial)

Will Rogers with *Follies* Girl Annette Bade, *Follies of 1922*.
(Will Rogers Memorial)

A Ben Ali Haggin tableau. (White Studio photo, Will Rogers Memorial)

and we couldn't figure out where to put it. Finally we decided it was Rents, so we put it in, "For Rent, of One Husband, two Thousand Dollars."

Of course while the girls had these tremendous salaries I was able to help on account of my technical knowledge of them (as I dress with their Chauffeurs), and on account of my equal knowledge of making out an Income Tax, with any man in the World. As none of us know a thing about it.

Look what I saved them on Bathing Suits! I had them all claim they bought various Suits. And I defy even a Congressional Investigating Committee (and you certainly can't pick any more useless Body of men than they are), I defy them to say that a Bathing Suit on a Beautiful Girl don't come under the heading of Legitimate Advertising.

Now, as I say, these Girls all wanted to do what was right as they could afford to but this Income Tax has not acted that way with the Men. The Income Tax has made more Liars out of the American people than Golf has.

Even when you make one out on the level, you don't know when it's through if you are a Crook or a Martyr.

Of course, people are getting smarter nowadays; they are letting Lawyers, instead of their conscience, be their Guide.

There is some talk of lowering it, and they will have to. People are not making enough to pay it.

And, by the way, the only way they will ever stop Bootlegging, too, is to make them pay an Income Tax. (At present it is a Tax exempt Industry.) Income Tax has stopped every other Industry, so there is no reason why it won't stop Bootlegging.

Of course, some of our more thrifty Girls have followed the example of their Male Tax Dodging friends and Incorporated (as the rate is lower on Corporations). Wall Street attended to that little matter when they were drawing the Tax Bill up in Washington.

These Girls had to do that, the same as men, to protect their Salaries. Of course, the big Gamble in buying into these Individual Corporations is the Lucky chance that she might make one or more wealthy marriages during the year. When of course, her being Incorporated, all she gets comes under the heading of Income, and you, as a Stockholder, get your Pro Rata Share. If she lands a big one you have struck Oil. Then, on the other hand, she may marry for love. In that case you have brought in a Duster.

For example, down on the Exchange you will find the Anastasia Reed, incorporated, along with General Motors and Blue Jay Corn Plasters. At the end of the year, the Stockholders, after adding up the Salary along with the accumulated Alimony, can either declare a dividend, or vote a Dinner and put the Undivided profits back into the growing Concern.

Now, I can't tell you the name but I was lucky enough to land 5 shares just before a Blond Corporation married a Multi-Millionaire who was over 70 years of age. Us Stockholders have figured out at our last meeting that if he dies when we think he will (and we have no reason to believe otherwise, unless the Poison acts as a Monkey Gland) why, just those 5 shares will make me independent for life.

I don't want to use this space as an ad, but I have been able for a small monetary fee to tip off my friends just what stock to buy. You see I am in a position to judge as I watch who is in the front row every night and I can just tell when Mendelssohn's Spring Song will start percolating for some particular Corporation. Now, at the present time, there is every night in the front row a Millionaire Oklahoma Oil Magnate and a Bootlegger, both angling for the same Corporation. If this Bootlegging person lands her, why her Stockholders are made for life, but if the Oil Magnate comes through (for sometimes these female Corporations are swayed by sentiment), why the stock won't be worth within a thousand Percent of what it will be if the Bootheel Party lands.

Now, take me personally; this Income Tax thing don't bother me at all. You are allowed 200 dollars for each Child, and my Children and my Income are just coming out even now.

THE AUDIENCE WANTED
TO SEE GIRLS AND ACTION

WELL, as I sat in a Compartment on the Special Train carrying the Company back from Atlantic City, where we had been trying out the new show, I just got to thinking of the heartaches and disappointments after the hopes and expectations of the same bunch of people going down this time one week ago. This does not only apply to Chorus; it applies to every Person in the Show. I don't mean by this that we have a show that is not up to our expectations, for it is said that it is the best. But what struck me is the hard work, the disappointments and the blasted hopes that the finished show is based on.

You people of the audience see the finished product with all hands laughing and doing their part as if they never had a worry. But you don't know how many were turned back—some discharged, some put in minor parts, and hundreds of things changed around from what you originally expected to do. Maybe lots of this was through no particular fault of theirs at all; lots of times just through unfortunate circumstances. Everybody is ambitious, in the theatrical profession, I think, more than in most any other business.

Every Chorus Girl dreams of the day when she will get a little Bit or Part to Do. Perhaps it has been promised to her in this show. They may have it handed to them at rehearsals, and work hard on trying to perfect it as the Stage Manager wants it. It may be with one of the Comedians. Opening night the Girl may do great, but the stunt doesn't appear funny to the audience, or maybe the comedian himself is bad in it and the whole thing is out, all through no fault of hers. She has to take her place back in the Chorus line or get out. It's just one of those tough breaks.

Ever since I came back East to join the show I have been thinking night and day on some novel little things to do and of course had built up great hopes on them. Well, I want to tell you honestly I didn't have a single one that turned out. Well—yes, they were turned OUT just as fast as I did them. The

"Blues that Spotlights Never Show," *New York Times*, 29 June 1924, sec. 8, p. 2.

first part would be in the Alley before I got through with the last part.

One of my marvelously bright Ideas was to put out a card which read, "Songs and Jokes we would like to forget but they won't let us." Well, another Comedian and myself went out doing the Songs which had been done to death lately and jokes which were not too old, but yet had been told a lot. I had the idea of doing this behind a woven net drop that came down to keep the Audience apparently from throwing and hitting us. It was the old Cherry Sisters stunt.

Well, the Songs we sang didn't seem to the Audience to be old enough to be funny or new enough to be good. So the net was given to a poor fisherman. One of the Actors said to me, "I think that net killed it. If you had done the act without the net I think it would have gone." I said: "Friend, I wouldn't do the same act again for a thousand dollars Without The Net. The next time we would have really needed it."

Then another one I had laid great stress on was an old-fashioned illustrated Song with slides. The Song was called "Men of Yesterday." It was a ballad lamenting the men who had passed and what great men they had been in their day. Now at the same time I was showing on the screen such prominent men as McAdoo, Al Smith, Charley Chaplin, Harold Lloyd, Dawes, Underwood, Jackie Coogan, and Ben Turpin. I leave it to you if that idea don't contain some humor, to be singing a sad song lamenting these Down and Outs and then showing the Pictures of these men, including a lot more equally prominent.

Well, if you think it's funny I wish you had been in the audience. You would have been a novelty. I never saw a Song that seemed so long to the end. It died standing up, sitting down and rolling over. I asked people about it later and they said "Why, McAdoo and those fellows you showed are not down and out." Now, will you tell me what's the use of trying?

Ann Pennington has worked for the last two years with Brooke Johns, who plays the banjo for her to dance by. Well, I conceived another bright idea of learning one Chorus of her dance, and, dressed as him, going out and doing it as the audience was accustomed to seeing him do it. I got a teacher and nearly drove everybody out of the Theatre for two weeks hammering on this Banjo. Got to Dress rehearsal night at Atlantic

City and found that her Dance come right ahead of my own Roping Specialty. I couldn't do it there and so that was another idea gone into the Ocean.

Going down last Sunday, I was Singing and Playing all the way. Today that Banjo is in a crepe bag in the Baggage Coach ahead. Two weeks of good banjo practice gone for nothing.

We started in with a plot. I had a scene with a little Girl who I was supposed to have raised, and she had won a beauty prize and was going on the stage and leave me. Well, I thought, here is where I will do some of my Moving Picture Acting. It is a pretty little scene, as I realized that she was going and that I had learned to love her. Everybody at rehearsals said, "Oh, that's great." I got so I could do it so good I cried—actually.

Well, opening night they listened for a few minutes and they didn't hear me pull any wise cracks, so they just made themselves up something to laugh at. They didn't want to hear me serious. They wanted to know what I thought of Coolidge, or what was going to become of the Democrats. Now, I don't mind telling you I had visions of that little Scene getting me in a Dramatic play, where I could leave the ropes in the Barn. The whole plot was pumped into the Atlantic.

The Audience didn't want to hear a lot of talk. They wanted to see Girls and action. So consequently all those whose parts pertained to the plot had to change to something else or get out. So you see we have all had our trials and worries. I came back with nothing that I went down with. Everything is something else that developed while there.

There is enough material thrown out of one of these Shows after the first performance to build Ringling Brothers' Circus. We had so much show I wanted to send the First act on the Road and take the second act into New York.

So a plot and a Corset are two things you will never see in our show.

You may have a scene and like it and think you are good in it, and they find it don't fit into the scheme of the show, or maybe it's not funny enough. Girls are disappointed about their Costumes and are crying. Maybe they have been taken out of numbers for some reason or other. Principals may have what they think are their best Songs or dances cut out, for this is one big machine and no little Cogs are supposed to mar the ultimate end. If you are ground under, it's just your hard luck; not one chance in a hundred that it was your fault, but things just broke bad for you.

The boss [Ziegfeld] has them himself more than anybody. He builds and plans all year to see big ideas go wrong at dress rehearsal or on opening night. So nothing that happens to us can we blame on him. He is gambling two hundred and fifty thousand dollars on each one of them, so what are our worries compared to his?

Of course, after we all get into New York and get started why we forget some of our disappointments, and others will get other jobs. But right at the time when we were speeding in, all on edge as to where New York would take us, I thought, here is a great advertised show, that is supposed to be a light-hearted and care-free organization, and supposed not to have a worry or a care. Yet I bet you there was more real downright Drama on that train than on any other that was going in.

But through it all they just gritted their teeth and stood it, rehearsed all night and half of the days, everybody trying their best without a murmur, Stage hands, Musicians, Actors, Owner and all the bosses, going all night and day, ready to gamble their future on one night's showing.

I want to tell you, folks, you will never know what a blow it was to me not to be able to sing about those Noble "Men of Yesterday" and play that Banjo for Ann Pennington.

If I am sad when you see the Show, you will know what it's from.

〰〰〰〰〰〰〰〰〰〰〰〰〰〰〰〰〰〰〰〰〰〰〰〰

GAGS

I wouldent come out here but Mr. Ziegfeld's Shows always abound in Novelties, and I am one here tonight, I am the only

"Original Follies Notes," TMs, OkClaW; "The Inimitable Will Rogers," clipping (1916), Scrapbook #20, OkClaW; Betty Rogers, *Will Rogers*, 140.

one on the Stage here fully clothed. I will be a disappointment probably as I am leaving everything in regard to the architecture of my Anatomy to your imagination. Remember you havent had to imagine all night.

And if any one should dash on and tear anything from off my person, I want you to know it was no plans of mine. I want to leave the stage with the same amount of clothes that I entered with.

Of course after the first show should there be a demand on the feminine part of the audience, for the same appeal to them that is made to the tired business man, I might be induced, I say I might be, for Arts sake to remove a couple of Ropes.

But I will say this for Mr. Ziegfeld, Artists say that the most beautiful thing in the world is the form divine, Well you must admit that since 8 PM yesterday you havent detected a knock knee, or a Bow leg. When he does show you something it's at least worth seeing. A 38 Bust or a big Ankle would have as much chance getting into this stage door as Hiram Johnson has of entering the White House.

That Ben Ali Haggin certainly can put on those Pictures, They say the true Artist is the man who can take little and do much with it, Well he is what I would call the Michelangelo of his day, you just give him 12 girls, and two wreaths, and he will group you a tintype that our old Fathers used to have to look through a hole in a pen knife to see. Boy what a tough Job he has.

No use to read the papers in the morning as I can tell you what they will say and have for years. Mr. Ziegfeld's glorification of the American Girl was unfolded last night, It's a beautiful show, as he alone knows how to do one. It is sadly lacking in Humor, Why cant we have humor in our American Revues.

As if a Follies audience ever paid attention to what some Comedian was doing in this show, It's just a question of when will the girls be back. No sir dear Critics we will never have a perfect Revue according to Follies standards until our Girls learn to do something out here in one while other girls are undressing for the next full stage number.

Follies opening night is like nothing else in the world, It's like a convention of old wives meeting the new, or wives viewing for the first time their Husbands' sweetheart.

I was supposed to have bought a pony from the Prince of Wales for $2500. I didn't buy him, I bought him for Mr. Ziegfeld. I wouldn't give $2500 for the Crown, much less a pony. Mr Ziegfeld bought him for his little girl. A short time afterwards I asked him how he liked the pony. "Fine, [my daughter] Patricia brought him right in the house." You know, Ziegfeld has a beautiful country estate up at Hastings-On-The-Hudson. Well, it's not exactly his. It belonged to Billie Burke, his wife, and he moved in. He says, "What do you know about the pony coming right in the house." I told him, "Lord the stables that pony's been used to, you are lucky to get him in your house. The pony thought he was slumming or he would never have gone in there." That's why I couldn't buy one. I knew I couldn't support him in the manner in which he had been accustomed.

Ziegfeld has a way of dressing a chorus girl so that you don't know whether she has or whether she hasn't, and you go away and wonder about it two or three days, and then you come back to have another look.

They say that a shark won't bite at a leg that has a stocking on it. These theatre goers must think they're sharks, the way they strain their eyes to determine whether they're being worn or not.

The girls of the Frolic wear a little less each year. I only ask that my life be spared until I see three more Frolics.

Well, the Summer is about over, and what will these butterflies do then? Some of these girls don't know where their next limousine is coming from.

People think that I can't be a real cowboy, or I wouldn't work in a show where there's nothing but calves.

We have a hard time keeping our girls together. Every time we get to a new town some of them marry millionaires, but in a few weeks they catch up with the show again.

~~~~~~

One reporter, curious about Will's feelings toward the Girls, visited his dressing room, which contained a special shower installed by Ziegfeld.

WHAT THE FOLLIES GIRLS HAVE DONE TO ME

WE went to see Will Rogers with a notebook, and a Waterman filled with scarlet ink.

Our Editor had dared us to ask Mr. Rogers what the Follies girls had done to him. Said Editor assured us that he would print what we got, either with or without apologies to Mister Sumner!

Well, we thought, as we set forth for the New Amsterdam Theatre, where the darling of the Follies and the darling of the Films is playing; well, *here* is where we get a Tale of Terror.

"We bet he's *scared* of 'em," we thought.

You know . . . here he is, poor Will Rogers, Westerner, family man, comedian, regular fellow . . . what will he think of the little pollies in the Follies with whom, nightly, he comes into scented contact? Will he blush when he speaks of 'em? Will he stammer and grow pale? Or will he be stern and disapproving and say that these girls are not like the Old Folks at Home, and that he wouldn't raise his gal for Mister Ziegfeld?

He did not.

We went to the theatre and were reluctantly admitted via the

Will Rogers as interviewed by Gladys Hall, "What the Follies Girls Have Done to Me," unidentified clipping [1922?], Scrapbook #20, OkClaW.

stage entrance. Probably the doorman thought we had hopes of becoming a Folly, and could plainly see that our hopes were doomed before entering.

We had to wait for Mister Rogers for quite some time, because he was on the stage with Messrs. Gallagher and Shean when we arrived. While we waited, we had several eyefulls of froufrous and suchlike. Visions of ladies of an appalling loveliness. "He needn't tell *us*," we told ourselves, "no Mere Man could hold his own against such as these." We thanked whatever gods there be that we hadn't a husband in the Follies. We began to feel sorry for Missis Rogers!

When Will finally appeared, he was clad in a baseball costume, and he told us that he had to make "a lightning change for the street," and that then we could "come up." He went up the stairs with a group of the Follies girls, laughing and talking. He was, of course, chewing gum, but the girls didn't seem to mind. If anything, they liked it.

In less time than it takes us to write it, he sent for us and we went into a dressing room the like of which we have never seen before. His valet apologized for it, but Mister Rogers didn't. We thought to ourself that one of the dear old Follies girls ought to have a heart and vacuum-clean it for him. One or two things were outstanding—for instance there was a strange appearing contrivance in one corner of the room which might have been an infernal machine, but which turned out to be a shower-bath. There was also a small, brand-new, pocket Corona typewriter, upon which Will Rogers writes the speeches that are making him famous. And there were sheafs of Mss. lying about, which made us feel that we had stumbled into an editorial office instead of into the Follies.

And there were letters . . . letters . . . letters . . . and telegrams . . . and telegrams . . . telegrams . . . We thought that half the world must spend its time writing or wiring Will Rogers.

We asked him, without further parley, what the Follies girls had done to him, and he stared and said he didn't know what we meant. He looked about for a possible exit and said that there had been a woman in to see him that morning from "some magazine or other," and she had asked him what he thought of "the new woman movement" or some such thing. "I don't," said Will Rogers, "know anything about such things.

They ain't in my line. I don't know what to say. I've never thought about it."

"Never thought about the Follies girls?" we reproached. "Why, every man has thought about the Follies girls!"

Will Rogers twisted upon his uneasy chair. "Why, folks is just folks," he said, "it all depends on the girl!"

"But what have they done to *you?*" we persisted.

"They've made me love 'em," said Will Rogers, "if that's what you mean.

"They're just old-fashioned girls at heart.

"Most of 'em are working for their livings and working darned hard, too. You ought to see 'em at rehearsals. They know how to work and there's no nonsense about it, either.

"There's not half of this stage door Johnny business you hear about, either. It's mostly the bunk.

"Just 'cause these girls are beautiful, they get panned. I don't get this association of beauty and evil. Most of the bad 'uns and criminals I've seen have been as ugly as all blazes.

"Real beauties can afford to be good.

"I tell you, ma'am, I'd rather have my daughter working in the Follies than troopin' around Hollywood, Cal., with her mother at her heels. Yes, sir! These movie mothers . . . gosh, they're the ones that cause the troubles!

"I'd just as soon as not have a girl of mine in the Follies. It's the girl every time. But if she ever does go in, she'll go alone. I think everything in this world of my wife, but I don't believe in this mother business on the stage or screen.

"Why, these Follies girls have hearts as big as their hat boxes.

"Why, do you know what they did? Just this last Christmas every girl in the place, from the scrub women up, banded together, and after the show they presented me with a silver thingumbob and silver candlebra for the table. I can tell you, I was touched. And pleased. It just shows what they are.

"Why, most of the small towns have more hot stuff on their Main Streets than the Follies have in their theatre.

"There's a lot of talk nowadays about the old-fashioned woman and the new-fashioned woman. I don't know. I take folks as I find 'em, and there's something to be said for all.

"I've been working in the Follies a good many years, and I've always found everything on the level inside and out. It's mostly girls who aren't in the Follies, who cause the trouble. Most every girl who goes to Hollywood, for instance, says she's been in the Follies. Nine times out of ten they ain't never been inside the stage door. The result is that most every time there's trouble out there, it's always a Follies girl . . . maybe!

"Yes, ma'am, the Follies girls have made me keep my faith in women-folk, rather than the other way around. They're all wool and a yard wide, these girls. They're great pals. And they know how to work. I couldn't say anything against 'em if I would, and I wouldn't if I could, which I can't. They've been sweet and dear and lovely to me.

"I've got the best wife in the world, as I've said, and she thinks a heap of the girls, too, and they think a heap of her. She's been on the road with us a lot, and when any of the girls are sick or in trouble, they go to her and she fixes 'em up and takes care of 'em."

"Isn't Mrs. Rogers ever jealous?" we asked.

"No, she's never jealous," said Will Rogers. "There's no occasion for such a thing. She knows me. She knows there ain't any of these girls going to lose their heads over *me*."

Mr. Rogers escorted us to the stage door. So the Follies girls are home folks!

Well . . . well . . . Interview and learn life, is all we have to say!

We don't know how our Editor will take it, when he filled our pen with crimson ink and all, nor how you fans will like it, but *what* a blow it will be to Signor Sumner!

SCENE 3

HORSEPLAY

A performance by Will Rogers in the *Follies* was always marked by considerable horseplay. Will would participate in zany skits, ludicrous dance routines, and often lasso prominent people in the audience. In the following article he describes the celebrities he introduced to the audience and the notables who visited him backstage.

ROPING THE BIG SHOTS

WELL, as The Illiterate Digest goes to press we are just getting over a day or so of very cold weather. For a couple of days there it looked like we were going to be able to KEEP KOOL WITH KOOLIDGE. In fact I like to froze with him the first cold day. If it is going to be a cold winter I would just as soon have kept WARM WITH WADSWORTH.

Well, prosperity must have hit us because of a lot of prominent men have suddenly got enough to get into the Follies on. We have had a disgraceful mess of them lately. One night last week we had the War Industries Board, 200 strong, all in one party. They were the famous $1.00 a year men during the War. Now, will you tell me how men who only got one dollar a year could afford the Follies? They still have their organization and once every year they meet and have a kind of a Reunion, and live over again the old prosperous days. Then, in between, they just sit and pine for another War.

They were all Republicans but one. That was Mr. Barney Baruch, the head of it during the War. With all the boasted Republican prosperity they made Baruch buy the Tickets. They keep this one Democrat in there so he can pay for everything.

You see, when President Wilson formed this Board during the War he told Baruch to go out and get all the prominent business men of every line together and see if they couldn't form some kind of Association to speed up supplies for the War. Well, he thought of course Baruch would come in with members of both Political Parties. But when they round them all up, why they are all Republicans!

"Election Over, Notables Relax," *Tulsa Daily World*, 30 November 1924.

Will Rogers with distinguished visitors backstage at a *Follies* performance in
Chicago, March 1922. *Left to right*, Mrs. Charles Fitzmorris, Police Chief
Charles Fitzmorris (Chicago), Mrs. John Hylan, Roy Keehn, Mayor John
Hylan (New York City), Mayor William Thompson (Chicago), and Will
Rogers. (Will Rogers Memorial)

So Mr. Wilson asked him why be so partial to one Party. And Mr. Baruch told him: "You told me to get prominent men from every Industry and I did. Now I can go and get you some Democrats but they won't be very prominent and won't have any Industries with them. Besides, I doubt if you can get a Democrat to work for $1.00 a Year. They are used to getting at least a $1.00 a day."

Well, they decided to use these Republicans and let the Democrats do the fighting. They knew they could do that.

Now you see Baruch took care of all these Political opponents and now that his Party is out and theirs is in, they have not done a thing for him. It is a shame they won't repay him. Why, they even make him pay their fare to these Reunions every year. But he is a game guy and don't squawk. He is, you know, the Sight Draft of the Democratic Party.

He comes back in my dressing room and sit and talked for an hour, and he complimented me on an Article of mine showing why the Democrats didn't do better in the last election. He said I had it absolutely right when I said that the Democrats had to get rid of the League of Nations Idea and get a Slush Fund in its place, and that if the Republicans had been kinder promiscuous in peddling our Oil, why it only showed that Voters admired personal preparedness in their Public officials.

So the Democrats should go out and get themselves some slick Candidates and not preach too much on their Party's honesty in the Campaign. Shrewdness in Public life all over the World is always honored, while honesty in Public Men is generally attributed to Dumbness and is seldom rewarded.

Among some of the many prominent ones I introduced to the audience was Eugene Meyers of some finance Board. They sent him out all over the west to loan money to the Banks to finance the Farmers until after election. He put the money in and the Republican Candidates for Senators in each State borrowed it all themselves, so they were the only Farmers benefited. I told this on him in the show and it got a big laugh and I have always noticed that people will never laugh at anything that is not based on truth.

Then they had the great Republican Leader, Charlie Otis, from Cleveland, an old Ex-Cowpuncher, by the way. He is such a strong political factor in Ohio Politics in Cleveland that La

Follette carried the city by a big majority. Too bad La Follette didn't have him working against him all over the country. He is a great old fellow even if he is a such a poor Politician.

Herbert Swope the enterprising Editor of the N.Y. World was among them. They had him along so, in case of a raid, they would have a Democratic name to give the Police. He is the first Democratic Editor to revive without stimulants after the election returns come in.

At their business meeting some man representing a Farmer's organization made a speech asking that the Farmer be given the same protection in financing by the Government that is given Eastern Industries. That got the biggest laugh of the meeting.

Al Smith, New York's popular Governor, was also in a few nights ago. Our show seems to be a relaxation from all the humor of Public office. They like to come in and be instructed and think seriously every once in a while. After all, most prominent men have sensible sides if you can only get their mind off themselves and the humor of their importance.

Al is a bear. He come up on the stage and I made him promise that he would run for President on the Democratic Ticket in 1928, provided they decided to enter a man by then. Al promised he would if I would be his Secretary of State. I wouldn't mind the job so much but, Lord, I would hate those Whiskers. Perhaps we can compromise on a Bobbed Mustache.

No kidding though, you just watch that Guy step in '28. If the voters still want "Plain Folks" by then, why here is a Bird that has got 'em all skinned for just old down to earth Horse Sense.

And, say, by the way, with that Industrial Board that night by mistake was another good Democrat. That was Governor Ritchie of Maryland. In looking for a Democratic Governor Candidate next time don't overlook this one. They sometimes nominate Men for geographical reasons. Well, here is a man that is nearer to the White House than any Governor living. Baltimore is only an hour from Washington over Bootleg Boulevard.

Governor Ritchie could be president and still run over and govern Maryland. That ought not to take over a couple of hours a week of his time to oversee a little patch of ground like that.

He could get those Stills systematized over there so he would only have to go over and check up and come back.

Another distinguished visitor we had last week was Sir Thomas Lipton, who I introduced and he made a very pretty little speech. I introduced him as the man who made more tea and drank less of it than any man living. I told him that he truly represented the British Isles, as he was Born in Ireland, weaned on Scotch Whiskey and made English Sportsmanship famous.

He is such a good loser it would be a shame for him to win; it might spoil him. He is, by the way, over here seeing something about running second again.

And last Saturday Matinee who should we have but Chauncy Depew! That was wonderful. It was the first time I had ever had the honor of talking for him. I did all the political stuff, which I thought he might enjoy, and then I introduced him to the audience and what an ovation he did get.

Just think, this wonderful old man who will soon be 91 years old, and has been making the world laugh and think for years. He is the most famous after-Dinner speaker we ever had. He made the loveliest and brightest little Speech for us, said he had been trying to amuse people for 70 years but never found it necessary to use a Rope to do it.

I told him that the Follies would get him. We might have to wait 91 years to get him but, we would nail him sooner or later.

Then a night or so ago, who should come back to see me in my dressing room but Mrs. Richard Croker, just over from Ireland on her way to Florida. You know, we are fellow Cherokees. Her folks are Cherokee Indians and so are mine and we are both mighty proud of it. I have known her for years. She is really a quite remarkable woman. There was no marrying this Man for money. They really loved each other and had a very happy married life, and when he left her this money and property he knew where it should go. She deserves every cent of it, and everybody I ever talked with is glad she got to keep it.

She told me they made a mistake by attacking her in Courts in Ireland. You can't buy Judges over there. They are appointed for life. Political promises don't interest them. She told me of that wonderful place outside Dublin, "Glencairn" his Irish Estate, and told me of the wonderful Horses and Stock. She had me all excited to go to Ireland. That is where some of my folks come from. There is a fine breed for you, Irish-Indian. Ziegfeld says I have a touch of Hebraic in me, too. Which would make me an Irish, Jewish, Indian.

My family crest would in that case be a Shillalah with a Tomahawk on one end, and a percent sign (%) on the other.

A famous Rogers trademark was chewing gum during his act, a custom he had developed in vaudeville. Will picked up the habit either from baseball players or to prevent nervousness on stage. One time he had accidentally walked on stage chewing gum and the audience broke into laughter. Soon he was using it as a comic device, sticking the gum on the proscenium arch or anywhere else on stage.

PROSPECTUS FOR "THE REMODELED CHEWING GUM CORPORATION"

LAST week I made, on account of my Movie work, a trip to Catalina Island and along with the Glass bottom Boat I had pointed out to me the home of Mr. William Wrigley on the top of the highest mountain. He also owns the Island. We were not allowed to go nearer than the gate as the Guide said some other Tourist had carried away a Grand Piano, and he had gotten discouraged at having them around. Another tourist was caught right on the Lawn Chewing an opposition Brand of Gum. That is really the thing that gummed up the Tourist Parade.

Then I remembered having seen his wonderful building in Chicago, all, mind you, accumulated on Chewing Gum at a Cent a Chew. Now I felt rather hurt at not being allowed to at

The Illiterate Digest (New York: Albert & Charles Boni, 1924) 87–95.

Comedian Ray Dooley clowns with Will Rogers in the 1925 *Follies*.
(White Studio photo, Will Rogers Memorial)

least walk through maybe the Kitchen, or the Cellar, because I know that I have contributed more to the Building of that Home than any one living. I have not only made Chewing Gum a pastime but I have made it an Art. I have brought it right out in Public and Chewed before some of the oldest Political Families of Massachusetts.

I have had Senator Lodge (who can take the poorest arguments in the World and dress them up in perfect English and sell them) after hearing my Act on the Stage, say: "William" (that's English for Will), "William, I could not comprehend a word of the Language you speak, but you do Masticate uncompromisingly excellent."

This reception which I received at the Wrigley Home was so in contrast to the one which I received at Mr. Adolphus Busch's in St. Louis. When he heard that one of his best Customers was at the outer Gate, Mr. Busch not only welcomed me, but sent me a fine German Police Dog to California, the stock of which had come direct from the Kaiser's Kennels in Pottsdam. The Dog did wonderful until some one here by mistake gave him a drink of Half of One Percent Beer. He would have been six years old next May.

After looking on Mr. Wrigley's home with much admiration and no little envy, the thought struck me: A man to succeed nowadays must have an Idea. Here I am, struggling along and wasting my time on trying to find something nice to say of our Public Men, when I should be doing Something with Dividends connected with it. So then the thought struck me: WHAT BECOMES OF ALL THE CHEWING GUM THAT IS USED IN THIS COUNTRY?

I just thought to myself, if Bill Wrigley can amass this colossal fortune, and pay the Manufacturing charges, why can't I do something with Second Hand Gum. I will have no expense, only the accumulation of the Gum after it is thoroughly masticated. Who would be the most beneficial to mankind, the man who invented Chewing Gum, or me who can find a use for it? Why, say, if I can take a wad of old Gum and graft it onto some other substance, I will be the modern Burbank. (With the ideas I have got for used Gum I may be honored by my Native State of Oklahoma by being made Governor, with the impeachment clause scratched out of the Contract.)

All Wrigley had was an Idea. He was the first man to discover that the American Jaws must wag. So why not give them something to wag against? That is, put in a kind of Shock Absorber. If it wasn't for Chewing Gum, Americans would wear their teeth off just hitting them against each other. Every Scientist has been figuring out who the different races descend from. I don't know about the other Tribes, but I do know that the American Race descended from the Cow. And Wrigley was smart enough to furnish the Cud. He has made the whole World chew for Democracy.

That's why this subject touches me so deeply. I have chewed more Gum than any living Man. My Act on the Stage depended on the grade of Gum I chewed. Lots of my readers have seen me and perhaps noted the poor quality of my jokes on that particular night. Now I was not personally responsible for that. I just happened to hit on a poor piece of Gum. One can't always go by the brand. There just may be a poor stick of Gum in what otherwise may be a perfect package. It may look like the others on the outside but after you get warmed up on it, why, you will find that it has a flaw in it. And hence my act would suffer. I have always maintained that big Manufacturers of America's greatest necessity should have a Taster—a man who personally tries every Piece of Gum put out.

Now lots of People don't figure the lasting quality of Gum. Why, I have had Gum that wouldn't last you over half a day, while there are others which are like Wine—they improve with Age.

I hit on a certain piece of Gum once, which I used to park on the Mirror of my dressing room after each show. Why, you don't know what a pleasure it was to chew that Gum. It had a kick, or spring to it, that you don't find once in a thousand Packages. I have always thought it must have been made for Wrigley himself.

And say, what jokes I thought of while chewing that Gum! Ziegfeld himself couldn't understand what had put such life and Humor into my Work.

Then one night it was stolen, and another piece was substituted in its place, but the minute I started in to work on this other Piece I knew that someone had made a switch. I knew this was a Fake. I hadn't been out on the Stage 3 minutes until half of the audience were asleep and the other half were hissing me. So I just want to say you can't exercise too much care and judgment in the selection of your Gum, because if it acts that way with me in my work, it must do the same with others, only they have not made the study of it that I have.

Now you take Bryan. I lay his downfall to Gum. You put that man on good Gum and he will be parking it right under the White House Dinner Table.

Now, some Gum won't stick easy. It's hard to transfer from your hand to the Chair. Other kinds are heavy and pull hard. It's almost impossible to remove them from Wood or Varnish without losing a certain amount of the Body of the Gum.

There is lots to be said for Gum. This pet Piece of mine I afterwards learned had been stolen by a Follies Show Girl, who two weeks later married an Oil Millionaire.

Gum is the only ingredient of our National Life of which no one knows how or of what it is made. We know that Sawdust makes our Breakfast food. We know that Tomato Cans constitute Ford Bodies. We know that old Second-hand Newspapers make our 15 dollar Shoes. We know that Cotton makes our All-Wool Suits. But no one knows yet what constitutes a mouthful of Chewing Gum.

But I claim if you can make it out of old Rubber Boots and Tires and every form of old junk, why can't I, after reassembling it, put it back into these same Commodities? No one has found a substitute for Concrete. Why not Gum? Harden the surface so the Pedestrians would not vacate with your street. What could be better for a Dam for a River than old Chewing Gum? Put one Female College on the banks of the Grand Canyon, and they will Dam it up in 2 years, provided they use discretion in their parking.

Now, as for my plans of accumulation, put a Man at every Gum selling place. The minute a Customer buys, he follows him. He don't have to watch where he throws it when through; all he has to do is to follow. He will step on it sooner or later no matter where they throw it.

When he feels it, he immediately cuts off the part of the shoe where it is stuck on, so he can save the entire piece. Then he goes back and awaits another buyer.

I have gone into the matter so thoroughly that I made a week's test at a friend of mine's Theatre. At one of Mr. Sid Grauman's Movie Theatres here, I gathered gum for one week and kept account of the intake every day. My statistics have proven that every Seat in every Movie Theatre will yield a half Pint of Gum every 2 days, some only just slightly used.

Now that gives us an average of a Pint and a Half every six days, not counting Sunday where the Pro Rata really increases. Now figure the seating capacity of the Theatre and you arrive at just what our Proposition will yield in a good solid commodity.

Of course, this thing is too big for me to handle personally. I can, myself, disrobe, after every Show, one Theatre and perhaps a Church on Sunday. But to make it National I have to form it into a Trust. We will call it the "Remodeled Chewing Gum Corporation."

Don't call it Second Hand; there is no Dignity in that name. If we say "remodeled" why every Bird in America falls for that.

Of course, it is my idea ultimately after we have assembled more than we can use for Concrete and Tires and Rubber Boots to get a Press of some kind and mash it up in different and odd shapes.

(You know there is nothing that takes at a Dinner like some Popular Juice Flavor to our Remodeled and overhauled Product. I would suggest Wood Alcohol. That would combine two Industries into one.)

I want to put flavors in there where we can take some of this colossal trade away from these Plutocratic Top Booted Gentlemen. If we can get just enough of this Wood Alcohol into our reassembled Gum to make them feel it and still not totally destroy our Customer we will have improved on the Modern Bootlegger as he can only sell to the same man once.

Now, Gentlemen and Ladies, you have my proposition. Get in early on, "Old Gum made as good as New." Think of the different brands that would be popular, "Peruna Flavor Gum," "Jamaica Ginger Gum," "Glover's Mange Gum," "Lysol Gum."

It looks like a great proposition to me. It will be the only Industry in the World where all we have to do is to just pick it up, already made, and flavor it.

I am going to put this thing up to my friend, Henry Ford.

Think, with no overhead, how he could keep the Cost down.
It's a better proposition than being President.

〰〰〰〰〰〰〰〰〰〰〰〰〰〰〰〰〰〰〰〰〰〰〰〰〰〰〰〰〰〰〰〰

Rogers acted in a *Follies* sketch playing a lady from the dance
halls of San Francisco. A burlesque of a western melodrama,
the skit parodied a current New York play starring actress
Lenore Ulric.

HOW I GOT INTO SKIRTS

MY little old act with the lasso was just put in to kill time while
the girls were changing their costumes. A male actor's monolog
in a girl show is just like an intermission. So I tried to make
my act attractive by telling a few jokes, and the audiences laugh,
and so Mr. Ziegfeld calls me a star.

Telling jokes was all right, but when Ned Wayburn came to
me a few weeks ago and said, "Bill, I'm adding a little dramatic
sketch to the Follies, and want you to act one of the roles," I
said, "Well, if this guy isn't kidding me, I haven't anything to
lose because I've got no reputation as an actor, if I can make a
hit, the critics will come out and say I am versatile and what
not." You know what makes a critic—two seats on the aisle—
but I kinder calculated I could make these critics sit up when
I came before them to do a John Barrymore. But then the
blow fell.

At the first rehearsal I learned they wanted me to wear skirts.

Now skirts is all right in their proper places. Girls wear them,
and sometimes the shortest ones are worn by old ladies. College
boys wear them when they indulge in amateur theatricals. But
to ask a he-man of the wild and woolly West to wear skirts in a

TMs, ca. 1922–23, OkClaW.

Will Rogers (*seated right*) dressed in skirts in the western melodrama sketch *Koo Koo Neil*, in the *Follies of 1922*. (Will Rogers Memorial)

burlesque show kinder flopped me. I thought Wayburn was kidding me, and so, to kid him back, I said, "yes."

But the darn fool meant it. He was in earnest. He brought out the manuscript of KOO KOO Nell, and gave me the title role. When I saw I was really expected to play a girl's role and wear skirts say, the howling of a prairie dog at midnight was deep silence to what I said. But Wayburn insisted, said I had agreed in front of the whole cast to play the role, and that my contract with Ziegfeld [compell]ed me to play any role of which I was cast, I was roped, tied and thrown—and that's how I got into skirts.

Since I had to wear the blamed things, I decided to make up as near like Lenore Ulric as KIKI as I possibly could, so I saw that little actress at a Thursday matinee and ordered my costume built just like her first-act dress. The audience gets the idea of the burlesque at once, especially since Brandon Tynan as David Belasco, is supposed to be rehearsing the act. I really tried at first to imitate Miss Ulric's voice, but no one could do that, so I imitated her mincing ways and cute little business with the powder puff, and, when I went on the first time, I thought the audience would throw things at me, but instead they howled. I didn't know whether they were laughing with me or agin me, but so long as they laughed and didn't throw things, I had no kick coming.

Now, after playing the darn fool role, I am getting used to the skirts and corset and the plumes on the hat, and am able to speak my lines without getting rattled. I am now studying the role of Ophelia, and hope to play Juliet next season, when all the other actresses have retired from the combat. Or if Miss Ulric ever gets tired of playing KIKI, I am willing to take her place if the public will let me. Meanwhile I will keep on throwing the rope and telling my little jokes in the Ziegfeld Follies, unless someone sends me poisoned candy for playing KOO KOO Nell in our little burlesque. It all goes to show that a real actor must be versatile. I never knew I was a real actor before, but it don't pay to quarrel with the critics, and since some of them called me an actor, I'm beginning to believe I am.

Many critics reviewed the *Follies* each year and commented on Rogers' unique style in the shows. The following selections describe the humorist's important contribution to the *Follies*.

OUR TALKING THACKERAY

WILL Rogers, the inimitable and unquenchable, says everyone flocks to the opening of the Follies [of 1918] and "brings his present wife to observe how his old one acts. Come," he adds, "and see where your alimony goes."

Whether or not that is the motive of attendance, everyone *does* flock to the opening of the Follies—the world and his wife, and his wife's sister, and the lady who will be his wife when the lady who is ceases to be. . . .

W. C. Fields, who used to be a juggler, as Will Rogers used to be a lariat-artist, before Mr. Ziegfeld discovered that both are comedians, leads the horseplay in "A Patent Attorney's Office." Eddie Cantor and Harry Kelly aid in the fun-making, which culminates with an amusing demonstration of a mouse-trap, in imitation of the legendary fly-catcher invented by Lew Kelly. Then Ann Pennington, making her entrance as a papoose on the back of a stalwart squaw, contributes an Indian dance; Lillian Lorraine follows a score of nearly nudes descending the stairs—those beautiful stairs of Mr. Urban's—and finally we reach Marilyn Miller, the freshest and most charming incarnation of youth and *joi de vivre* since the early days of Annette Kellermann. When it comes to chicken, my preference is for Chicken a la Marilyn. . . .

Ann Pennington dances again, and Mr. Rogers appears, *in propria persona*, to chat of timely topics. At this sort of thing Mr. Rogers is without an equal. He is more than a monologist; he is a talking Thackeray. Mr. Rogers threatens to write a book called "My Four Years with the Follies, or Prominent Men I've

Channing Pollock, "Our Follies and Mr. Ziegfeld's," *The Green Book Magazine*, September 1918, 392–395.

Will Rogers with *Follies* star Ann Pennington, *Follies of 1918*.
(Will Rogers Memorial)

Met at the Stage Door." Also, he confides that from now on, the Government's going to be "more strict with these spies. When they catch 'em doing anything, they're going to publish their names." Women are like elephants, according to the wise Mr. Rogers. He likes to look at 'em, but he wouldn't want to own one. Then he speaks of a girl acquaintance who has sent five sweethearts to France, and is still recruiting, and suggests giving home rule to Ireland and reserving the motion-picture rights. He and Ann Pennington wind up jointly with a lariat-dance—a Rocky Mountain bacchanal.

THE FOLLIES OF 1924

THE last night we were in New York I paid the usual small fortune to see Will Rogers in the Follies. Twelve dollars and the tax to see any show, even with Will Rogers, in it, is too much. I went back to Will's dressing room to see him and invite him to Tulsa sometime when he wasn't counting the gate receipts from some of his various sources of income, and stayed and chatted with him so long that I missed one of the best acts and made him late getting on for his own specialty. You know there must be something to Will Rogers' stuff or it would not stand up like it does. He keeps his audience in an uproar of laughter from the minute he comes on stage until he leaves it.

He asked where I was sitting in the audience and intimated that he would lasso me for his usual hit of horseplay, there being no real notables present, but I was too far out of his reach and aside from the fact that I had been one of a half a dozen Oklahomans who thought they were running for the United States Senate, there wasn't anything funny he could say about me.

One of his acts is to come on the stage as the new United States senator from Oklahoma and hold a conversation with another pseudo-senator caricaturing a cross between the late

Eugene Lorton, "Lorton Missed One Act of Follies Talking to Will Rogers," *Tulsa Daily World*, 5 February 1925, clipping, OkClaW.

Senator Henry Cabot Lodge and Charles Evans Hughes. The skit is his own creation and brings the house down with laughter and applause.

Another act of his is an investigating committee of the senate to investigate the various investigating committees of that body.

The chief witness is a politician who convulses the audience for 15 minutes with a monolog that begins nowhere and ends at the same place without completing a single connected sentence. As chairman of the committee Rogers then tells the witness that his statement is the most lucid and comprehensive explanation that has ever been made concerning the subject under investigation but that there was a small part of his statement that the committee would like to have made a little clearer, beginning with the second word and ending with the last. As he starts in a gas machine on the stage, which has been charged during his testimony, blows and the act is over.

The literary critic Edmund Wilson once saw Will rehearse the finale of act 1 in the 1924 *Follies*. Several numbers in this show were largely built around Rogers, who, with W. C. Fields, was the star of this edition. Rogers joined the Tiller Girls, noted for their precision dancing, and the rest of the cast in a rousing western dance closing.

I WOULD LIKE TO CORRAL

WILL Rogers mounts the block, about which the Tiller girls are wheeling. *Say: he's going to whirl the lasso around the whole thing. Yeah: he's clever!* They crowd the wings. Behind them, the negro wardrobe woman waits, patient and with a shade of sullenness—knowing herself handsome in another kind, she bides blinking at all that white beauty—those open-eyed confident white girls in their paradise of bright dress: turquoise

Edmund Wilson, "The Finale at the *Follies* (Dress Rehearsal)," *New Republic*, 25 March 1925, 126.

Will Rogers in a rope dance act in the 1924–25 *Follies*.
(White Studio photo, Will Rogers Memorial)

skirts and canary-yellow cloaks, pink bodies hung with dark
green leaves, white flower-stalks blooming into hats of purple
and orange—all excited by the costumes and the music, proud
to have been picked out by Ziegfeld, happy to look like magazine
covers—brown-eyed, clear-skinned, straight-backed, straight-
browed. A touch of the hand in flight: *Tomorrow at 11 o'clock?*

The comic thin girl, a little strained: *How long has this been going on? The curtains close: you're turning. They open: you're still turning. They close again: you close in and you stop! Now, go through it again from the beginning!*

The Tenor takes the stage: *Although I stand here singing, A rope I should be swinging, but I've really got to get it off my chest!* The long flower-like shapes of the show-girls, blooming in enormous sombreros: black, white, green, white, orange, white, purple, green, orange, black, white, green. *You'll find it rough but gentle, Romantic, sentimental, Though I'm not a butter and egg man from the West!* The showgirls droop away. *I would LIKE to corRAL, A very merry necessary little gal!* At the signal, the Tiller girls burst in: white with orange leggings and sombreros, white with purple leggings and sombreros. They make a swinging line: all together, with the strong urgent beats of their kicking they tell the strong urgent beats of the music. *I would LIKE to corRAL!* They crack whips, all at once. Will Rogers mounts the pedestal: the tall girl drops to a sitting pose, hugging one knee, hanging the other. The Tiller girls wheel about the pedestal, two circles flying against each other: he whirls his lariat down about them: he keeps it turning against the outer circle. *I would LIKE to corRAL!* The beat has mastered everything: it pounds fast in a crash of orange. Two minutes, in wheeling speed, mastered by the crashing beat, focussed in the green-gilt proscenium frame, they concentrate the pulse of the city. The brown-gilt curtains close: they are turning. They open: they are still turning. They close: they close in and stop. They close.

SCENE 4

TIMELY TOPICS

Will Rogers' participation in the *Frolic* and the *Follies* was a pivotal turning point in the humorist's career. On the stage of the New Amsterdam Theatre he started making jokes about world affairs and celebrities. The daily newspapers were an endless source of material for him. After two years with Ziegfeld, Will wrote the following article explaining his "extemporaneous" technique. The 1917 piece is one of Will's earliest published pieces and signifies his growing interest in getting his writings published.

THE EXTEMPORANEOUS LINE

THE question that every guy asked who used to come to interview me was: "Did you really come from out West?" I got so tired of hearing it that I used to tell them: "No, I'm from New Jersey, but don't you tell anybody." The next question invariably would be: "How did you get on the stage?" Say, anything can get on the stage. Its keeping them off that's hard. A fellow can be the champion soup eater and if he can locate a manager that will set him up behind a bowl, and tell him to go to it—if he can keep the audience amused and the soup holds out—why he's on the stage.

Of late all I am asked is: "Who writes your stuff and where do you get it?" And the surprising answer is: The newspapers write it! All I do is to get all the papers I can carry and then read all that is going on and try to figure out the main things that the audience has just read, and talk on that. I have found out two things. One is that the more up-to-date a subject is the more credit you are given for talking on it, even if you really haven't anything very funny. But if it is an old subject, your gags must be funny to get over.

The first thing is the remark you make must be founded on facts. You can exaggerate and make it ridiculous, but it must have the plain facts in it. Then you will hear the audience say: "Well, that's pretty near right."

Lots of good subjects have been in the papers for days and I

"The Extemporaneous Line," *Theatre Magazine*, July 1917, 12.

Will Rogers in a classic *Follies* pose.
(White Studio photo, Will Rogers Memorial)

can't think of a thing on them. Some of the best things come to me when I am out on the stage. I figure out the few subjects that I will touch on and always have a few gags on each one, but the thing I go out to say may fall flat, and some other gag I just happen to put in out there goes great. For instance, here is an example! "Mr. Edison is perfecting a submarine destroyer. Well they say he only sleeps three or four hours out of the twenty-four. That gives him plenty of time to invent."—That was only a little laugh, but I used it to show the audience that I had read about the invention which had only been announced that day. It happened that at this time New York cafés were closed at one o'clock so I casually added to the remark my sudden thought: "Suppose Mr. Edison lived in New York and Mayor Mitchel made him go to bed at one o'clock; where would our invention come from?" And that was a big laugh.

This illustrates my work. I have to have my idea—all extemporaneous speakers do—but my laugh comes quickly and apparently out of nowhere.

Another thing I read, was that submarines could not operate in the warm Gulf Stream—so I said: "If we can only heat the ocean we will have them licked." That didn't get much of a laugh and I was kinda stuck—but I happened to add, "Of course, that is only a rough idea. I haven't worked it out yet." This last went big and covered up the other.

I was talking of the income tax and how hard it hit our girls in the show, and just happened to mention, "A lot of them have figured out it would be cheaper to lay off."

I start in on a subject and if it is no good then I have to switch quick and lots of times when I come off of the stage I have done an entirely different act from what I intended when I went on. Sometimes an audience is not so good and my stuff that night may not be very good, so it is then you see the old ropes commence to do something. It gets their mind off the bum stuff I am telling and as I often say to the folks in the show, I reach away back in my hip pocket and dig up a sure fine gag, as I always try to save some of my best gags—just like a prohibition State man will his last drink.

In the two and a half years I have been with Mr. Ziegfeld in his Follies and Midnight Frolic where we play to a great many repeaters, I have never done the same act any two nights. I have always changed parts of it and in the Frolics a great many times I have done an entirely new act.

Another thing, I think I do the shortest act of any monologue man and that recommends it. On the Amsterdam Roof I never do over six minutes and in the Follies nine or ten, generally eight.

Picking out and talking about distinguished people in the audience I use quite a little, but never unless I know them personally and know that they will take a joke as it is meant. The late Diamond Jim Brady I always spoke of, as I knew him and he always seemed to take an interest in my little act. Once at a big banquet Mr. Brady recited a little poem which he had written himself. I learned the piece and shortly afterwards one night when he was in the audience I did his poem. This made a great hit with Mr. Brady. My best one on him was: "I always get to go to all the first nights, yes I do. I go with Mr. Brady. He sits in the front row and I stand at the back and if any body cops a diamond I am supposed to rope 'em before they get away with it." He was certainly a wonderfully fine man.

On the opening night of the New Midnight Frolic, Lieut. Vernon Castle had just returned from France and was then with Mrs. Castle. Vernon and I had played polo together and he is a regular fellow. I walked over to them, shook hands and said: "Here is one old Tango Bird that has made good," and then I told about how Fred Stone and I got Vernon on a bucking horse once and that was where he got his idea of aviating. I said: "Vernon, we worried about you when you were out there at the front, but not half as much as we worried about Irene in the pictures. Boy you don't know what war is, you should see what your wife has been giving them in 'Patria.'"

ORIGINAL FOLLIES ROUTINE NOTES

Politics is the ruination of the Country. Elect me for life, then they wont have to cater to any interest. If you elect one party to power, why the other party dont do any useful work for the next 4 years, only try to work some scheme to get back in. But if they were elected for life they wouldent have to worry. The minute a man knows he cant get a political Job, he may turn to something useful. A Business that's doing well dont change people every 4 years. A Man dont no more than get into the White House and learn where the Ice Box is than he has to get out again, Then he is never any good for hard work again.

Taxes, Why make the other fellow pay, It aint why it has been proven to work, Dont a rich man buy Non Taxable Bonds, and not have to pay any taxes and dont the litle fellow put his in his business and have to pay, Well let him be as smart as the big fellow.

What would you do with Traffic, that is the Big problem nowadays, Simply make every body going east go Mondays and everybody west Tuesdays.

Now if some man in Jail was nominated for the U S Senate he would be elected, People would figure well in there he cant talk us to death.

Since Hair Tonic developed such a kick Dandruff has increased 300 percent.

"Original Follies Routine Notes," TMs, OkClaW.

Will had chosen to become a topical humorist at an opportune time. With World War I raging in Europe, more Americans were reading the news and wondering if the United States would be forced into the war. America's neutrality, preparedness, and diplomatic negotiations were often subjects of Rogers' humor in 1915 and 1916.

When the United States entered the war in April 1917, Rogers feared that he would be unable to joke about such a serious matter and would have to change the style of his routine. But he soon learned that laughter was important during the war both as a morale booster and to relieve tensions. "Why, they laughed better during the war than any other time," he recalled. "And the more serious the situation, the better they laughed if you happened to hit the right angle of it" (Donald Day, *Will Rogers*, 87).

Rogers wholeheartedly supported the war effort and especially enjoyed poking fun at the Germans. The father of three children, Will was exempted from the draft, but he helped raise money for the war effort through benefit appearances and donated 10 percent of his income to the American Red Cross. As this article by Rogers from 1918 suggests, the news from the war front often dominated his routines at this time.

WORLD WAR I

THE Follies give men an opportunity to come here with their new wives to see what their old wives are doing. If they come early they can see just where their alimony is going to!

Anybody who does anything nowadays writes about it, like my four years here or there. When I round out this season I'm going to write a book on "My Four Years in the Follies and Prominent Men I Have Met at the Stage Door!"

I hear that Charley Chaplin is going to war. Now I can see the Kaiser hit with a custard pie square in the face! There sure is good news from the front nowadays. There's one thing about the Italians. They're either coming or going! There's no stand-

"Some of Will Rogers' Fund of Fun at the Follies," 1918, clipping in scrapbook #20, OkClaW.

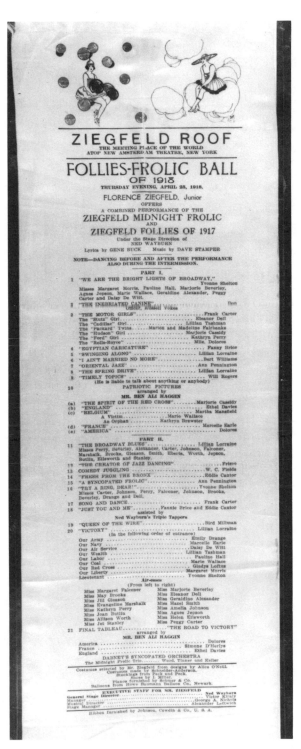

Playbill for the *Follies-Frolic* Ball of 1918. Will Rogers' "Timely Topics" monologue is featured in scene 9. (Will Rogers Memorial)

Will Rogers and chorines in the *Follies of 1917*. (UPI/Bettmann)

ing still with them! Austria and Germany are priding themselves on the many substitutes they have found. But somehow they can't find a substitute for the most important thing, food. It was Austria's war in the first place, but Germany took it away from her. Now let Germany suffer!

I see where Ham Lewis got up in the Senate the other day and made a long speech on Russia. Whenever anybody wants to make an impression in the Senate and wants to make sure that the rest of the members don't know whether he's right or wrong he speaks on Russia!

If the United States had sent Roosevelt to Russia instead of Root, you can bet your bottom dollar the Russians would be fighting somebody now! According to a report somebody shot at Lenin the other day, but missed him. We ought to send over a few American wives. There hasn't been a husband missed in this country in the last three years! But don't be sore at Russia. She'll soon be in the fight. They're rehearsing among themselves now!

England is debating about giving Ireland home rule. Somebody should tip England off to give Ireland home rule, but reserve the moving picture rights! There's one thing about an Irish Parliament. There's never going to be a dull moment there!

A U-boat sunk a Norwegian vessel last week. I guess Norway, Sweden and Denmark intend to remain neutral down to the last ship! But you've got to hand it to Uruguay. That country's got the right idea. It declared war on Germany without much fuss. Germany hasn't sunk any of her ships, you bet. But she's building one now!

Our shipping board is going to do some active work now and turn out one ship after the other. Schwab is already wearing his uniform! I see where they appointed Ford to the Shipping Board, too. I hope if he builds any ships that he'll change the front! They've got an awful time in Washington over this here prohibition fight. I read that Wilson doesn't want to do away with the two per cent alcoholic drinks. What good is this drink anyway? Who wants to drink fifty bottles to get 100 per cent drunk?

The Republicans are jealous over the way the Democrats are running the war. I bet when peace is declared and the Republicans get in power they'll start another war to show how much better they can run one! Still there's one thing we can say about Wilson; he's not partial in handing out jobs. Just look at all the one dollar a year men. They're all Republicans! Look at Colonel House. Some people fight their way into fame, others walk into fame, but for the first time in history a man has listened his way into fame!

The Government wants 2,000,000 more men, but they're not going to be gotten from the draft. They want more officers! After they're in, they're going to reduce 'em! Down in Washington the other day I met an honest to goodness private! Poor fellow, he saluted so much he was all in!

You can't kick about the women in this war. They're all doing their bit. Some of them can't wait until they get into a crowd to knit! You know, women are wonderful things. To me they're like an elephant. I like to look at 'em, but hate to own one! The girls in this show are patriotic all right. One of the girls came up to me yesterday and said: "Will, I've already sent five sweethearts to France and am still out recruiting!"

THE COWBOY PHILOSOPHER
ON THE PEACE CONFERENCE

Once the war ended in November 1918, the news focused on the Peace Conference held at Versailles, France, during the first six months of 1919. In his *Follies* routines Rogers frequently joked about the Conference's proceedings and its leading participants, including President Woodrow Wilson. The president viewed the war as a "Great Crusade" for democracy and an opportunity to create a just and lasting peace. In his Fourteen Points address in January 1918, Wilson outlined his vision of the postwar world, calling for the political self-determination of all peoples, the limitation of armaments, and the creation of a League of Nations to guarantee territorial integrity and to perpetuate world peace.

Wilson believed that the Peace Conference offered an opportunity to implement his grand design and a nonpunitive settlement. Before he left for the conference, he made some serious blunders. Ignoring the importance of bipartisanship, he failed to appoint a prominent Republican to the American Peace Commission at Versailles and failed to consult with the Republican-controlled Senate, which would have to ratify the treaty. Thus Wilson made the treaty a party issue. He also did not appoint a senator to the American Peace Commission at the conference. The delegation included Wilson; Robert Lansing, secretary of state; Colonel Edward House, Wilson's assistant; General Tasker Howard Bliss, chief of staff; and the diplomat Henry White.

At the conference Wilson found the representatives of England, France, and Italy quarreling over the spoils of war, demanding territory and reparations from Germany. Major decisions were made secretly behind closed doors by the "Big Four"; Wilson, France's Premier Georges Clemenceau, Britain's Prime Minister David Lloyd George, and Italy's Premier Vittorio Orlando. Although Wilson was able to institute a few points from his peace program in the treaty, including the League of Nations, he was forced to compromise on most of his demands. Wilson's final defeat came when the Senate

Rogers-isms: The Cowboy Philosopher on the Peace Conference (New York: Harper & Brothers, 1919).

failed to ratify the treaty. The League of Nations was seriously weakened without United States participation.

Rogers found the deliberations at the Peace Conference to be a great sideshow. The conflict between the quixotic idealism of Wilson and the political motives of the other leading delegates provided considerable material for the humorist's monologue. A shrewd observer of politics, Rogers was quick to expose the hypocrisy of the world powers and the "follies" of the delegates. He was personally disappointed with the conference's outcome, feeling that the proceedings resembled a "remnant sale," with the European victors stealing territory from the vanquished.

Audiences at the *Follies* enjoyed Rogers' witty sayings about the conference, and the gags were so popular they were published in newspapers. In 1919 the jokes were assembled and published by Harper and Brothers in book form as *Rogersisms: The Cowboy Philosopher on the Peace Conference*.

The volume illustrates Rogers' idiosyncratic writing style, which relies for comic effect on irregular punctuation and capitalization, run-on sentences, haphazard spelling, tangled tenses, humorous puns, new words, and a liberal dose of southwestern dialect and American slang. Rogers crafted this style and voice to convey a "common man" persona as he had on the stage. The folksy language and familiarity had become his trademarks.

The Cowboy Philosopher on the Peace Conference was the first of six books Rogers published during his lifetime. "You can't tell *Peace* from *War* without this Book," Will proclaimed on the cover. "I made this book so short you could finish it before the next war."

In the Five times I have appeared before President Wilson I have used dozens of these same jokes, about him, And he has the best sense of humor and is the best audience I ever played too, Which bears out the theory I work on, That you can always joke about a big Man that is really big, But dont ever kid about the little fellow that thinks he is something, cause he will get sore Thats why hes little,

W.R.

ALIBI

THERE is no particular reason why I should horn in on you Public with a Book, But thats just when they seem to write them, When theres no need or reason for them,

The shorter white Paper gets the more careless these Pen Hounds get with it,

All my friends advise me to go ahead Will and write it cause you wont annoy people with it like these other Writers do with theirs, Nobody will read yours

When a Guy has never grazed educationally any further than McGuffeys fourth Reader his ravings aint liable to throw any jealous scare into Literary Circles,

Grammar and I get along like a Russian and a BathTub,

In fact Americans are getting to dote too much on Grammar and Good Manners, They say the most perfect English in this country is spoken in Sing Sing, And at the Federal Prison in Atlanta, They claim a Knife never touched a Lip, So you see where that junk leads you too,

I was going to write a Book on the War, But I heard some fellow had already done it,

In fact I figure that the fellow who dont write on the war will be a novelty, **There is so many Books on the War that no two people will have to read the same Book.**

Then the War was too serious a subject I could not write on it, But the Peace Feast, That seemed to offer a better field for Humor provided you stick to the *facts*,

I have some inside facts procured from the most reliable source, And as I dont want to see the World grow up in ignorance on this historical subject I would really feel selfish and mean too withold it,

Heres how I got it, There is a fellow I know, Who had a friend, And this friends Sister had a sweetheart and he was a Soldier in France and his cousins pal was a Bunkie of Col Houses Chouffer, The Col told his Chouffer So you see my information comes from the same place Pres Wilsons does,

So Here Goes Under The Bottom With THE FIRST PEACE BOOK,

THE PEACE CONFERENCE

OF course this whole Peace Conference talk started from the time Pres Wilson said to Germany "We wont deal with you as long as you occupy invaded Territory." Well the Kaiser come right back at him and said, "If you can show us how we can give it up any faster than we are I wish you would do it,"

Now the Armistace was signed, and Germany agreed to quit running at eleven oclock on a certain day,

Of course we got the word a couple of days before it was really signed, Making everybody have TWO DRUNKS where one would have done just as well,

It would have been signed on this first day But the German Generals whom they sent out to sign up, had never been to the front and dident know just where it was,

The Kaiser was on the verge at one time of visiting the western front then he said, "No I will just wait a few days till it comes to me,"

Our Show was playing in Philadelphia when the first Armistace was signed, (*The one the saloon man framed up*) I was a bit leary of it all the time as I had been there once before when the Union League Club had paraded for a Mr Hughes, Then later they had to put the Parade back,

I HAD ALWAYS BELIEVED PHILA TO BE SLOW AND HERE IT WAS 2 DAYS AHEAD OF THE FACTS

At that time everybody wondered what to do with the Kaiser, I thought he should have been brought to this Country and made to clean the streets after that first Armistace day,

A funny thing the Armistace was signed about the time the returns of the last election come in. The Germans and the Democrats learned their fate on the same day,

When the war was over the Kaiser called his 6 sons to him and said, "Now boys we better duck Cause this war is over and you boys can get hurt *Now*,"

The thing that hurt the Kaiser worse than losing the war, Was that in all the Armistace terms they dident even mention his name,

Everybody commence talking about the Peace Conference and who was to go, Some Republican Senators went so far as to engage a lower birth,

There was so much argument about who was to go, That Pres Wilson says I tell you what, "We will split 50–50 I will go and you fellows can stay,"

At last we were going to get even with them for all their commissions coming over here,

You know for a while COMMISSIONS were coming so fast, That we were lucky to find a fellow who knew what Flag to put out each day,

We were meeting Servian Commissions with Romanian Flags,

Of course there were nations coming at that time who had not enough to support a flag, Thats why the commission were here to place a Flag Contract,

Now to get to my Peace trip, About three months are supposed to have elapsed between the last Paragraph and this one, All of which time was taken up by Congress talking, (*see congressional Record*) Finally Pres Wilson got tired listening to them and walked out on them,

If it had not been to get away from Congress, I have my doubts if he would have gone to Europe,

Now for the Number 2 Peace trip,

This Peace trip is not an original Idea, (It was originated by some obscure MANUFACTURER OF KNICK NACKS,) *Name furnished at advertising rates,*

Its always the same, the fellow who originates anything or starts something new is generally called a nut, The next fellow comes along takes his Idea improves on it and of course is a smart man,

Of Course this No 2 Company used better Judgement than the first one. This one waited till the war was over to Go,

This is the only case in Theatrical History where the No 2 Company was better than the original,

Of corse I claim this Manafacturer in some middle west town (I cant seem to recall that fellows name) made one mistake, There were people on his Boat that should never have had a return trip ticket,

Through Holland receiving them is where the Kaiser got his idea of going there,

Of course there was a lot of dissatisfaction against the Pres going, Mostly by people whom he did not take along,

I was in favor of his going because I thought it would give us a chance to find out who was Vice President, But it Dident,

I also felt confident that he was the only man that could explain the 14 points –––––––––––––

We were especially lucky in having him represent us in England as he is the only one we could have sent that spoke good enough english that they could understand,

He would have taken a Senator but couldent find one that had a dress Suit

A congressman of course was out of the question   He couldent have eaten off a 15 million dollar plate   He would have starved to death looking at it,

For awhile it looked like Mr Hughes would get to go, While the others were signing up he could have been investigating, his report would have been ready the day before the next election,

Also asked a manafacturer from some lake town (I cant think of that Birds name) But he said "No thank you one trip cured me"

The Sectry of Agriculture was named to go for a while, It was thought that if we were fortunate enough to be assigned any loose Islands at the meeting He could immediately advise what to plant thereby getting in a crop next year,

MR ROOT was named then some one happened to think of RUSSIA and that was off,

Wanted BRYAN *to go but nobody knew where he was,*

I wanted to go along as *JESTER* Pres Wilson will miss his comedy when he gets away from Congress,

I wanted to represent the United Press (the one that sent in that prematur peace report)   I could have had them there before they started,

See they took one Republican with them, But I have never read any thing in the papers about him landing, Just about chucked that guy overboard,

Took a republican along to argue with on the way over,

They will about make him Wait on the Peace Table,

See where Admiral Dr Grayson stood his Maiden voyage well,

Mr Creel went along to suppress any SCANDAL that may crop up

On arriving they found they had forgotten something after searching they found it was the *Industrial Committee,*

Now Mr Barney Baruch is going in case we land a few Shekels, why Barney will count up for us,

Also Mr Garfield "said he wasent going to stay in this Country and FREEZE another winter,"

If they keep on sending for them, Talk about getting the boys back, it will take a couple of years to get all these Peace Guys back,

We may not have had as many Nations in the war as these other Nations but we are going to Swamp them at the Peace Table,

Col House was there to meet the Boat in a *listening Capacity,*

Lot of men have *fought* their way into fame and *talked* their way into fame but Col House is the only man that ever just LISTENED HIMSELF IN,

After looking over Paris the troop went to London, Can you imagine how sore these Republicans got when they read about a Democrat sleeping in Buckingham Palace,

Kaiser and Czar used to kid King George and tell him he dident have any power   He can get back at them now and say "No I havent got much power but I am still *Kinging* aint I,"

Pres left London passed through Paris got an earfull from Col House and played a week of one Night stands through Italy,

He had a letter of recomendation from Caruso so he met some of the best people in Italy,

Every time the Pres wanted applause in his speeches in Italy he would mention GARIBALDI which sounds same in English as Italian,

Belgium wanted to book him there but the Pres got wise that they were holding so many Banquets they were trying to wear him out before the Peace Feast started,

King of Italy also the King of England have agreed with him up to now But unfortunately they neither one will be at the Peace signing,

England is orally in accord but there has been nothing signed,

They are a little late starting as they were waiting to find someone who knew what freedom of the Seas mean,

NOW IF HE CAN ONLY HANDLE THAT MEETING AS HE DOES CONGRESS WE NEED HAVE NO FEAR OF THE RESULT,

You know a lot of people think he is liable to be too easy with them   dont you believe it he can be pretty stern when he wants to   remember last fall when he sent Germany their

Questionaire, Said GIVE ME YOUR REAL NAME AND PERMANENT ADDRESS,

Lets hope the Turkish Deligation dont bring all their WIVES or we never will get *PEACE*,

And lets make those Russians shave before they sign up we want to know who we are dealing with,

If Ireland sends a deligation I can hear France say bring us back war,

Now the Pres says we are going to recognize the CZECHO SLOVAKS we may recognize them but we will never pronounce them,

That Nation has caused Readers more trouble than any other one in war,

They cant make the Peace terms much worse than those Armistace terms for they read like a 2nd mortgage, Party of the second part has no more chance than a Democrat in the next Congress,

We are handicapped at this meeting, England and France both have their Prime Ministers there while *BILLY SUNDAY* dident go for us,

Each Nation is supposed to share in the Peace terms according to what they have done in the war, Holland gets the KAISER, Mexico the CROWN PRINCE,

Now the Pres has to get back here before Mar 1st when the Country goes in into the hands of the Republicans or they are liable to want to charge him a tarriff to get in again,

OF COURSE WE DONT RECEIVE MUCH NEWS OF THE PEACE CONFERENCE. FIRST FEW WEEKS THEY ARE ALL JUST COMPLIMENTING EACH

OTHER. WAIT TILL THEY GO TO DIVIDE UP SOME-
THING. (What a truth that turned out to be)

Well by this time Congress was getting pretty rough so Pres
W grabbed his boat and commuted back home,

Said I think I will land in BOSTON the old Pilgrim Fathers
had pretty fair luck, and *nobody has ever landed there since*,

Germany couldent figure out how America could get troops
over there and get them trained so quick they dident know
that in our manual there is nothing about **RETREATING** and
when you only got to teach an Army to go one way you can do
it in half the time,

I feel pretty proud over that last little gag, As I used it be
fore Pres Wilson in Washington and he repeated it in his Boston speech, Saying "as one of our AMERICAN HUMORISTS
says," Up to then I had only been an ordinary Rope thrower,

Pretty tough when the Pres cops your act,

Pres had pretty good luck on that 1st trip they saw his 14
points and raised him ————————— more

Says in there, "There is to be no more wars" and then there
was a Paragraph a little further down told you where to get
your AMMUNITION in case there was one,

Now he come's back to Washington to explain the *LEAGUE
OF NATIONS* to Congress You know those guys cant read
anything and understand it,

But after eating out of 15 million dollar Gold Plates and
hobnobbing with Kings and Dukes can you imagine how Congress looked to him when he come back,

Had All the Senators up to dinner at White House Took
Ham Lewis three days to dress for it,

Not much news from the Dinner　*Burleson copped the Phones,*

On last day went up to Capitol to sign all the bills Congress had passed Well after he had signed the *bill,*

Then he went before Congress and balled out the WILFUL 37, he was busier than Mcadoo with a new train,

HE and Taft both spoke on same stage first time Pres and x-pres ever *agreed,*

I still wanted to go along but he said: "wait Will till some other trip and I will take you,"

You know *13* is his lucky number   if they dont sign this up on this trip he knows they will on his 13th trip,

You see Congress got sore cause he did not call them in extra session, You know the next Con, is *Republican,* Be a good joke on them if he dident call them at all wouldent it,

Back to Paris to meet Col House the only man the Pres ever listened too,

MR DANIELS went over. First time they have ever taken Josephus anywhere, He will be allright in a crowd,

Made Mr Hoover food DICTATOR for all the Allies That means that *BELG   FRANCE* and *ENG,* are not going to get any *more* to eat than we do,

Conference at 1st gave America Japan Italy France 5 deligates each and England including her Colonies fourteen, Thats all right to allow England for each one of her *Foreign Relations,* But they did not allow us a single one for *Wisconsin,*

How would you like to have been on a committee of Englishman *to inform Ireland they dident get any Deligates,* OH BOY,

Finally got it down to the big TEN now theres only FOUR, speaking to each other,

America dident know till they got over there that those European Nations have had a disease for years called the **Gimmes.**

England and Japan had a secret Treaty where England was to get everything south of the equator and Japan everything North,   Guess they were going to leave the equator for Ireland,

Japan wanted to put in the contract that she was as good as anybody else If she *admitted* it why put it in, If a man is a Gentleman he don't have a *sign* on him telling it,

'Tell Japan we will recognize them as soon as they recognize China,

Peace Table is turning out like all Banquets   the speeches are too long,

Everybody at the Table wants a second helping, And Germany the cook hasent got enough to go around,

They agreed on one of the 14 points that was that America went in for *nothing* and *expects nothing*   they are all UNANIMOUS WE GET IT,

Wanted to put the LEAGUE of nations in with Peace Treaty, thats like a fellow going into a store and the Merchant wont sell him a Suit unless he uses a Gillette Razor,

Its been a great thing for these Senators   if it had not been for this to *knock* they would not have gotten all these Lecture Dates,

The way a lot Of Senators talk you would think Pres W was going to trade America off for a couple of Golf Clubs,

They seem to think the Pres took the **Monroe Doctrine** in his pocket and is liable to lose it over there,

Pres Wilson threatened he would start the war over again, Be terrible if they found out this war was fixed and they had to fight it over again,

They cant let the Russians in this league or they would make a Bush League out of it,

Best time to have formed this League of Nations was during the war when all these Nations needed each other,

Everybody is for something to prevent War, but they are afraid it is like Prohibition it dont prohibit,

League of Nations just as clear as the Income Tax blanks,

One thing we got to be thankful for our Soldiers can win wars faster than our Diplomats can talk us into them,

Pres Wilson finally got discouraged at the stalling and told them that if they dident hurry up and do something the Americans would pick up their Wives and come home,

Pres says "JAMES BRING MY BOAT"

They then got busy and decided that Belgium could try the Kaiser,   Belgium said "how do we get him,"   Allies said "thats it if we could get him we would try him ourselves,"

Some Nations got so tired waiting for Peace they went back to fighting again,

Been working on this League of Nations all winter,   Finally one of the deligates said "What about Peace with Germany"   The others all said "thats right   we never thought of that,"

Went to call in Germany and they said "Why we had give you all up thought you wasent coming,   We got a better offer from the Bolsheveki"

They offer us no indemnities and no Baths,

If they ever have another war lets have it understood before they start what each Nation wants at the finish,

All those Nations claim they were fighting for freedom, But of course a little more land would make a little more Freedom,

One thing about this League, The last war there were only 10 to 15 nations in it   now if they all sign this they can all be in the next one,   It wont be near so exclusive,

Course its hard to please everybody Taft tried that,

If Pres Wilson had any doubts about this League of Nations being put through he should have taken some of these Prohibitionist. They would have shown him how to get it through whether people wanted it or not,

France says they would have more confidence in this League if they would slip a couple of Nations in between them and Germany,

I WONDER IF WE QUIT FIGHTING TOO QUICK AND DIDENT SIGN PEACE QUICK ENOUGH,

Dont get impatient. It has been just this hard at the end of every war to try and prevent another one,

Pres on his last voyage home said the Monroe Doctrine was fully protected already   And to show them that it was, He has now put it in,

The Monroe thing the Republicans talk so much of and know so little about, Protects us again everything but VILLA.

And in the whole History of America he is the only *Nation* that ever attacked us,

Italy says they will pick up their Marbles and go home

Pres Wilson says you may Fiume, But you will never get it,

Today is Japans day to threaten to pack their kimonas and leave,

Italy bases her claim on an old treaty, She cant afford to trace her Treatys back too far,   *If I remember she originally was signed up with Germany*,

Pres Wilson certainly used good judgement in visiting Italy when he first went over,

Sectry BAKER has gone back over to France again   think old Newt, kinder likes PARIS,

They wanted Mcadoo to go but the salary wasent right,

Can you imagine a guy that couldent make a living out of all the jobs he held, I would love to have just half what one Republican would have made out of all that,

Lot of Reps dont want this League Gag to pass they are jealous cause the Democrats ran the last war, And they want to have another one to show how much better they could run one than the Democrats,

Even the Big 4 seem to be losing confidence,   They have removed the words High Contracting Parties, which appeared 418 times in the original and now speak of it meekly as members of the League,

We know Pres Wilson had a lot to do with drafting it, Cause it has so many WORDS

Now it will take longer to explain it than it did to write it,

If Mr Lodge and Mr Lowell debate on these new amendments Boston has applied for a change of Venue,

Only debate ever held where both men agreed,

Pres is up to his old tricks has sent a NOTE to Italy,

His appeal to the Italian People caused as much of a furore as the one to the voters last fall,

Italy says they know Fiume was not in their secret treaty with other Allies   But its a nice town and they hate to see it fall into bad hands,

Get all those Nations sore enough to start telling the truth about each other, We will hear something,

Italy claims Fiume because there is more Italians there than anybody else,   according to that Look whod get NEW YORK

Japans claims are sorter novel   "They want pay for capturing part of China one of our own Allies"

They have offered to protect Siberia if they have to stay there forever to do it,

If Japan gets all her claims China will pay more indemnities than Germany who lost the war,

Imagine Japan, Pres Wilson, and Italy, All talking at once, Good thing they cant understand each other or this Conference would never have lasted this long,

AND THEY CALL THAT A PEACE CONFERENCE,

Guess those CZECHO POLOKS have gotten their freedom, I see where they are at *war*.

Wish I could find a man who had read this LEAGUE OF

NATIONS, And could tell which was the *Assembly* and which was the *Council*,

Thats a good clause in there "where any Allied Nation must give three months notice before it jumps onto any other Allied Nation,"

Now the Women want to send Deligates, They forget this is a Peace Conference,

See where the German Deligates to the Peace Table brought their Golf Clubs   We can see now how Admiral Graysons Pupil stacks up against opposition,

See where Pres Wilson and Italy have compromised on that town down there   *Italy got it*,

Its kinder new wrinkle in Diplomacy, The Slovaks can play with it four years till they begin to like it, And then they take it away from them,

AS I UNDERSTAND IT ITALY IS TO HAVE IT TUESDAYS AND SATURDAYS,

But they are going to build those other People (*with that terrible name*)   A little young town just as much like this one as they can, down the river aways

Guess the reason they put a four year limit on it, Was that they figured that would about cover the existence of any of those new Nations,

The Idea over there now seems to be lets get something ready to sign up, Whether its any good or not,

See where Pres Wilson and Japan *compromised* on that CHOW CHOW PLACE   JAPAN GETS IT,

I dont know how much money Indemnity Japan will demand from China,

You know CHINA *has one of the best* JAPANESE *Armies in the World*,

See where Pres Wilson and England compromised on Freedom of the Seas   England got it,

Italy left the Conference and got what she wanted, Japan threatened to leave and got what she wanted,   If Pres Wilson had left some Republican Senators would have gotten what they wanted,

Seems several Nations were like Jesse Willard *they wanted to know what they were to get before they entered the Arena*,

Well they finally handed Germany the Peace terms   80 thousand words   only thing ever written longer than a Lafollette Speech

HAD TO BE THAT LONG TO TELL THE GERMANS WHAT THEY THOUGHT OF THEM

Imagine what a document for Lawers to pick flaws in,

Could have settled the whole thing in one sentence, "IF YOU BIRDS START ANYTHING AGAIN WE WILL GIVE YOU THE OTHER BARREL,"

RUSSIA cant get in on this Peace   There is not enough Paper in the World to print 80 thousand Russian words on,

If they want to get even with Germany they ought to let them keep their Cables And appoint Burleson to run them

I thought the Armistace terms read like a second Mortgage, But this reads like a FORECLOSURE,

If Germany ever wants to go to war again she will have to fight with *BEER STEINS*

If Germany stops to read those 80 thousand words before

they sign them, We needent expect Peace to be signed for years yet,

Now Folks with all this kidding and foolishness aside, for I just say in here whatever I think anybody might laugh at, But of course my real sentiments are the same as everybody else, anything to prevent war   If He puts this thing through and there is no more wars, His address will be WHITE HOUSE WASHINGTON D C till his whiskers are as long as the Peace Treaty   If it should be a Fliv, (which it wont) Why then a letter would reach him at ALABI NEW JERSEY. So all Credit to Pres Wilson it took some game Guy to go through with it.

THE COWBOY PHILOSOPHER ON PROHIBITION

The crusade for Prohibition was one of Rogers' favorite subjects at the *Follies*. The movement to outlaw the manufacture, sale, and transportation of intoxicating beverages through a constitutional amendment started with the formation of the Woman's Christian Temperance Union in 1874 and continued with the Anti-Saloon League in 1895. Anglo-Protestant reformers feared that the new wave of Catholic and Jewish immigrants from southern and eastern Europe undermined traditional American values. They viewed drinking as a source of social evil and the saloon as the center of urban political machines. The crusaders saw Prohibition as a tool to clean up corruption, control crime and the liquor trade, and improve working conditions.

At the time Rogers joined the *Frolic* in 1915, fifteen states had enacted their own Prohibition laws, and in 1917 Congress approved the Eighteenth Amendment authorizing federal Prohibition. The ratification struggle made daily headlines, and Rogers often joked about the debate in his monologue. By 1919 enough states had approved the amendment, and that year Congress passed the Volstead Act to enforce Prohibition. But the law proved unenforceable and generated widespread violations and crimes, ranging from home-made distilleries and illegal speakeasies to bootlegging and gang violence. The amendment was repealed finally in 1933.

Rogers believed that the so-called "noble experiment" to regulate drinking was a preposterous joke and an invasion of government into people's lives. The law, he felt, was hypocritical and instead of improving society increased crime and corruption. He regularly kidded the moral reformers and the drys, feeling that Prohibition was a huge folly.

His wry, tongue-in-cheek comments in his stage act and notes were published in his second book, *Rogers-isms: The Cowboy Philosopher on Prohibition* (1919). "You won't find the Country any drier than this Book," the author wrote on the cover. The book is a witty exposé and satire of a unique period in American history.

Rogers-isms: The Cowboy Philosopher on Prohibition (New York: Harper & Brothers, 1919).

THE 14 POINTS OF THE PREAMBLE

ALL high class Literary Lizzards when they start assembling a book have some fellow that is better known than they are to dash off a kind of an introduction,   Well I was afraid if I had someone do that they would just be liable to say something funny And out side of the book being SHORT the one thing I guarantee it to be free from is humor, I dont want anybody spoiling the Book with some Komical remarks,

Besides I carry my own introductions with me, For I figure that no man can give you as good a boost as you can give yourself,

I would not have written this Book but My Publishers (get that, my Publishers) Harper and Brothers, (by mentioning their name they wont cut this out) Big firms love advertising just as much as us little punks do,

My Publishers asked me to write another Book as they had a sale on the last one, (Which was called Will Rogers on the Peace Conference) Dont hurt to slip in a little Add for yourself once in awhile Especially when it is done in a clever way like this and dont look like one,

They said write another book as we have traced the sale of the last one, And the fellow who bought it has a friend in the same institution, And we feel sure we can double the sale of your last book with this one,

In tracing this sale they found the party who bought the book was the same one who voted annually for Bryan, And his friend who we hope to land as a prospective purchaser, Holds the proud distinction of being the only man in the United States who found no fault with Burleson,

I said to them what will I write about, And they said by all means pick out a subject that is different, Something that nobody else has written on, Get something where you have no

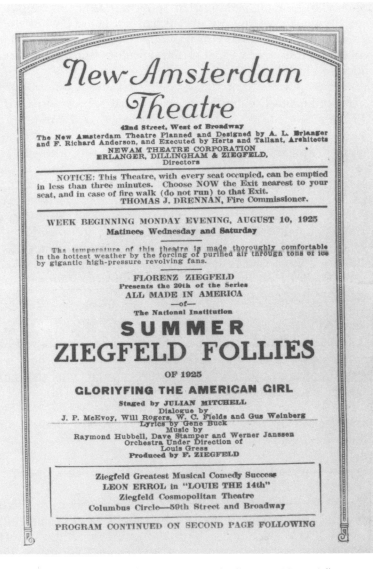

New Amsterdam Theatre

42nd Street, West of Broadway

The New Amsterdam Theatre Planned and Designed by A. L. Erlanger and F. Richard Anderson, and Executed by Herts and Tallant, Architects

NEWAM THEATRE CORPORATION
ERLANGER, DILLINGHAM & ZIEGFELD,
Directors

NOTICE: This Theatre, with every seat occupied, can be emptied in less than three minutes. Choose NOW the Exit nearest to your seat, and in case of fire walk (do not run) to that Exit.
THOMAS J. DRENNAN, Fire Commissioner.

WEEK BEGINNING MONDAY EVENING, AUGUST 10, 1925
Matinees Wednesday and Saturday

The temperature of this theatre is made thoroughly comfortable in the hottest weather by the forcing of purified air through tons of ice by gigantic high-pressure revolving fans.

FLORENZ ZIEGFELD
Presents the 20th of the Series
ALL MADE IN AMERICA
—of—
The National Institution

SUMMER
ZIEGFELD FOLLIES

OF 1925

GLORIYFING THE AMERICAN GIRL

Staged by JULIAN MITCHELL
Dialogue by
J. P. McEvoy, Will Rogers, W. C. Fields and Gus Weinberg
Lyrics by Gene Buck
Music by
Raymond Hubbell, Dave Stamper and Werner Janssen
Orchestra Under Direction of
Louis Gress
Produced by F. ZIEGFELD

Ziegfeld Greatest Musical Comedy Success
LEON ERROL in "LOUIE THE 14th"
Ziegfeld Cosmopolitan Theatre
Columbus Circle—59th Street and Broadway

PROGRAM CONTINUED ON SECOND PAGE FOLLOWING

Summer *Follies of 1925* program. (Will Rogers Memorial)

opposition, Well I started to thinking, then one night it came to me, I give you my word I had not heard a word about it, neither had I read anything in any papers about it, I dont know myself how I happened to think of it, But I got right up and wired my Publishers

"Have-hit-on-just-the-thing,-an-original-subject,-PROHI-BITION"

Aint it wonderful how I just happened to hit on this out of the way subject, and Title, Of course a writer must not let his Title interfere with what he is writing about, Look at that Spaniard he wrote a Book called the "Four Horse men of the Apothecary" I read it plum through and there wasent a thing about Horses or Drug Stores or anybody riding, In fact there is no town or Country on the map where these four fellows are supposed to come from, Then he has another book called Blood and Sand and its all about Horses and Cattle,

Now the Title of this little Gem of Free Thought is PRO-HIBITION But I will be like the Spaniard, The more I can keep my readers away from the Title, And keep them just on the opposite from the Title (about 95 proof) why the more chance I got getting away with it,

I want also to regretfully announce that this Book is not subsidized by any Liquor Concern,

You wont find the Country any drier than this Book,

All Stage rights of material in this Book reserved for Senators and Congressmen to tell at Chautauquas as original,

Want to thank Proffessor Lowell of Harvard for the English Translation

Want also to thank the Writers of the Old and new Testament for furnishing facts for some of my strongest Arguments against Prohibition,

PROHIBITION

NOW before I start in I want it distinctly understood I dont knock Prohibition through any personal grudge as I do not drink myself, But I do love to play to an audience who have had a few nips, just enough so they can see the joke and still sober enough to applaud it,

You all who have had no experience have no Idea of the difference, the Prohibitionists just seem to be sore on the World,

How they got the thing through, Senators and Congressmen were all in Washington waiting for the next pay day, When one member come in and says lets vote on Prohibition, The others all said, Why we cant vote on Prohibition our people back home dident tell us to come here and vote Prohibition, The old desciple of Bryan democracy that had proposed it says No I know they dident tell us to vote on it but its a good day and I just feel like voting on something,

So they sent around to all the various Bars in Washington and collected a quorum and voted everybody dry,

They did not know when they were doing it that they were killing off the thing that a Senator or Congressman holds dearer than anything in the World And that is an Audience in the Galleries in Washington, For no one ever goes to hear them any more, In fact no man living can sit in the Gallery and listen to them without a certain amount of Liquor in him,

They dident want to vote dry but they were so afraid of the way the Political Breeze seemed to be headed at the time, Never figuring it might change,

There is an old Legend that years ago there was a man elected to Washington *who* voted according to his own conscience,

Congressmens short sightedness is what put it through, then Bryan modestly claimed the credit,

They claim it was necessary to put it through as a war measure, how about this? Now France fought quite a bit in the war and trained on Wine, England did her part on Scotch and Polly and Ale,   Canadian Club furnished its Quota from Canada, Italy Chiantied over the Alps into Austria,   Womens clothes and Scotch Whiskey dident keep the Highlanders back much Guinnesses Stout kept the Irish fighting as usual, The American Troops dident retreat any further than you can run your hand in a **Paper Bag,** And they had been used to old Crow and Kentucky Bourbon,   Russia was doing fine till some nut took their Vodka away from them and thay went back to look for it and nobody has ever heard of them since, Germany the Country with the smallest percentage of Alcahol in their National drink (which is beer) and Turkey who are totally prohibition,—why they lose the war,

Looks to me like if Germany and Turkey ever wanted to win a war they better start drinking a MANS SIZE DRINK,

Now a Prohibitionist is a man or woman, Who is so self satisfied with himself that he presents himself with a Medal, called the "CROIX DE PERFECT HE"

He gives himself this Medal because he is now going to start to meddle in everybodys business but his own,

Look at these Towns and people after Prohibition has hit them, Everybody looks like they had just had a puncture and no extra tire,

Streets that used to be lighted up at nights and thousands of people on them are now used for robbing purposes only,

If you drop into a Café after the Theater in a Prohibition town, They will wake up the Night watchman to cook you something,

Watch a crowd clustered around a couple of water pitchers in the center of the Table, They look like they had just heard the Kaiser had invaded Belgium again,

It will take some men two years solid rehersing to learn how to order a soft drink without blushing,

I knew one man in a dry town when he took his first Grape Juice high ball; it took three Doctors to revive him,

Somebody ought to get out a book "**How to learn to drink soft drinks in 20 lessons,**"

Soda Fountains will all have to go to the extra expense now of putting in a foot rail,

There will be people among the coming generation that can name 12 different Phosphates that couldent name 2 Presidents,

The first six ice cream sodas served to six pinockle players mean six more Bolshevikis,

One good thing in favor of the soda squirt bartender, His trade dont start coming in as early in the morning as the old hard stuff ones did,

The new ice cream dipper hound at the fountain will have another advantage over the old bartender, he wont have to listen to the same story over and over again,

If prohibition will just stop some men trying to repeat stories they have heard, It will not have been in vain,

Once they claim a fellow repeated a story he had heard and got it right, but this has never been verified,

If they will bring the ice cream into the drug stores in kegs instead of tins, They will make a lot of men seem more at home,

They will soon be listing Jamaica Ginger stock on the exchange,

They are trading Bethleham steel shares now for Peruna stock and paying the difference,

When a man drives up to a Gasoline filling station he will say, Give me 10 gallons in the tank and fill up this pint bottle,

The worst crime a child at home can commit now is to eat up the raisins that Dad brought home for fermenting purposes,

If I was California I would not claim the credit for making the wine they are serving nowadays,

Just look at the industries that will be put out of business, Getting bit by a snake will be a lost art,

You know no man is going to let a snake bite him after Liquor goes out,

Then there is the woman who used to faint and Brandy seemed to be the only thing that would revive her, now she will have to struggle along without fainting,

But the saddest case of all will be the loss of the Kentucky Colonel industry (They received their title through owning the widest brimmed black hat and having the largest Bourbon capacity of any man in the county Sah,)

When they go to dig up his Mint bed, He will say just dig it a little deeper and I will get in myself, we are both nonessentials,

---

Of course on the other hand it has introduced a lot of new methods especially in regard to getting it in to dry territory, There are people who if they put in half the time studying on some mechanical invention that they do how to smuggle in booze, Why they would be as great as Edison,

They put it in extra tires and even in the ones they were running on, One day a fellow had a couple of blow outs on the way into Oklahoma and lost all the profits,

But there is really only one successful way to bring it into dry territory and after all it is the most satisfactory, You drink it just before you get to the state line, in this way you are allowed to bring in all you can carry,

I saw a box of Armours Meat drop off an express wagon and broke every bottle,

Prohibition has done some very good things in the road building line, It has been the cause of more road improvement between dry and wet towns than any other thing,

If you want good roads leading out of your town vote it wet and the surrounding towns will fix up your roads,

Bad roads have broke more bottles of booze than the authorities,

The Prohibitionists put the bill through as a food saving device, And it has certainly been a success, Its made food so high people cant eat it,

The poorer people will have to go to Europe this summer to escape the high prices over here,

It looks like we would have to have another war for things to get cheap like they used to be during the last one,

And they still allow these Prohibitionists to eat, You know a drinking man he dont eat much and the more he drinks the less he eats but these Prohibitionists they just naturally ruin a meal,

Prohibitionists dispose of enough food just before speaking engagements to feed all the starving Armenians in the world,

The amount of time and energy consumed by Prohibitionists in speaking if put to a legitimate business would cut everybodys average work day down to 4 hours,

But the minute they get Prohibition they will hop on to something else it will be Cigarettes or room and bath, or something

See where they propose to stop Cigarettes first and then profanity,　They are going to have a tough time with that profanity, cause as long as there is a prohibitionist living there will be profanity, !ZR-Z*??ZIZ,!R-R-R-Z!!!

You have seen millions and millions of dollars worth of Liberty Bonds sold in Cafes where everybody is drinking and jolly, Did you ever see any sold in an Ice cream Parlor,

The government said a man in Uniform couldent get a drink, Guess the government figured that the ones who dident have the nerve to go needed the liquor worse than the soldiers did,

Headlines in papers last year said **"Government stopped Brewries making beer"**　The brewries had stopped making BEER years ago of their own accord,

On account of the bartenders diluting the drinks people were ready for prohibition before they knew it,

If they stall off Prohibition from July to january some bars will have to get another bottle of booze,

Mighty good thing we have had a nice warm winter this year or people would not have had any room in their Cellars for their coal,

Next winter there will be husbands tending to furnaces that never knew where they were before,

What is life without a cellar

If a residence gets on fire nowadays the fireman dont run to save the children or the valuables but to the cellar to save the booze,

There has been more underground building in the last year than there has been on top,

Prohibition has been a big saving for a lot of fellows. Where they used to have to go to the corner, now they only have to go down stairs,

If you ever see this add in the papers they would have to call out all the police reserves to keep back the applicants, "FOR SALE ONE HOUSE FULLY STOCKED,"

Bout the only thing left for a poor man that cant afford his own house with a cellar is to move to a Republic,

Personally I think the saloon men put this prohibition through as they have sold more in the last year than in any ten previous years before,

Every time the Government would put on an extra tax the liquor people would put two extra on for themselves,

Industries that switched to making ammunition during the war are now trying to see if they cant manufacture some drink called NO KICKO, or PRETTY NEAR O,

Everybody wonders what to do with the Kaiser, I think he should be brought over here and made to sample every soft drink made,

Maine and Kansas were the first Prohibition states, now look at them,

Maine was noted for two things, one was drinking awful whiskey and the other was shooting another hunter,

Will Rogers
measures the length
of his rope.
(White Studio
photo, Will Rogers
Memorial)

If it had not been for the hunting season in Maine and the early deaths from bad whiskey, Maine would have had a population now almost equal to Rhode Island,

The principal industry of Kansas was bootlegging,

The only way you could tell a **Citizen** from a **Bootlegger** in Kansas was the **Bootlegger** would be sober,

"There was so many bl nd P gs n Kansas for years that the Nat ve hog of that State today s born w thout eyes,"

The Booze they sold was so strong they had to dilute it with Alcahol,

Light Wines and Beers were as little known there, as Bevo is in a wet state,

Champaigne was as rare as a bathtub,

The liquor was made from corn without either shucking or shelling it,

This high explosive they used in the war called T N T, was originally Bootleg Whisky,

If a Bootlegger finds his supply running low he adds a hand full of Giant Powder and a few bottles of red ink and serves,

If a state ever once goes dry it will stay, as there is enough Whisky peddlers to keep it voted that way,

Imagine voting the Nation dry when the Allies owe all their success now to Haig and the Tanks,

They say the Tanks over there would go through anything, Well we have Tanks over here that have gone through all they ever had,

Convict in Toronto Canada waiting to be hung gave his guard some coffee, had a powder in it that put him to sleep and the fellow escaped, prohibitionists now use that against coffee drinking habit,

I just want to sight a case what a wrong prohibition coming into a country will do and the pleasures and amusements it will knock people out of seeing, I got a friend Bill Rice runs a Carnival Company had the first one of these diving girl shows, Well he went to a little town in Arizona to play and got all ready, dug the hole and put his tank in and was all ready for the water when they told him why there wasent that much water in the whole county, and was just about to crab the show when an old saloon man said he could fill it up with CORN WHISKY, it would look like water, so they did and that afternoon when the act went on Bill himself was the first out on the diving board, nobody up to then knew Bill could dive but he sho did, and went off that board mighty pretty but dident come up so they all waited and finally ran to the edge and looked over and there lay Bill high and dry on the bottom just sucking up the last that was in the tank, Now those people away out there if prohibition had been in would have been denied that exhibition, and diving was an awful big novelty to them, and it also taught Bill a lesson, If he ever went back to Arizona again to get a bigger tank,

Did you know that a prohibitionist could be arrested for treason, Treason means anything that gives annoyance to your own people thereby giving aid to the enemy,

Outside of profiteers I cant think of anything that has given more annoyance,

Prohibitionists are the originators of Camouflage, They made drinking look worse than it is,

The minute prohibition goes in, I can see Cincinnati ceceeding from the Union

Ohio was voted wet by the people and dry by their missrepresentatives,

She was supposed to go dry a month ahead of the National ammendment   She did that so it would give them a month to reherse in,

Pretty tough on the Columbus Ohio saloon men they have to close just when that big Methodist Conference meets there,

The minute Prohibition went in my friend Luke Mcgluke claimed exemption,

Billy Sunday (by the way I wonder what ever become of him) said when we get prohibition that there wont be any more jails,   Kansas and Maine have more in them than out,

Another thing it wouldent be right by those jailers to throw them out of a job, those prohibitionists never have any regard for the other people   Just think of it the minute we get prohibition hundreds and hundreds of jailers and guards are thrown out of work,

Of course the only way we have to prove anything is by the Bible,   I find Genesis 9th Chapter 20 verse, "Noah began to be an Husbandman and planted a vineyard,"

The minute he got to be a husband he started in right away to raise the necessary ingredients to make what goez with married life,

Now Californians followed Noahs example, But fortunately in Noahs time there was no one to tell him he couldent have a vineyard,

Why dont they pick on the Marrying thats in the same verse, why single out the poor old vineyard

Next Verse "And he drank of the wine and was drunken and was within his tent"

Now here is what shows the prohibitionist up so bad, for Noah was a chosen man, If the lord dident punish him where do they come in to tell somebody what to do,

The prohibitionists *rave* about water,   Now Noah knew more about water than all of them put togeather, He was the **WATER COMMISSIONER** of his time,   He was an expert on water and the first man smart enough *not* to drink it,

He was the first one to discover a use for it, that was to float a boat on, But as a beverage he knew it was a total failure,

Now everything happens for the best through Noah partaking of too much wine, and going on this little spree is why the lord picked him to gather these Animals into the Ark,   He was the only one who had ever seen them,

You see if Noah had not drank we would today perhaps be without menageries,

Other men of later generations have claimed that they have seen animals that Noah dident take on the ark, But perhaps their Vineyards too were of a different variety,

Noah was told to collect two of every variety of animal and take them on board   I defy any man to show me where he took a prohibitionist and his mate aboard,

The only thing we can liken in this day to the ark was the first commuting trip of the George Washington,   There was two of every kind of peace deligate with the exception of the Republican, there was only one of that specie, as there seemed to be at that time no especial desire on the part of the organizers of the expedition to populate the earth in the future with that kind of animal, As they propagate very fast,

It is not even recorded in the history of the conference that they even landed there with this lone specimen, As theres been no mention made of him whatever,

In the next verse we find "Ham saw his father and told his bretheren"

There was the foundation of the first prohibitionist, butting in where he had no business,

He made such a bad job out of it thats why all bad actors are called hams.

In the next verse Noah awakes, puts a curse on Hams son Cannan, "and told him a servant of servants shall ye be"

Little did Noah think when he told him he would be a servant that some day servants would rule the house as they do today,

This wine had such ill effects on Noahs health that it was all he could do to live 950 years,

Just 19 years short of Methusalah who held the long distance age record of his and all time,

Show me a total abstainer that ever lived that long,

And on the 40th day Noah sent out a dove and unlike Bryans, Noahs came back,

Now later on in the **14** chapter when Abram was returning from victorious battle it says Melchizedek king of salem met them with bread and wine,

What did we meet our victorious troops with Huylers Chocolate and spearmint chewing gum,

Also, shows that no matter what a long name a king may have there is some good in him,

What did Moses say when he took all the philistines up on top of the mountain   He said "Corinthians what will you have"

And Rebecca with the pitcher who was it told her "fillem up again"

You only hear wine spoken of in there and that is as it should be now, Light wines and Beers, that was what they had in Biblical days and that is what President Wilson says we should have, do away with the Hard Stuff, Also, can the saloons,

They used to say, drive the saloons out of politics, Why not go further and drive politics out of Congress,

I agree with the prohibitionists about doing away with Saloons and Whisky, But let people who want to, buy beer and light wines and take it to their homes and have it when they like,

If they would make all these fat saloon owners go to work, that would solve the labor question,

Doing away with saloons will certainly crab the diamond stud and ring industry, as about all other male species has gotten wise and quit wearing them,

President Wilson in his last note to the Americans said: Keep light wines and beers,

Many a politician now wishes he had had the nerve to have said the same thing,

Now are you going to follow Bryans advice or Pres Wilsons,   I will string along with the one who has done something,

Simply take their two batting average, Pres Wilson has been right a lot of times   But W J has yet to guess his first winner,

President says give us light wines and beers, if they can get beer any lighter than it is they will have to get a prop to hold it up,

Have to turn your glass upside down now to keep it from flying away,

After drinking a bottle of this weak beer you have to take a glass of water as a stimulant,

That is what they fill these dirigible baloons with now, its lighter than air,

You cant drink enough to get drunk on, But you can drink enough to fly,

That peculiar taste that beer has nowadays is the aniline dye they use to make it look like beer,

A bartenders apology goes with every bottle,

The only thing heavy about wine is the price,

There is a reward offered for a waiter that can make a cork pop like it used to,

Michigan has the natural ingredients of one of the best jags in the world, Take a bottle of any near beer and pour it over a bowl of grape nuts (michigans second commodity) eat this hurriedly then take a five mile ride over one of their roads in a Ford and you have as good results as any souse would want,

They talk of shipping it in dry territory in coffins, Why my state of Okla, did that years ago, the way they got on to them was, There had been more bodies shipped to this town than the combined population of the whole state, One man got rich breaking up the coffins and selling the lumber as a byproduct,

Now the bootleggers use aeroplanes to bring it in, The town marshal of my home Claremore Okla is rated as the leading Ace, he has brought down over 3000 quarts,

You dont have to go any farther than our best ancient writers to prove that prohibition was unnecessary, look at old OMAR KHAYHAM "The Pickled Philosopher of Persia" do you think Billy Sundays SLANG will live as long as Omars Philosophy has,

In that verse something about "a loaf of bread a jug of Wine and Thou," Look how they have jagged those three things up on him, Bread,——they voted wheat so high nobody can eat bread, Wine will soon be gone and the wine they have got, if it had ever been handed to Omar I would hate to have read his book, Thou——I guess he meant a woman, Well she has the vote and she aint the same thou any more,

He says he divorced old Barren reason and took the daughter of the Vine to spouse, Have you ever heard a dry say anything that smart,

I am against Divorces but there was a good legitimate reason and the first divorce case in history,

Not only Omar but all the great men of the past had something on their hip all the time, Caesar carried a canteen of Chianti that would make an Italian Restaurant proprietor envious, Shakespear, history says, when writing always had two bottles in front of him, now you know there was only one of them had Ink in it. He is the originator of the line "Bring on another Flagon of Ale,"

History says Nero fiddled while Rome burned, Now any man has got to drink to fiddle, and whoever listens to him fiddle has to drink more,

I have visited Washingtons old home at Mount Vernon, There are glasses in a case there that were never meant to drink water out of, Have a grape orchard there and I know they dident eat that many raisins, a basement down stairs and there were no furnaces in those days, What was in it?

The New York Times gave a prize for the best editorial on the war   guess you would think some Teetotalar got it. WELL if Marse Henry Waterson is a total abstainer Mcadoo is a good railroad man,

The Romans were the first people to discover after Noah any other reason for water, they put it in those beautiful Roman Baths then built marble slabs to lay on and watch it, You never saw a picture of a Roman in the water in your life,

Look at the mince pie, goodbye to it, We dident kick what all they put in it (and they put everything but mince) but when the old brandy is shy why so long pie,

Speaking of prohibition we played in Baltimore which was wet the week the armistice was signed, Washington was dry, Well Baltimore had such a big celebration and run so short of stuff that they had to send over to Washington for some more,

I had a friend who wanted a drink awful bad when we were in Washington but he couldent borrow a uniform from anybody,

The janitor who cleans up the Senators and Congressmens rooms at the Capitol pays a big price just for the empty bottle privilege,

The foreign Embassys are supposed to be the only wet spots,   If I was a drinking man I would stop at the Oklahoma Embassy while there,

Big interests used to maintain a lobby with plenty of money there, Now they maintain a bar and get the same results,

Now you often hear a Wall Street man say "It cost me 6 quarts and over 100 cocktails to get that bill through,"

Now Congress says the women can vote,   They use to could drink and not vote now they can vote and not drink,

Ziegfeld Follies playbill from 1925. (Will Rogers Memorial)

It will take them, just as long to make up their minds who to vote for as it did to tell what to order to drink,

Most of them will vote for some guy named Martini just through force of habit,

If those women think they are going to get as much of a thrill around a voting booth; as they did around the old Punch Bowl they are going to be fooled,

Thats why the Anti Suffs fought it so hard They knew that the old cocktail served in a teacup at the afternoon tea, carried more real authority than all the primaries ever held,

Prohibition takes all the joy out of voting, Who wants to vote if theres no place to stop on the way home, Besides one has to be about half drunk to vote for most of the candidates they run nowadays,

If some politicians wait for the sober vote to elect them they are sunk,

At first its going to feel kinder embarrassing to sell your vote while you are sober,

If they add the cost of the drinks a man used to have to buy while dickering for your vote to the price of the vote, It ought to bring a fellow more real money now than it did,

Votes will be higher as men wont be able to sell them as often as they used to,

In the old days if you could keep the politician who was buying, drinking with you, You could sometimes sell several times to him alone,

And its going to make an awful difference in counting them, More men have lost office through bad counting than through bad political policies,

A man with nothing on his hip but a patch aint liable to mistake one hundred for one thousand,

And if he is sober he aint near as liable to be asked to make said mistake,

A quart of old crow in the counting room at night has put more men in office than voters ever did,

If a man had to drink for every vote that has been torn up, or missplaced he wouldent have to worry about prohibition coming,

They lay all the divorces on to liquor, When its only bad judgement in picking em,

Some men have to drink to live with a woman some women have to drink to live with a man, most generally though they both have to drink to live with each other,

The drys as usual have it just wrong,   It wont stop divorces it will stop marriages,

A couple sitting opposite at a table dont look near so good to each other over a water decanter as they do over two just emptied Champaign glasses,

Instead of weddings being jolly parties, From now on they are going to be as they should, very solemn affairs,

The old fashioned Justice or Minister that used to be woke up at three in the A M by a couple coming from some gay party wanting to get married, will have to look for some other occupation now,

If it will only cause better food and shorter speeches at banquets it will make up for all the bad it does,

And Poetry, they claim liquor is responsible for most all the poetry, and I believe it for it sounded like it,

See we have Russian Boomb throwing, if we have to take it to get that other Russian evil prohibition why I am in favor of giving them both back,

These secret societies will be harder hit by it than anybody, As what they are taking away was their secret,

These reformers are always wanting to save you and if it wasent for them people wouldent need saving,

They cant lay Bolshevism on to booze, As at the late prices none of them could afford to buy it,

If you saw a man drunk in the old days it was a sign of no will power, But if you see one drunk now its a sure sign of wealth,

Somebody asked an old cattleman down home where I live if he was going to buy an Automobile (he was only worth a couple of hundred thousand)   He said "No I aint, there are men in this county now who own automobiles that havent got a pint of whiskey in their house,"

Why not settle this Prohibition Fifty-Fifty,   Let the Prohibitionists quit drinking,

Any time a dry is up talking just mention one word and he is through, — Russia,

If Pres Wilson wanted to get this League of Nations through he should have taken some Prohibitionists with him they would have showed him how to get it through whether the people wanted it or not,

Some bird named Sheppard put this bill through congress, Leave it to a Texas Sheep herder to crab it,

Turkey is the only other prohibition country in the world, If we enjoyed some of their other privaleges it wouldent be so bad,

Somebody figured out now that we can have 2 and three quarter percent beer, But who wants to drink 37 and a half bottles to be 100 percent drunk,

Well I will jarr loose now, that is about enough of this nonsense, I want to apologize to the drys and say that maby I will write another one on their side and have better arguments, I dont drink and it dont make any difference to me which side I am on,

I get paid for getting laughs and I found out that the majority of the people would laugh more if I kidded the drys,

BUT LOTS OF PEOPLE LAUGH ONE WAY AND VOTE THE OTHER.

LOOK AT CONGRESS IT VOTED DRY AND DRINKS WET.

SCENE 5

ROASTING THE NATION'S CHIEF EXECUTIVES

Both on the stage and in his writing Rogers roasted the leading politicians of his time. By pretending to be an unbiased observer of the political scene, neither a Republican or Democrat, Rogers could lampoon members of both parties. He discovered that he could even poke fun at the nation's leading executives. In May 1916 Will appeared in a Friars Club revue in Baltimore, and seated in a box was President Woodrow Wilson. The president laughed at his quips about preparedness, William Jennings Bryan, and the presence of American troops in Mexico. The event gave the humorist confidence to take on any subject. Rogers recalled this memorable evening when he wrote the following tribute to Wilson at the time of his death in February 1924.

WILSON COULD LAUGH AT A JOKE ON HIMSELF

SOME of the most glowing and deserved tributes ever paid to the memory of an American have been paid in the last few days to our past President Woodrow Wilson. They have been paid by learned men of this and all Nations, who knew what to say and how to express their feelings. They spoke of their close association and personal contact with him. Now I want to add my little mite, even though it be of no importance.

I want to speak and tell of him as I knew him, for he was my friend. We of the stage know that our audiences are our best friends, and he was the greatest Audience of any Public Man we ever had. I want to tell of him as I knew him across the footlights. A great many Actors and Professional people have appeared before him, on various occasions, in wonderful high-class endeavors. But I don't think that any person met him across the footlights in exactly the personal way that I did on five different occasions.

Every other Performer or Actor did before him exactly what

"Wilson Could Laugh at a Joke on Himself," New York Times, 17 February 1924, sec. 8, p. 2.

Will Rogers gained fame when he performed before President Woodrow Wilson in the *Friars' Frolic* in Baltimore, May 1916. *Standing, left to right,* Andrew Mack, Neil O'Brien, James J. Corbett, Harry Kelly, Felix Adler, Harlan Dixon, George Daugherty, Vaughn Comfort, Johnny King, Tom Dingle, Eddie Garvey, Julius Tannen, George Sidney, Tommy Gray, Bert Levy; *seated, left to right,* Max Figman, Laddie Cliff, Will Rogers, Sam Harris, Jerry J. Cohan, Louis Mann, Fred Niblo, George M. Cohan, Lew Dockstader, Frank Tinney. (Will Rogers Memorial)

they had done before other audiences on the night previous. But I gave a great deal of time and thought to an Act for him, most of which would never be used again and had never been used before. Owing to the style of Act I used, my stuff depended a great deal on what had happened that particular day or week. It just seemed by an odd chance for me every time I played before President Wilson that on that particular day there had been something of great importance that he had just been dealing with. For you must remember that each day was a day of great stress with him. He had no easy days. So when I could go into a Theatre and get laughs out of our President by poking fun at some turn in our National affairs, I don't mind telling you it was the happiest moments of my entire career on the stage.

The first time I shall never forget, for it was the most impressive and for me the most nervous one of them all. The Friars Club, one of the biggest Theatrical Social Clubs in New York, had decided to make a whirlwind Tour of the principal Cities of the East all in one week. We played a different City every night. We made a one-night stand out of Chicago and New York. We were billed for Baltimore but not for Washington. President Wilson came over from Washington to see the performance. It was the first time in Theatrical History, that the President of the United States coming over to Baltimore just to see a comedy.

It was just at the time we were having our little Set-to with Mexico, and when we were at the height of our Note Exchanging career with Germany and Austria. The house was packed with the Elite of Baltimore.

The Show was going great. It was a collection of clever Skits, written mostly by our stage's greatest Man, George M. Cohan, and even down to the minor bits was played by Stars with big Reputations. I was the least known member of the entire Aggregation, doing my little speciality with a Rope and telling Jokes on National affairs, just a very ordinary little Vaudeville act by chance sandwiched in among this great array.

I was on late, and as the show went along I would walk out of the Stage door and out on the Street and try to kill the time and nervousness until it was time to dress and go on. I had never told Jokes even to a President, much less about one, especially to his face. Well, I am not kidding you when I tell you that I was scared to death. I am always nervous. I never saw an Audience that I ever faced with any confidence. For no man can ever tell how a given Audience will ever take anything.

But here I was, nothing but a very ordinary Oklahoma Cowpuncher who had learned to spin a Rope a little and who had learned to read the daily Papers a little, going out before the Aristocracy of Baltimore, and the President of the United States, and kid about some of the Policies with which he was shaping the Destinies of Nations.

How was I to know but what the audience would rise up in mass and resent it. I had never heard, and I don't think any one else had ever heard, of a President being joked personally in a Public Theatre about the Policies of his administration.

The nearer the time come the worse scared I got. George Cohan, and Willie Collier and Frank Tinney and others, knowing how I felt, would pat me on the back and tell me, "Why he is just a Human Being; go on out and do your stuff." Well, if somebody had come through the dressing room and hollered "Train for Claremore, Oklahoma leaving at once," I would have been on it. This may sound strange, but any who have had the experience know that a Presidential appearance in a Theatre, especially outside Washington, D.C., is a very Rare and unique feeling even to the Audience. They are keyed up almost as much as the Actors.

At the time of his entrance into the House, everybody stood up, and there were Plain Clothes men all over the place, back stage and behind his Box. How was I to know but what one of them might not take a shot at me if I said anything about him personally?

Finally a Warden knocked at my dressing room door and said, "You die in 5 more minutes for kidding your Country." They just literally shoved me out on the Stage.

Now, by a stroke of what I call good fortune (for I will keep them always), I have a copy of the entire Acts that I did for President Wilson on the Five times I worked for him. My first remark in Baltimore was, "I am kinder nervous here tonight." Now that is not an especially bright remark, and I don't hope to go down in History on the strength of it, but it was so apparent to the audience that I was speaking the truth that they laughed heartily at it. After all, we all love honesty.

Then I said "I shouldn't be nervous, for this is really my second Presidential appearance. The first time was when Bryan spoke in our town once, and I was to follow his speech and do my little Roping Act." Well, I heard them laughing, so I took a sly glance at the President's Box and sure enough he was laughing just as big as any one. So I went on, "As I say, I was to follow him, but he spoke so long that it was so dark when he finished, they couldn't see my Roping." That went over great, so I said "I wonder what ever became of him." That was all right, it got over, but still I had made no direct reference to the President.

Now Pershing was in Mexico at the time, and there was a lot in the Papers for and against the invasion. I said "I see where they have captured Villa. Yes, they got him in the morning Editions and the Afternoon ones let him get away." Now everybody in the house before they would laugh looked at the President, to see how he was going to take it. Well, he started laughing and they all followed suit.

"Villa raided Columbus, New Mexico. We had a man on guard that night at the Post. But to show you how crooked this Villa is, he sneaked up on the opposite side." "We chased him over the line 5 miles, but run into a lot of Government Red Tape and had to come back." "There is some talk of getting a Machine Gun if we can borrow one." "The one we have now they are using to train our Army with in Plattsburg. If we go to war we will just have to go to the trouble of getting another Gun."

Now, mind you, he was being rode on all sides for lack of preparedness, yet he sat there and led that entire audience in laughing at the ones on himself.

At that time there was talk of forming an Army of 2 hundred thousand men, so I said, "We are going to have an Army of 2 hundred thousand men. Mr. Ford makes 3 hundred thousand Cars every year. I think, Mr. President, we ought to at least have a Man to every Car." "See where they got Villa hemmed in between the Atlantic and Pacific. Now all we got to do is to stop up both ends." "Pershing located him at a Town called, Los Quas Ka Jasbo. Now all we have to do is to locate Los Quas Ka Jasbo." "I see by a headline that Villa escapes Net and Flees. We will never catch him then. Any Mexican that can escape Fleas is

beyond catching." "But we are doing better toward preparedness now, as one of my Senators from Oklahoma has sent home
a double portion of Garden Seed."

After various other ones on Mexico I started in on European
affairs which at that time was long before we entered the war.
"We are facing another Crisis tonight, but our President here
has had so many of them lately that he can just lay right down
and sleep beside one of those things."

Then I first pulled the one which I am proud to say he afterwards repeated to various friends as the best one told on him
during the War. I said, "President Wilson is getting along fine
now to what he was a few months ago. Do you realize, People,
that at one time in our negotiations with Germany that he was
5 Notes behind."

How he did laugh at that! Well, due to him being a good
fellow and setting a real example, I had the proudest and most
successful night I ever had on the stage. I had lots of Gags on
other subjects, but the ones on him were the heartiest laughs
with him, and so it was on all the other occasions I played
for him. He come back Stage at intermission and chatted and
shook hands with all.

Some time I would like to tell of things he laughed at during
the most serious stages of the Great War. Just think there were
hundreds of millions of Human Beings interested directly in
that terrible War, and yet out of all of them he stands, 5 years
after it's over, as the greatest man connected with it. What he
stood for and died for, will be strived after for years.

But it will take time, for with all our advancement and
boasted Civilization, it's hard to stamp out selfishness and
Greed. For after all, Nations are nothing but Individuals, and
you can't stop even Brothers from fighting sometimes. But he
helped it along a lot. And what a wonderful cause to have laid
down your life for! The World lost a friend. The Theatre lost its
greatest supporter. And I lost the most distinguished Person
who ever laughed at my little nonsensical jokes. I looked forward to it every year. Now I have only to look back on it as my
greatest memory.

As the following two articles illustrate, Rogers received considerable press coverage of his performance before Wilson. The publicity undoubtedly boosted his reputation, because two months later Ziegfeld hired him for the *Follies of 1916*.

PRESIDENT WILSON JOINS WITH FROLICKING FRIARS

"I want to thank you for all the fun I have had to-night. I am in need of fellows like you."

In these words Woodrow Wilson greeted the Friars during the intermission on the Academy of Music stage, Baltimore, Tuesday night. . . .

Never in the history of the Academy of Music has the historic old edifice held such a large audience. Every record was smashed. The house was jammed to suffocation, every inch of available space being occupied. . . .

The President occupied a lower box. The President's party included Mrs. Woodrow Wilson, Secretary Joseph P. Tumulty and wife, Ray Baker, Miss Margaret Wilson, the President's daughter; Miss Helen Bones, a niece of the President, and Mr. and Mrs. Joseph Wilson of Baltimore, the President's brother and wife. The show proved a smashing success. The President was pie for Will Rogers, every point or gag Rogers pulled bringing a hand or a laugh from the President. When Rogers asked what became of Bryan the house roared and when he said that at one time things looked serious for the country, that was when we were five notes behind, Wilson laughed right out loud.

WHEN WILSON MET THEM

THERE are numerous incidents in all Friar trips, and this one is not an exception, although it is just starting on the long itinerary. The Friars are telling of two incidents at Baltimore

Clippings [May 1916], in scrapbook entitled "Clippings from Rogers' Tenure with the Ziegfeld Follies and Midnight Frolic (1916–1917)," CPpR.

when the President and Mrs. Wilson motored from Washington to that city to attend the performance. Will Rogers, who throws a lariat while doing a monologue turn, happened not to be on stage when the President went back to congratulate the Friars. Later it was arranged so that he could meet the Nation's Executive. He was summoned to the President's box and as Mr. Wilson arose to greet him, Rogers still had chewing gum in his mouth— he chews all through his act—and as he was presented to Mrs. Wilson he was in a predicament. By as dexterous a twist as ever he gave a lariat, Rogers transferred the gum to the band of his hat, then went through the formalities of meeting Mrs. Wilson. Afterward he put on his hat forgetting the gum. It took three or four Friars to pry loose the bonnet.

〰〰〰〰〰〰〰〰〰〰〰〰〰〰〰〰〰〰〰〰〰〰〰〰〰

The only president who took offense at Will's jokes was Warren G. Harding. The incident occurred in Washington, D.C., in February 1922 when Will was touring with the *Ziegfeld Frolic*. Will performed in a skit called *The Disagreement Conference*, a takeoff on the Washington Naval Conference held between November 1921 and February 1922. Delegates representing the leading military powers met to discuss the reduction of naval armaments and signed a treaty limiting warships. Rogers, who played Secretary of State Charles Evans Hughes in the sketch, made some innocuous jokes about Harding's golf game. The president had planned to attend the show, but when Harding learned about the remarks he promptly canceled his tickets.

From then on, Harding became the butt of Rogers' humor, especially when corruption, such as the Teapot Dome scandal, plagued the president's administration. Harding's troubles gave Rogers abundant material for his gags, but he basically viewed him as a president victimized by his political cronies. When Harding died suddenly in August 1923, Rogers called him "the most human of any of our late Presidents. There was more of the real 'Every Day Man' in him. If he had a weakness, it was trusting his friends, and the man that don't do that, then there is something the matter with him. Betrayed by friendship is not a bad memorial to leave" (Betty Rogers, *Will Rogers*, 168–169).

THE DISAGREEMENT CONFERENCE

SECRETARY Hughes: The first disagreement conference is now called to order. . . . When Mr. Harding appointed this commission, for some unknown reason he put a democrat on it. Nobody knows why unless it was to wait on a peace table. So, Mr. Underwood, you kindly act as Interpreter, or do any odd chores around here, you see. I have also a wire from Henry Ford, saying in case the Navies are scrapped he wanted to buy them. Somebody ought to tell him that those boats are made of steel. Now you foreigners don't know who I am, do you? I'm Secretary of State. Secretary of State is a kind of consolation prize—when you're not quite good enough to be President, why they make you Secretary of State and all you do is the work. I am one of the few men who was not Secretary of State under the Wilson Administration. . . . I will never forget the one time I was President for one day. And if some smart Alex democrat had not thought of the idea of counting the votes, I would have stayed President that term. Now I brought you Bohunks over here to talk Turkey to you. Now we made a mistake in the last war by fighting it on credit. The next war has got to be C.O.D. Now, listen, I am going to tell you guys something—there ain't going to be any more wars till you fellows pay me for the last one. If you can't pay the principal, peddle some of those Buckingham Palaces and pay the interest. This is not as a lot of people think, a peace conference, to do away with all wars. What we are here for is to make wars cheaper. We've got to get wars down to a paying basis. We made a great mistake in the last war by fighting it on credit—what we got to do is to have the next war C.O.D. And another thing, you are not going to have any more wars until you pay me for the last one. We have stalled our boys along enough about that bonus, and I don't want any of you birds to wind up this conference by trying to borrow any money. From now on this government is going to be run as a government, and not as a pawn shop. . . .

(Phone rings. Sit) Hello, Mr. Harding. You lost by two holes.

The Disagreement Conference in "Original Scripts for Stage," TMs [1922], OkClaW.

Will Rogers (*standing center*) impersonates Secretary of State Charles Evans Hughes in *The Disagreement Conference* sketch, *Follies of 1922.* (White Studio photo, Will Rogers Memorial)

Well, you can't win every day. I would like to get out on the old links again, but I guess by the time I finish the conference, I will be too old to play. Now don't worry, Mr. Harding, I won't call it a League of Nations. I will call it something else.

WILL ROGERS TURNS DEMOCRAT

WASHINGTON, Feb. 14.—Will Rogers, film star and noted comedian, wanted President Harding to see his show when it played here.

President Harding didn't care to see it and went to another show instead.

So Rogers has sent the following message to Secretary Christian at the White House:

"From now on I'm a Democrat."

And this is how the Republicans lost a vote.

Rogers, in his show had an act, "The Disagreement Conference," a satire on the arms conference. He thought Harding would get a good laugh out of it. He went to the White House and offered President Harding a box at the show or, if the President was unable to attend, offered to bring the arms conference skit over and hold a private show in the White House for the executive family.

Instead of accepting either offer, the President went to another show that night. Rogers, miffed, sent the above-mentioned. But that wasn't all.

At the close of the show Rogers does a lot of fancy rope swinging, dancing and monologing. The latter consists largely of pithy remarks about timely news topics. He added to his repertoire two utterances that enhanced the high dudgeon of White House officials.

"Will Rogers, Miffed as Harding Refuses to See his Act, Turns Democrat," United News clipping," February 14 [1922], Scrapbook #20, p. 47, OkClaW.

1. "Heard the President's treaty message yesterday," said Rogers. "I thought it about the best speech Secretary Hughes ever wrote."
2. During a curtain call speech, Rogers voiced his feelings thus:

"You folks know I never mean anything by the cracks I make here on politics. I generally hit the fellow that's on top because it isn't fair to hit a fellow that's down. I played here five times during the Wilson administration and every time Mr. Wilson came and laughed at the cracks I made at him more than he did at those I made against the other fellow. It makes a fellow feel good and sort of at home to find a man like that. If a big man laughs at jokes on him, he's all right."

WILL KIDS HARDING

YOU know, I have been speaking around here at so many of these Banquets and Luncheons that I got to be a sort of Pest, so a couple of days ago they got a Speaker and brought him on here. They got him from the front Porch of Ohio, Warren Gamaliel something; I forgot the other. Well, he wasn't bad. He has a Lecture Tour booked through the West and didn't know just what to talk on. So he came here to try out an Act. I guess it is the one he will use. Anyway, I guess he didn't make good as a speaker here in N.Y., as I see they didn't keep him; they let him go back, and invited me to take up where I had left off before. He didn't come to hear me in the Follies. I went to hear him. I am broad minded that way.

Now I don't want to make any play for favor, or throw Bouquets at myself but just want to show you the kind of a Patriot I am.

Mr. Harding wants to see the Follies, but, on account of the humorous relations between the White House and myself being rather strained, he naturally feels a kind of hesitancy about coming, for at the present time you can't see the American Girl

"Slipping the Lariat Over," *New York Times*, 6 May 1923, sec. 8, p. 2.

being glorified without being annoyed by a jarring presence among them which I am free to admit is myself.

So, on the first of June, I am leaving; not because I want to (for, speaking candidly, it's not the worst position in the World, as my surroundings here have been most beautiful). But, even though you wouldn't judge it by my writings or Grammar, I have some politeness and courtesy, and, being a fair American Citizen, (I won't say "good," as I think I have heard that used before), I certainly have a high regard for the Chief Executive of this great Commonwealth, and I won't do a thing to stand in the way of any pleasure that he may wish to enjoy, no matter how small. So I am willing to get out, and sacrifice a living wage.

There is no reason why a National Institution that is viewed night after night by the best Male members of our Government should not be seen in its mission of Glorifying Young Womanhood by the leading Citizen of our Land at least once. Now, if this is Treason, make the most of it. . . .

〰〰〰〰〰〰〰〰〰〰〰〰〰〰〰〰〰〰〰〰〰〰〰〰〰〰〰〰

In contrast to Harding, Will got along well with Calvin Coolidge and visited the president several times at the White House. Rogers enjoyed making fun of Coolidge and once did an imitation of him on the radio in 1927. Coolidge accepted Will's ribbing as good fun. The president had been in office only one month when Will wrote this article about him.

POKING FUN AT SILENT CAL

THE Masterpiece of Literature this week is on the failure of President Coolidge. From what I have read about what people

"Slipping the Lariat Over," *New York Times*, 2 September 1923, sec. 7, p. 2.

want him to do he seems to be about the most colossal flop of any President we ever had. Now, I will just enumerate a very few of the reasons why he has been a failure.

First, you take the Farmers. There has been no rain in a great many States where they have growing crops, and if rain don't come pretty soon it will just about be the ruination of them. Then, on the other hand, there are States where they were trying to harvest their crops and they have had too much rain. Now, you see, he has been in there over a month now and it's time he was declaring himself.

Of course it wouldn't look so bad, but it's been the Republican States that have had the rain when they needed it and the Democratic ones have been left dry, and even Papers that ordinarily want to be fair have commenced to comment on it.

Not only the Rain, but you just look at the Boll Weevil on the Cotton. He has had plenty of time to say what he was going to do with the Weevils. Other Presidents have settled the thing by coming out against them, and why don't he?

Personally, I have always advocated taking those Boll Weevils, as long as the South has to feed them and nourish them, and getting some way of using them after they are mature. Get a Guy like Burbank to cross them with some other animal that is short-sighted and see if he can't train them to live off Cuckle Burrs instead of the Cotton Stalk.

Or get some famous New York Chef to frame up a dish made of them. Just tell the New Yorkers it was eaten in Paris and they would go wild over it and pay any price.

Or get some Breakfast Food Co. to use them. They are using everything else. Just think what wonderful advertising possibilities the name has: "Eat a Bowl of Boll Weevil before Breakfast." Of course, they could stop raising cotton for one year and starve them out and then, when they started growing again in the next year, there would be none to bother them, but nobody ever thought of that.

It's not my place to tell People what to do. That's what we pay Mr. Coolidge 75 thousand a year for. I can't think of everything. I am not getting paid for looking after the Nation's affairs, so it's not for me to settle the Boll Weevil. I simply tell you how it can be done; but why don't he do something?

Now take Skiatook, Oklahoma, near my home town of Clare-

Will Rogers performs, circa March 1925, in the sketch *A Country Store*, playing a Vermonter who recounts his experiences visiting President Calvin Coolidge. (White Studio photo, Will Rogers Memorial)

Will Rogers dancing at the conclusion of *A Country Store*. (White Studio photo, Will Rogers Memorial)

more, Oklahoma, (the home of the greatest Magic Water in Rogers County). Well, do you know that Mr. Coolidge has not yet come out in the open and appointed a new Postmaster?

I am not knocking, mind you; I am a tolerant taxpayer, but why don't he say who is to be Postmaster in Skiatook?

Right here in Beverly Hills close to where I live, Charlie Chaplin has built a Home. He is outside the City limits and can't get City Water, and he can't find any by digging. Now, what is Coolidge going to do about it?

Of course, I will admit that Charlie never thought of needing water, but that don't excuse Mr. Coolidge for not doing something about it. If he don't, the first thing you know, we will have a Dry Comedian on our hands.

Wheat is only worth 90 cents a Bushel. He has been in a month and it's still 90 cents. Why don't he issue a message and say wheat from now on is $1.50 a Bushel?

For the last few days out here it has been foggy and cloudy until almost noon and we couldn't shoot any Pictures. Now that never happened during any other Administration that I can ever remember. So why don't he do something?

France and England are about to go to War over how much they owe each other. Why don't he (President Coolidge) come out at once for the League of Nations and stop this coming war?

All of Europe looks on the verge of war. Why don't he come out against any entangling alliance for America, and stop any chance of us getting into European affairs? He could very well do both of these things if he only would, so why don't he do it?

France owes us a bunch of Dough. All he has to do is make them pay it. Why don't he come out and do it? He has been in for over a month now.

The Railroads are in terrible shape (really worse than usual, which don't seem possible). Now, what has he done to remedy the situation? Not a thing! It's funny to me he can't remedy these things when other Presidents have always coped with them so readily and satisfactorily.

The Coal situation has been dragging along ever since he first took the office. Still he has not done a thing to settle it to the satisfaction of both sides.

Louis Firpo hasn't smiled since he come to this country. We have been mighty good to him in a financial way, so why should

he look on us with a sneer on his face? Still, he has been doing
this for over a month now and not a statement has Mr. Coolidge
issued in regard to it. You let things like that go and it will
gradually bring on International complications.

What has he done for Capital? Nothing! What has he done for
Labor? Nothing! As I say, I don't like to complain and won't;
nobody ever heard me utter a word against the management of
our Government; but when a men is neglecting his duty and
failing to come out and settle things once and for all it's simply
more than even my Patience can stand.

Now, they are trying to make Babe Ruth change the style of
bat he uses. Can you imagine a President standing idly by and
not doing a thing?

Russia wants to be recognized, and you know if a man can't
recognize you in a month's time, why, the chances are you don't
know him at all.

He should have come out on all these problems the night he
was sworn in up in Vermont. Why, if he had been the right kind
of President, do you suppose he would stand idly by and see all
the Negroes going North (even if they hadn't been doing anything down there)? Why didn't he stop them?

What about the German Mark? Is he just going to sit there
and let them get cheaper than Fords?

I see by the papers that Valentino is wearing suspenders and
his hair is getting bald. Now, what has Mr. Coolidge done about
it? That's a National Calamity, and still, for the last month, he
has just let it drop till the first thing we know we will all be
worshipping a Toupee.

Now, what makes it harder is that when Mr. Coolidge went
in I had a lot of confidence in him; he always struck me as a
quiet, competent man, and I can't understand why he is not
doing a thing in settling these various questions which I have
enumerated.

Look at Mary Miles Minter! What has he done for that poor
downtrodden Girl? I tell you the time is coming when these
Picture Stars will come into their own, and if Mr. Coolidge don't
take their part we will elect some other man that will. They
have been getting the worst of it long enough.

What has he done for the drinking man? Why, Liquor never
was so high, from what the papers say. He hasn't done a thing

to bring the necessities of life down to the reach of the Common people. I tell you, you can look up the history of the world and you won't find a single Nation that ever amounted to anything on 15-dollar-a-quart Liquor. The poor man simply can't pay rent and do it.

What he has been doing these 4 weeks is more than I can figure out. Everybody is wondering if he is going to call Congress in extra session. About the only way I know of for him to make himself solid, after all these colossal failures is to not only not call Congress now, but not call them at all. I tell you if he did that he would go down in History as another Lincoln.

SCENE 6

BRANCHING OUT IN
NEW DIRECTIONS

Success in the *Ziegfeld Follies* generated new careers for Rogers as a film star, banquet speaker, radio entertainer, and syndicated columnist. Charles V. McAdam and Virgil V. McNitt, owners of the McNaught Newspaper Syndicate, enjoyed Will's performance on the Ziegfeld stage. They suggested that he write a weekly newspaper column discussing the news in a humorous vein similar to his routine in the *Follies*. McAdam recalled:

> Our office was in the old Times building in New York at 42d Street. It was right across the street from the Ziegfeld Follies show. He was the star and at the same time was writing his daily telegram for McNaught. Many a day he would come into my office and chat. He had a habit of asking the office girls to come in and listen to what he would say that same evening in his show—it was a sort of rehearsal. The public relations man at the theatre would tell him what important person was going to be in the audience and he would do a little researching and really give him the works humorously that evening. If the girls thought he was funny so much the better. (Preface to Will Rogers, *The Illiterate Digest* [1974], xix)

Rogers' first syndicated column was published on 31 December 1922. At this time he was performing in the *Follies of 1922*.

FIRST SYNDICATED WEEKLY COLUMN

EVERYBODY is writing something nowadays. It used to be just the Literary or Newspaper men who were supposed to know what they were writing about that did all the writing. But nowadays all a man goes into office for is so he can try to find out something and then write it when he comes out.

Now, being in Ziegfeld Follies for almost a solid year in New York has given me an inside track on some of our biggest men in this country whom I meet nightly at the stage door.

So I am breaking out in a rash right here in this paper every Sunday. I will cite an example to prove to you what you are

"Slipping the Lariat Over," *New York Times*, 31 December 1922, sec. 8, p. 1.

going to get. Last week there was a mess of Governors here from various Provinces. And a good friend of mine brought back to the stage and dressing room Governor Allen of Kansas. (Hurry up and print this story or he wont be Governor). Well, I stood him in the wings, and he was supposed to be looking at my act, but he wasn't. He was a watching what really is the Backbone of our Show. He anyway heard some of my Gags about our Government and all who are elected to help mis-run it.

So at the finish of my act I dragged him out on the stage and introduced him to the audience. He made a mighty pretty little speech, and said he enjoyed Will's Impertinences, and got a big laugh on that. Said I was the only man in America who was able to tell the truth about our Men and Affairs.

When he finished, I explained to the audience why I was able to tell the truth. It is because I have never mixed up in Politics. So you all are going from time to time to get the real Low Down on some of those Birds who are sending home the Radish Seed.

You know, the more you read and observe about this Politics thing, the more you've got to admit that each party is worse than the other. The one that's out always looks the best. My only solution would be to keep 'em both out one term and hire my good friend Henry Ford to run the whole thing and give him a commission on what he saves us. Put his factory in with the Government and instead of Seeds every Spring mail out those Things of his.

Mail Newberry one, every morning Special Delivery.

I tell you, Folks, all Politics is Apple Sauce.

The President gave a Luncheon for the visiting Governors, where they discussed but didn't *try* prohibition.

It was the consensus of opinion of all their speeches that there was a lot of drinking going on, and that if it wasn't stopped by January, that they would hold another meeting and try and get rid of some of the stuff.

Senator Curtis proposed a bill this week to stop Bootlegging in the Senate, making it unlawful for any member to be caught selling to another member while on Government property. While the bill was being read, a Government employee fell just outside the Senate door and broke a Bottle of Pre-War Stuff (made just before last week's Turkish War). Now they are carpeting all the halls with a heavy material so, in case of a fall, there will be no serious loss.

Well, New Year's is here now, and I suppose we will have to hear and read all those big men's New Year greetings, such men as Schwab and Gary and Rockefeller and all of them. Saying the same old Apple Sauce. That they are Optimistic of the coming year, and everybody must put their shoulder to the wheel and produce more, and they predict a great year. Say, if we had those Birds' Dough, we could all be just as Optimistic as they are. But it's a good Joke, and it's got in the papers every year, and I suppose always will.

Now the Ku Klux is coming into New York, and kinder o' got it in for the Jewish People. Now they are wrong. I am against that. If the Jewish People here in New York hadn't jumped in and made themselves good fellows and helped us celebrate our Christmas, the thing would have fell flat. They sold us every Present.

The Ku Klux couldn't get much of a footing here in New York. If there was some man they wanted to take out and Tar and Feather, they wouldn't know where he lived. People move so often here their own folks don't know where they live.

And even if they found out, the Elevator man in the Apartment wouldn't let 'em up.

See where there is a bill up in Congress now to change the Constitution all around, elect the President in a different way, and have Congress meet at a different time. It seems the men who drew up this thing years ago didn't know much, and we are just now getting a bunch of real fellows who can take that old Parchment and fix it up like it should have been all these years. It seems it's just been luck that's got us by so far. Now, when they get the Constitution all fixed up, they are going to start in on the Ten Commandments, just as soon as they find somebody in Washington who has read them.

See where they are talking about another Conference over here. The Social Season in Washington must be lagging.

Well, I think they ought to have it. These Conferences don't really do any harm, and they give certain Delegates pleasure. Of course, nothing they ever pass on is ever carried out. (Except in Greece, where they are all carried out.) But each Nation gets a certain amount of Publicity out of it, and us masses that read of it get a certain amount of amusement out of it.

Borah himself admits he don't know what it's for or what they should do. But it looks like a good Conference season and there is no reason why we shouldn't get in on one.

Besides, did you ever realize this country is four conferences behind now?

Next Sunday I will tell you about Ambassador Harvey. I am going down to *hear* him land, and see if he has on his Knee Breeches.

Beginning in 1920, Will started covering the Democratic and Republican conventions for newspapers. Coincidentally, both the *Ziegfeld Follies of 1924* and the 1924 Democratic Convention opened on the same day in New York City. Many of the conventioneers went to hear him at the *Follies*. On stage the humorist joked about the events of the meeting and used some of the same material in his convention articles.

TWO SHOWS OF EQUAL MAGNITUDE

SUNDAY morning at the depot at Atlantic City, two special trains were standing side by side. One was our train carrying the Ziegfeld Follies Company back to New York after a week's tryout of the new show. The other was for a bunch of Delegates going to the Democratic Convention in New York. Nobody seemed to know which to take, so, being an accommodating kind of a person, I called out:

"On your left for the Ziegfeld Follies show and on your right for the Democratic Consolation Show."

"Will Rogers Fears the Madison Square Show May Rival His in Magnitude of Its Appeal," *New York Times*, 24 June 1924, p. 4.

Now both shows open Tuesday. The Democrats go to Madison Square Garden, where Ringling Brothers' Circus always plays, and we go to the New Amsterdam Theatre, a beautiful theatre consecrated solely to Art.

We think we have the best show we have ever had. They think they have the best show they ever had.

It's the first time in the theatrical history of New York City where two shows of equal magnitude both opened on the same night.

It means "Men versus Women." They are featuring Men, and we are featuring Women.

I don't mean to appear partisan, just because I am with the Woman Show, but I think Women will outdraw Men as an attraction every time.

Can you imagine any one going into a big barn of a place to see Al Smith, Oscar Underwood, or that old Gentlemen Ralston, when they can go into a comfortable theatre and see 100 of the most beautiful Creatures on earth? I tell you it's not in the cards.

Now, take Bill McAdoo; he is a dandy, nice fellow, and I like him personally, but do you think I would go into a place to look at him when I could see Ann Pennington's knees?

Of course, they may get a few of the riff raff, because some people will go to see anything. There are some people so old-fashioned that they still listen to the radio.

But the class won't be there. They have got to get the class in their show to draw them in. Why, we have Imogene Wilson in our show, and she is better known than all their candidates put together.

And the costuming: to compare that is a joke! Can you imagine my old friend William J. Bryan's old alpaca coat staked up against the creations Evelyn Law and Martha Lauber will have on?

Mind you, I am not criticizing any man's grooming (in fact, I couldn't). But when you come into New York to open, you naturally have to compete with what New York rival attractions have to offer.

Now, these politicians' suits are all right in the Chautauquas (they know they are, for they have tried them for years), but not for New York.

The only thing they have on us is the badges. We are simply outbadged. Now, if you just want to look at badges and no beauty, why there is where you want to go, for as a badge display it is a total success.

Of course, we could put badges on our girls, but who wants to see a Follies' girl overdressed.

By an odd coincidence, both shows carry monologists. I have my little monologue in the Follies, and they are featuring in their consolation show another friend of mine, Pat Harrison of Mississippi.

Now I can modestly and truthfully say that in comparing us two—why they have the advantage, for Pat will not only beat me for humor, but he will lay it all over me for distance.

There is only one point where I will beat him, and that is on account of his being a politician. I don't think he has had a chance to learn anything about it, and that is sound logic.

Then another overwhelming advantage he has over me is, I only had one week in Atlantic City to break in my monologue and he has had years doing this same one in the Senate.

There is no race of people in the world that can compete with a Senator for talking. Why, if I went to the Senate, I bet I couldn't talk fast enough to answer roll call.

Both shows are holding dress rehearsals Monday night. They are trying out their platform, the one they are to speak from, not the one they are supposed to stand on after nomination, as of course that one won't be strong enough to hold up Carter Glass.

The city is doing all it can to make their stay here remembered. The Mayor issued orders that no delegate was to be robbed until after the convention was called to order.

It was a beautiful Sunday here. The New York churches were crowded with New Yorkers. Coney Island was crowded with delegates.

It may have been a coincidence, but every preacher in town preached on "Honesty in Government."

My side kick, Mr. Bryan, arrived and sent his three trunks full of resolutions direct to the stage door. One trunk was leaking.

In 1923, Will started recording some of his *Follies* routines on Victor Records. These phonographic records provided an opportunity for people who had never seen Will perform on stage to hear him, and the well-publicized recordings gave him a much wider audience.

A NEW SLANT ON WAR

HELLO folks. I've looked out at you from the movie screen and the stage but I've never got a chance to talk to you at home before. I'm not going to tell you any jokes. I just want to get acquainted with you. Talk over the affairs of the day with you.

Now you take wars. A very terrible thing. But as long as women are crazy over an officer's uniform there's going to be war. If we ever have another war it's going to be right here on the home ground. No use paying transportation going to Europe hunting a war. Just think how cheap we could put on a war without a shipping board. Instead of paying rich men a dollar a year to help run it why pay them what they're worth. That would be a big saving. Foreign nations wonder how we can train our soldiers to quit. That's because we only train them to go one way. Of course what they need in the next war and should have had it in the last one is a referee. The minute the war is over let him announce who won how much.

Right now we couldn't go into another war—we haven't got any slogan. Couldn't go into a war, anyhow, we're two bonuses behind as it is. Besides we might win it. We couldn't afford to win another one. I got a plan that will stop all war. When you can't agree with your neighbor, you move away. If you can't agree with your wife, she either shoots you, or moves away from you. Well, that's my plan, move nations away from each other. Take France and Germany, when they can't agree, take France and trade places with Japan. Let Japan live there by Germany. If those two want to fight—why let 'em fight. Who cares.

We don't always agree with Mexico. Well, trade Mexico off

"A New Slant on War," 6 February 1923, Victor Records 45347.

with Turkey, harems and all. Now we got men in this country that would get on great with Turkey. And that would solve the Irish problem. Take England and move them away from Ireland. Take them over to Canada, and let 'em live off their son-in-law. But when you move England away from Ireland don't you let Ireland know where you're taking 'em, or they'll follow 'em and get 'em.

NEW YORK

YOU know these talking machines are great things. When you go to the theater or movies and see some of us and don't like our act just kind of out of courtesy you have to stay and see it through. But on one of these if you don't like us you stop the machine, take the record off and accidentally drop it on the floor. Then the only annoyance we cause you is sweeping up.

Now folks, all I know is just what little news I read every day in the papers. I see where another wife out on Long Island here in New York shot her husband. Season opened a month earlier this year. Prohibition caused all that. There is just as many husbands shot at as in the old days, but women were missing 'em. Prohibition improved their marksmanship 90 per cent.

Never a day passes in New York, without some innocent bystander being shot. You just stand around this town long enough, and be innocent, and somebody is going to shoot you. One day there was four shot. That's the best shooting ever done in this town. Hard to find four innocent people in New York, even if you don't stop to shoot them. That's why a policeman never had to aim here; he just shoots up a street anywhere. No matter who he hits—it's the right one.

Robberies! Did you ever read about so many robbers? I see where some of our cities and towns are talking about being

"Timely Topics," 6 February 1923, Victor Records 45347.

more strict with these robbers. When they catch 'em from now on, they're going to publish their names.

They've been having every kind of a week here in New York. Smile Week, Apple Week, and one called Don't-Get-Hurt-Week. Taxi cab drivers couldn't hardly wait till the following Monday to run over you.

Everybody is talking about what's the matter with this country, and what the country needs. What this country needs, worse than anything else is a place to park your car. What our big cities need is another orange in these orangeade stands.

I read where a New York society woman is suing her ex-husband again. Claims she can't properly support their child on $50,000 a year alimony. Somebody's been feeding that young one meat.

Lots of people wonder why we left our soldiers in Germany so long. That's so they can get the mail sent to them during war. We had to leave them over there, two of them hadn't married yet.

I'm off Ireland for home rule from now on. I read an Irish paper the other day, and it says that liquor is 18 cents a quart. Can you imagine a nation wanting more freedom than that?

See where the Ku Klux Klan is coming into New York. Yes Sir. they're here. I'm no fool, you ain't going to get me telling no jokes about them.

NOMINATES HENRY FORD FOR PRESIDENT

TOASTMASTER. Gentlemen. You too Politicians. The Democrats are the middle-of-the-road party, Republicans are the straddle-of-the-road party, so I hereby nominate Mr Henry Ford for president, and christen the party, the all-over-the-road party.

"Will Rogers Nominates Henry Ford for President," 31 May 1923, Victor Records 45369.

In the first place it is too bad he is so competent, that is the only thing that will beat him. Mr. Ford is a good friend of mine, and years ago he overlooked a suggestion that would have made him immortal. It was when he went over to stop the war. I wanted him to take the girls we had in the Follies, and let them wear the same costumes they wore in the show and march them down between the trenches. Believe me, the boys would have been out before Christmas!

He has made more money than any man in the world by paying the highest wages. Yet he don't even manufacture a necessity, neither would you call it a luxury. It just kinder comes under the heading of knick-knacks.

I was at his home last year and happened to ask him that in case of stiff opposition just how cheap he could sell his cars. He said, "Will, by controlling the selling of the parts, I could give the cars away." He said, "Why those things will shake off enough bolts in a year to pay for themselves. The second year, that's just clear profit."

People think that Dr. Coué was the originator of autosuggestion. But Mr. Ford is! He originated auto suggestion when he made the synopsis of a car. He just recently lowered the price fifty dollars. That's done to discourage thievery.

He is the first man that ever took a joke and made it practical. So let's let him take this country, maybe he can repeat. He should make a good political race, he carries two thirds of this country now. There is no reason why there shouldn't be a Ford in the White House. They are everywhere else.

He is the only man that could make Congress earn their salary. He would start a bill through, and give each one something to tack on to it, and when it comes out, it would be ready to use. He is the only man that when Congress started stalling, could lift up the hood and see what was the matter with it. Some are against him because he don't know history. What we need in there is a man that can make history, not recite it.

Now if Mr. Ford will just take another one of my suggestions, he can be elected. If he would just make one speech and say: "Voters, if I am elected, I will change the front on 'em!"

During his years with the *Follies*, Rogers frequently was engaged as an after-dinner banquet speaker and convention orator. Many of his talks are classics of American humor. In his address to the Bankers' Association, Rogers displayed one of his favorite comical devices, which was to satirize the group which he addressed.

LAMPOONING THE BANKERS

LOAN sharks and interest hounds! I have addressed every form of organized graft in the United States, excepting Congress. So it's naturally a pleasure to me to appear before the biggest.

You are without a doubt, the most disgustingly rich audi ence I ever talked to, with the possible exception of the Bootleggers Union, Local Number 1, combined with the enforcement officers.

Now I understand you hold this convention every year to announce what the annual gyp will be. I have often wondered where the depositors hold their convention. I had an account once in the bank and the banker withdrew it. Said I used more ink than the account was worth. I see your wives come with you. You notice I say "come" not "were brought." I see where your convention was opened by a prayer, and you had to send outside your ranks to get somebody that knew how to pray. You should have had one creditor here, he would have shown you how to pray!

I noticed in the prayer the clergyman announced to the Almighty that the bankers were here. Well, it wasn't exactly an announcement, it was more in the nature of a warning. He didn't tell the devil, as he figured he knew where you were all the time anyhow.

I see by your speeches that you are very optimistic of the business conditions of the coming year. Boy, I don't blame you. If I had your dough, I would be optimistic, too.

Will you please tell me what you do with all the vice presi-

"Will Rogers Talks to the Bankers," 31 May 1923, Victor Records 45374.

dents a bank has? I guess that's to get anybody more discouraged before you can see the main guy. Why, the United States is the biggest business institution in the world, and they have only got one vice president. Nobody has ever found anything for him to do.

I have met most of you, as I come out of the stage door of the Follies every night. I want to tell you that any of you that are capitalized under a million dollars, needn't hang around there. Our girls may not know their Latin and Greek, but they certainly know their Dun and Bradstreet.

You have a wonderful organization. I understand you have ten thousand here, and with what you have in the various federal prisons, brings your membership up to around thirty thousand.

So, goodbye paupers, you are the finest bunch of shylocks that ever foreclosed a mortgage on a widow's home.

SCENE 7

THE THREE MUSKETEERS

Florenz Ziegfeld called his star comedians—Will Rogers, W. C. Fields, and Eddie Cantor—the Three Musketeers. They were featured together in the *Follies* of 1917 and 1918, two of Ziegfeld's most popular productions. All three rose from the vaudeville circuit to become *Follies* headliners and film stars. Yet each came from a different background and had his distinct comedic style. Eddie Cantor was raised by his grandmother in the bustling lower East Side of New York; W. C. Fields, the son of a commission merchant, grew up in Philadelphia. In the *Follies*, Cantor did a boisterous song-and-dance act while Fields performed his comic juggling routine and famous billiard ball and drugstore sketches.

The three became good friends during their years together in the *Follies*. "Probably at no time in theatrical history did three comedians in the same show work so harmoniously together," recalled Cantor. "In a business where a laugh to a comedian is life itself and he usually begrudges every chuckle another comic gets, the Three Musketeers of the Follies were ready to lay down their laughs for one another." Cantor remembers that the Three Musketeers often helped each other out. "Will Rogers would watch my act from the wings or W. C. Fields' skit and offer changes in the lines or situations that invariably improved the original material. We tried to do the same for him whenever possible" (Cantor, *My Life Is in Your Hands*, 197).

Cantor and Rogers had earlier toured together on the Orpheum vaudeville circuit. They appeared on the same bill in Winnipeg, Canada, around 1912. Rogers did his lariat tricks while Cantor performed in Gus Edwards' *Kid Kabaret*. During their years together in the *Follies*, Cantor grew to admire Rogers' integrity and concern about dishonesty in government. "It was through Will that I became aware of the importance of the individual as a citizen, and the working of government and politics," Cantor wrote. He felt Will's sudden death deeply. "I had grown so dependent on his wisdom that when he died, I was like a man suddenly gone blind with no one to guide him. When I could think more coherently, I concluded that the next best thing to asking Will what to do was to ask myself what Will would do. This has helped me make decisions ever since" (Cantor, *As I Remember Them*, 140).

The following excerpt from Cantor's autobiography, *Take My Life*, illustrates his lifelong affection for Will Rogers.

MR. AMERICAN CITIZEN

THE happiest engagement I ever played was at the Orpheum Theatre, Winnipeg, Canada, 1912. *Kid Kabaret* closed the show and fourth from closing was a cowboy who did the best roping act you've ever seen. He carried with him a man and a horse. He'd toss two lassos and rope the man's head and the horse's hooves at the same time. Once he missed. He came ambling off the stage with that grin of his, chawed his wad of gum and said, "If that horse'd been smart enough to stick out his tongue, I'd have gotten him." He didn't talk on stage, he was still a little too nervous to try that, but his off-stage talk was the wittiest, his interests the broadest. This cowboy was the first guy I'd ever met from west of the Bronx and I worshiped him—Will Rogers. We called him Bill.

He started teaching me a few simple roping tricks and briefed me about Oklahoma and his Indian heritage. His dad had been one eighth [one-quarter] Cherokee and his mother one fourth; and he was proud of the fact that his ancestors hadn't come over on the *Mayflower* but were there to meet the boat. His big ambition was not to let Oklahoma down. He wanted his state to be proud of him.

Until I met Rogers my world was the stage, my idols were the headliners, my ambition was to be rich and famous. Knowing the man from Claremont [Claremore], Oklahoma, was to gradually change all that. He was an entertainer and a great one, but his ambitions and talent went far beyond the theater. To him success meant being a good citizen and he opened a new world to me, a world in which you took major pride in being a working member of the United States of America.

Rogers was my grammar school, high school, and college. He taught me that the world doesn't end at the stage door and that politics are every man's business, actors not excluded. He kept

Eddie Cantor with Jane Kesner Ardmore, *Take My Life* (New York: Doubleday & Co., 1957), 104–115. Reprinted by permission of McIntosh and Otis, Inc.

on giving me an education as long as he lived; and since his death his writings are still my source book.

You understand, Will Rogers didn't set himself up as any teacher, he just lived the way he believed. As early as 1915 he was preparing for his future career. He'd joined the *Ziegfeld Follies* that year after a success with Blanche Ring in *The Wall Street Girl*. He'd added a monologue to his act and he wasn't satisfied to joke, the jokes must have substance. Every morning he read the papers, the *Morning World*, the New York *Times*, the *American*, the *Tribune*. Then he'd sit down at his little portable typewriter and peck out his commentaries on the news. He'd never had much education; he used to kid about it. "Eddie, I stayed in fourth grade so long I got to know more about McGuffey's Reader than Mr. McGuffey." But he had a built-in shrewdness and he worked at it, edited it, until it became 99.9 per cent pure wisdom.

When we were reunited in the *Follies of 1917* I found a great change in Bill. Not only had he become a top star, the only comedian who actually outdrew Ziegfeld's girls—he had begun to be a spokesman of the people. He never looked up to the mighty or spoke down to the masses. He called a spade a spade and made the spade like it. To a troubled world he brought a little peace of mind with a little piece of rope. Night after night, Bill Fields, Fanny Brice, Bert Williams and I would stand in the wings listening:

"Don't worry if a man kicks you from behind, it only proves you're ahead of him."

"Congress is so strange. A man gets up to speak and says nothing. Nobody listens. Then everybody disagrees."

"I know an Oklahoma rancher who's so rich he doesn't brand his cattle, he has 'em engraved."

The opening night of the 1917 *Follies*, I did what every actor dreams of—stopped the show. "That's the Kind of Baby for Me" was the song, and the audience applauded and kept on applauding; Tom Richards, who came on next, had to play through the din. Rogers wasn't on until next to closing and he dropped by my dressing room to pat me on the back. I didn't see him. My head was down on the dressing table.

"What are you crying about, Eddie? They're still clapping downstairs."

But my grandmother had died a few months before and I was wondering why, of all the people in the world, why couldn't my grandmother have been there tonight to see me finally make it?

"Now, Eddie, what makes you think she *didn't* see you?" Bill said. "And from a very good seat?"

I've never forgotten that. In fact, I've come to think the same way. We were together in the *Follies of 1917* and *1918*; and Rogers, Bill Fields and I were such buddies. Ziegfeld called us his three musketeers. Three such different guys! I the fresh East Side kid, Rogers the homespun westerner, Fields the man of the world. He used to love to kid Rogers. There was a girl in the show named Allyn King. A gorgeous face, a gorgeous figure, she could sing and act, she was a big thing in the *Follies*. Well, Allyn had one change that was so fast, she couldn't even stop to close her dressing-room door. Fields would see her running in and roar, "Hey, Injun, come out here quick!" Rogers would dash from his dressing room, Fields would put an arm about his shoulders and turn him so he was in full view of Allyn in panties and garters, struggling into costume. Rogers bit on that gag a dozen times, always turned red and fell all over himself escaping, while Fields'd bellow, "What's the matter, Bill? A very pretty girl!"

But one joke of Fields', meant in good fun, became a cruel jest. We were in Pittsburgh, the Wednesday before Thanksgiving, 1918, the Nixon Theatre. There were probably never three people who loved the theater more than Rogers, Fields and I. Days we had no matinee, we'd go to the theater anyhow to practice. Over at the Nixon this afternoon, Rogers started talking about this old friend, Clay McGonigle [McConagill]. . . . Rogers had told us the same story a hundred times and he always ended with, "I don't know what's happened to old Clay but if he were around, there's nothing I have in the world he couldn't have half or all of. That's how I feel about Clay McGonigle." Rogers left us about five-thirty and Fields and I went to an Italian restaurant for spaghetti.

"Eddie," Fields said, "we're gonna fix up that Oklahoma cowboy but good." He called over a waiter and dictated a note which the waiter transcribed in a crude hand.

"Bill. I'm going to see your show out front tonight and it's gonna be a thrill to know my old buddy is in the Ziegfield Follies. Clay McGonigle."

Fields deliberately had the waiter misspell "Ziegfeld." We put the note in an envelope, and back at the theater Fields handed it to the doorman with a dollar tip.

While we're dressing Rogers comes in choked with emotion. "Whitey, Eddie, guess who's in town and catching the show tonight—Clay McGonigle!"

He goes out on the stage this night and for once in his life doesn't stop the show. He addresses his ten-minute monologue to one man, Clay McGonigle. The audience doesn't know what he's talking about. "Clay," he says, "do you remember Mrs. Hennigan's pies?" No one in the theater knows who Mrs. Hennigan is! "And, Clay, when we were on that cattle boat, remember . . ." On and on.

Then Rogers rushes backstage, takes off his chaps, slicks his hair, and when the show breaks he's in the lobby waiting for Clay McGonigle. The people file out. No Clay. Rogers rushes to his hotel to see if there's a message. He checks every hotel in town where his friend might be registered. At 2 A.M. he's at the railway station still hunting for Clay. When he gets back to the hotel, he's white-faced and miserable.

"Fellas, you heard me tonight. Did I say anything that could possibly have offended Clay McGonigle? I can't understand . . . I wouldn't have said anything to hurt him."

We assured Bill he'd said nothing that could've given offense. By now we were so sorry for Rogers we could have killed ourselves; but if we'd told him the truth, he'd have killed us. Eight years later he walked into the Astor Hotel dining room and slapped me on the back of the neck so hard I almost fell into my soup. He'd just read a story of mine in the *Saturday Evening Post* and in the story was the truth about the note from Clay McGonigle.

The incident shows the sort of affection Rogers had, not only for Clay, but for every one who ever was his friend. He used to wire me every time I got a good notice: *"These critics are a little late. I knew this in Winnipeg."* Once his friend, you were his friend forever. He was very close to Flo Ziegfeld. In all the years Rogers worked for Flo, they never had a contract between

Will Rogers roping Eddie Cantor during their vaudeville days, Winnipeg, Canada, circa 1912 or 1913. (Will Rogers Memorial)

them. Rogers had asked for five hundred dollars in the *Follies of 1915* [*1916*].

"Flo, when I left Oklahoma I promised my wife and children that someday I'd make five hundred dollars a week. That was our dream." Ziegfeld fulfilled the dream, but a few months later Rogers asked for six hundred.

"What's the big idea?" Flo said, "I thought your wife and children were satisfied with five hundred dollars."

"They were, but since then we've had another child and he's kicking."

Bill was a family man and he worked at it. He was deeply religious and absolutely straight. From time to time his wife Betty would come on to visit him, and whenever he had a few days layoff, he'd fly home. He often came home with me to our little apartment in the Bronx, and at the first opportunity he dragged me back to Oklahoma to meet his family. His wife Betty was one of the darlings of the world; you never saw a couple more compatible. Betty understood that Rogers belonged to the public and she was willing to share him. She brought the children up to understand this too. They lived in a simple home adjoining that of his sister, Mrs. Spade [McSpadden], in Claremont [Claremore]. It was a warm and happy family and I enjoyed knowing them. But Oklahoma and the West, of which Bill bragged so much, left me cold that first trip. All I saw was a very big, empty, lonesome place. And to him our Bronx apartment must have seemed like a jail.

When we were on tour we always palled together, and gradually Bill got wise to me. Having been brought up by a very orthodox grandmother, for me certain foods were forbidden: pork, lobster, crab, oysters—so I'd try to find kosher restaurants. Bill'd ask me to have dinner with him, I'd always have an excuse; "I've got friends in this town." Bill finally figured that nobody could have that many friends. One night when I was turning him down, he said, "Eddie, you kosherin' up some place?" I confessed that I was.

"Well, why don't you ask me to go with you?"

Half an hour later we were seated across the table at a kosher restaurant on Euclid Avenue in Cleveland. Bill scanned the menu a little puzzled and I translated for him. He tried chopped chicken liver first, asked for a second portion and then a third. All the time he kept muttering, "Too late, I guess it's too late."

"Too late for what, Bill?"

"For me to turn Jewish," sighed the cowboy.

Years later when he was operated on for gall-bladder trouble, he blamed the whole thing on me. "That's what I get for going to all those kosher restaurants with Eddie Cantor."

But the truth was it was tit for tat. I introduced him to liver and herring, but he introduced me to his favorite food—chili. I used to tell him it was an internal hotfoot; but the fact remained that this man who dined with presidents and kings, even when he was earning twenty thousand dollars a week, loved nothing more than to eat in the most awful-looking chili joints. I remember going with him to one near the depot in Pittsburgh. It was the worst, I was afraid to go in it looked so spidery. But Rogers was crazy about chili and I was crazy about Rogers. There was a place in Chicago run by a Hungarian! That tickled Bill. "Think of it, Eddie, a Hungarian, and he makes the best Mexican food in the world!" With it, he'd take a bottle of beer. Sometimes, if he were devilish, on the town, he'd drink two bottles. He never drank anything stronger.

The night the *Follies* opened at the National Theatre in Washington, Rogers was invited to the White House. From midnight until sunrise he talked with Woodrow Wilson, with Secretary of the Navy Josephus Daniels, Secretary of War Newton Baker, England's Lord Balfour and France's M. Viviani. Finally he got up to take his leave. "Mr. President," he drawled, "Congress is gonna ask you how you can train an army so fast. Well, sir you tell 'em that when you teach an army to go one way, you can do it in half the time." With America in the war, his shrewd comments gained more and more attention. Henry Ford had sent a peace shipment of diplomats to Europe. Rogers said, "I think Henry made a big mistake in sending those long-hairs over. What he ought to have done was fill up that boat with Ziegfeld's pippins. He'd have the Kaiser and Mohammed V shooting crap over who was going to be first in the receiving line."

When we opened in Baltimore the evening papers carried a story of how the Kaiser, standing up in a small boat, had fallen overboard and they'd had to fish him out. "Well," said Bill, "I see where the old Kaiser tried walking on the waters. Guess he heard that someone else had once done it very successfully."

The beauty of Rogers' quips was that everything he said was basically true, and the great men of the world came to respect that. As time went on, there were few big men whom Rogers didn't know well: Mussolini, the Pope, the royal family of England, the Prince of Japan, Lady Astor, the Prince of Wales, the presidents: Wilson, Harding, Coolidge, Hoover, Roosevelt. He was perfectly at home with all of them because he was always exactly himself.

Alice Longworth once bet Will Rogers that he couldn't make Coolidge laugh. That was before Bill'd met the President. Alice wagered a box of candy against a modish new hat. Rogers went to the White House, was introduced to Coolidge, and said, "What was that name again, please?" He won the bet. Coolidge was to hear more of Rogers. Most astute were his published *Letters of a Self-Made Diplomat to His President*, in which he told Coolidge what he was hearing and seeing in foreign countries.

Rogers' comments had common sense and something more, the quality of prophecy. I went with him to not less than a hundred dinners just to hear him speak, to watch him analyze and psychoanalyze people and events. You see, I'd never enjoyed school, I'd never cared about dates and facts, I just wanted to know if I was going to have something to eat at night. But by the time I met Rogers and Fields (Fields educated me in a different way, I'll tell you about that), I new I was going to eat and I was learning, not by having facts pounded in my head but by enjoying the wisdom of men whom I loved. Rogers reached me on politics because it was wisdom with a smile.

"The United States is a great country, Eddie; we never lost a war and never won a conference."

"Everyone knows the world is round, but if it weren't for the United States, the world'd be flat."

"Talk about presidential timber (this in 1924) . . . Why man, they have whole lumberyards of it here at the convention. There were so many being nominated that some of the men making the nominating speeches had never met the men they were nominating. I know they hadn't from the nice things they said about 'em."

He begged Alfred E. Smith not to accept the nomination in 1928. He wrote in his column: "Al, give it four more years. Then the Democrats will definitely be in. But now . . . The day after election, you and the Democrats are going to find out how big a country this is west of New York." And when Smith did run he urged him to take off his derby while campaigning. "It makes you look like a city slicker, which you certainly are not." Bill tried out these lines on me. He'd often type out a column or a speech and then read it to me for a reaction. I was New Haven, New York, Atlantic City, and the Bronx. He wanted to see how a westerner's point of view would register.

They once made him mayor of Beverly Hills. "I guess I'll make a good mayor," he said," because I'm for the common people. And inasmuch as there are no common people in Beverly Hills, I'll make a good mayor."

The one speech from which I can't quote was one he made in 1925 at the Solax Club in New York. This is a Jewish charitable club and they were giving me a testimonial dinner. Rogers asked to be toastmaster. He was, at that time, the most talked-of humorist in the world. Imagine everyone's surprise when Rogers got up and started speaking—in Yiddish. It was the most hilarious evening I ever spent. It seems the minute he asked to be toastmaster, he got hold of a young student who in six weeks taught him enough of the language so that he could conduct the program.

What a great guy he was for benefits! He was always there, always on time, always the hit of the show. Once when I was handling the annual event for Surprise Lake Camp, the house was packed at eight-thirty, but Rogers was the only actor backstage. Actors hate to go on first, so they stall and arrive after a benefit has started. At eight forty-five, with the audience stomping and clapping, I asked Bill if he'd mind opening the show. He went on and stayed out there until the other actors started showing up at nine-thirty.

At a benefit in 1925 I told how, a few nights earlier, I'd entertained the Prince of Wales out on Long Island. It was after midnight when I'd arrived and everyone was very jolly, they'd had a few drinks, I said. Rogers followed me on the benefit. "The only difference between little Eddie and myself is—the Prince of Wales sends for me when he's sober."

The personal jokes between us were endless. When I opened in *Kid Boots* he presented me with a gorgeous silver gun and holster. I had to wear it, too. When Ida gave birth to Janet he sent us a Western Union telegram, but in gold, a gold plaque. In raised letters it said, *"If you wanta boy, send for Western Union."* This, in 1927, started a gag that became a classic.

When we built the mansion in Great Neck, Bill came out to see it. Now this place wasn't just a house. The man who'd built it specialized in *banks*; the steps he had leading up to our library had the sweep of a public monument. Rogers took one look and started to laugh. "You sure you want me in here?" he said. "Is this a reservation for Indians?" Later, when he built his beautiful home in California, he could have put the whole Great Neck place in his bathroom.

Rogers started writing his column in 1921 [1922], and it became the most widely read printed word in the country. In 1929, [Arthur] Brisbane asked me to write a daily column for the Hearst papers. There'd been a second fire at the White House and I'd cracked, "Golly, I didn't know business was that *bad*." Brisbane decided to have me do a commentary on finance. I'm no columnist, but with Bill as an inspiration I agreed to try. Rogers, in his column, welcomed me to the ancient and honorable profession. "Eddie and I spent our literary apprenticeship in the same school of hard knocks, Mr. Ziegfeld's *Follies*. We eked out a bare existence among the bare backs . . . Eddie specializes in Wall Street and the financial news. He's another Roger Babson . . . "

"Roger Babson" Cantor kept advising Will Rogers to get into the stock market. But he couldn't understand why any company would take in a total stranger, let him be partners in the business, and give him a share of the profits when they didn't know him. I tried to explain the facts of life about Wall Street and finally, in desperation, said:

"Bill, let me buy you a couple of hundred shares of stock. You don't have to spend a penny. I'll buy it, we'll let it lay and watch it climb. I'll sell at any time you say and give you a check for the profits."

He didn't object too strenuously, so I did exactly that. The first day the stock went up five points. Then it went up three points, then four. For ten days. On the eleventh day the stock dropped two points and Rogers phoned.

"Hey, I thought you said that stock was going up!"

"It's gone up, Bill. It's just dropped a couple of points."

"Get rid of it. I don't want any stock that drops."

I sold the stock and sent him the profits. A few nights later we both spoke at a dinner and Rogers slipped the same check under my plate. "For your boys' camp, Eddie." Sixty-five hundred dollars.

He kept on distrusting the stock market: "A holding company's an arrangement where you hand an accomplice the goods while a policeman searches *you*." And he had the last laugh again because in a matter of months "Roger Babson Cantor" was financially a bum. Those were the days when comedians had such long faces, barbers charged them double for a shave. I was no exception. I couldn't eat or sleep, the blood pressure was high and the stocks were low. One day I ran into Rogers on Broadway. He gave me a big bear hug.

"Eddie, saw *Whoopee* again last night and you're pretty lucky, you know. You're young, you're healthy, you'll get all that gravy back—just keep workin'." I must have looked pretty doleful. "Look here, Eddie," he said. "You have a *salable commodity*. It's as good as jewels or government bonds—you can make people laugh!" It was the best of advice. Ida'd told me the same thing; but a wife is always trying to smooth things for you and you feel she's prejudiced. Getting it from Rogers was different. It gave me renewed confidence.

In his scheme of things, what was money anyhow? Just something to do something with. He'd never given a damn about money and he was the most generous man I ever knew. I'd learned this back as far as 1917 when the *Follies* hit Detroit. We took a walk one day shortly before Christmas and dropped in at the *Detroit Free Press*. Rogers walked up to the Good Fellow Fund window and laid down ten one-hundred-dollar bills.

"Get some toys for the kids," he said, turning away.

"Wait a minute," the girl said. "What's your name?"

"My name won't help the toys any."

In the thirties when acting jobs were scarce I'd meet actors at Bank of America in Beverly Hills—and they weren't taking out, they were putting in—checks from Will Rogers. He was sending out weekly checks to down-and-out actors as if they were relatives. There were actors who turned down extra jobs because they were getting better pay from Rogers for nothing.

When Ziegfeld was ill and broke he was Bill's house guest. No one actually knew where Zieggy was, but he and Billie Burke were living at the Rogers' big ranch in the style to which they'd always been accustomed.

When Bill'd walk out of the commissary at the studio, he'd leave fifty dollars to pay for lunch for a group of secretaries or a group of extras.

This was just how he was. He was a guy who really meant: "I've never met a man I didn't like." He believed in people and he had a great hold on people. I think that if Bill had lived, Hitler might never have become the menace he was to the world. Rogers, with his great influence, would have fought the persecution of German Jews from the beginning. He would have appealed to the Christians of America. There would have been no breakdown of Christianity, no timorous laissez-faire policy. He tolerated no intolerance against any people. Of first importance to him always was his role as Mr. Citizen. The minute he wasn't needed before the cameras, you'd find him out in his car, glasses perched on his nose, one earpiece always busted, pecking at his typewriter. He had a voice, he was using it.

Once Bill and I ran against each other for President. The citizens of the District of Columbia can't vote, so they had a gag election. I won, but the fact is, Rogers could have been President. If he'd lived he might have been.

So strange, his tragic death. He'd been an enthusiastic air traveler since about 1915. He even got me up in a plane as early as 1919, an open cockpit. He did more flying for this country than anyone save Rickenbacker, Lindbergh, and Wiley Post. He believed in flying to the extent that when Knute Rockne was killed in a plane crash Rogers, in the middle of a picture, begged permission to take off at once to prove that flying wasn't dangerous. He had no interest in parachutes. "If the plane goes, I want to go with it."

He did. Unbelievably, the world was still here and Will Rogers wasn't.

The governor of Oklahoma phoned me soon after. "Would you speak for us at Skelly Stadium in Tulsa? Your friend Will Rogers was to do it, we feel he'd want you to take his place."

It was Citizenship Day and I tried to speak as Bill would have. To this day, I so often stop and think, "What would Bill do in this situation?" You see, I feel that to live and let live is not enough. You've got to live and *help* live. That's the meaning of citizenship in a democracy. That's what I learned from Mr. American Citizen himself, Will Rogers.

Rogers once spoofed Cantor at a dinner honoring the singer-comedian. Will made inside jokes about Cantor, fellow comics, and the Friars Club, an organization of show business professionals.

DINNER SPEECH FOR EDDIE CANTOR

EDDIE was born near Norvich in Russia [actually New York City]. He was such an ugly little devil the other children wouldn't play with him so they blacked him up and then the other children thought he was funny. His family were very poor and they wanted to get him some glasses. They couldn't afford the glasses so they just got the rims.

He was a very bright little fellow so he got a hold of some old sheepskins and made him a suit for himself buttonholes and all. When the people saw what he had done they put him in a club they had there called the Friars. So the club left Russia and emigrated to this country. The club kinder died out for awhile because at that time you could gamble anywhere. Eddie was about five years old, just old enough to join one of Gus Edwards' acts. He was born where it was very cold in Russia and to keep warm he had to run and jump around so he kept that up. When Gus brought him out to help sing the 18th encore of "School Days" why the audience got to throwing things at him but on account of his running and jumping tactics they couldn't hit him. So it afterwards become a nightly feature to see if you

"Speech at Dinner for Eddie Cantor," TMs, OkClaW. The talk could have been at a Friars Club dinner or the speech Rogers gave on 10 March 1929 at a testimonial dinner for Eddie Cantor at the Commodore Hotel in New York City for the Jewish Theatrical Guild of America.

could hit him while he was singing. But to this day he is one of the hardest performers to hit with anything we have.

He stayed with Gus until another Friar who had the drinking water privileges on the boat coming over come along and suggested that he get paid for his jumping. Well Gus couldn't see paying him. He didn't mind raising them but not paying them. Max Hart got this idea of having them pay Eddie and that was the start of what is called agents.

An agent was a man that figured out that though you might have intelligence enough to talk to an audience of thousands of people that you did not know enough to speak to a manager. So they conceived the idea of getting an office with a couch in it. Up till bootlegging come into vogue agenting was the most prosperous industry in the world. Now a great many of them have combined the two.

An actor could not ask for a salary without laughing. So these agents stood before a mirror and rehearsed for hours saying $500 and never smiling. They are the first to say "no" over a telephone, "I have tried to get him to take it out but he won't."

It was Eddie who was responsible for the tide of emigration which started from the lower east side and five cents-sed their way to the Bronx. He issued that slogan which will go down in history along side of Horace Greeley's. Eddie's was "Go North, young Hebrew."

The Friars about this time decided to take in a few pay members. They decided they needed a clubhouse where they would owe debts and have bonds and mortgages and everything. So they built this place Felix Adler and Dave Furgeson would have a place to lay off in. This club has brought laying off up to a fine art.

Then they said we need some good big name for an abbot so they elected George M. Cohan and every three years he'd drive up this very street by the club on his way to Long Island.

There is this thing about Eddie. He took no Irish name.

You remember Joe Welch? Vot a comedian. Ve had Jewish comedians in those days, and his brother, Benny Welch, vot a comedian. Ve had Jewish comedians in those days. "I go in the lion's den. Course can't stay in all day you know," Daniel entering the lion's den. Ve had Jewish comedians in those days. Ve had Jews in those days. Course ve got Jews now, but vot Jews!

Stars of the 1918 *Follies: left to right*, W. C. Fields, Will Rogers,
Lillian Lorraine, Eddie Cantor, and Harry Kelly.
(Will Rogers Memorial)

Another great Jewish comedian ve had vas Frank Bush. "I was
going down the street, I met two Jews. The little Hebe says to
the big turkey, 'vot a low life.' Vot an Irisher, and Cliff Gordon,
vot a comedian, vot a comedian. You don't dink so? Vy he had
all Cliff Gordon's stuff, he vas so clever. Vell Joe Schenck is
laughing yet."

Now who have ve got as Jewish comedians? Not a soul. Sam
Goldwyn is de only one left. De last of de old school. De new
school.

And Christian comedians, ve had some great Christian comedians too. Course dey vasn't Christians but dey vas comedians. Dem monologue guys in dem days, Nat Vills, excuse me
from laughing, Honey Boy George Evans, vit de cegar, "In De
Good Old Summer Time, In de Good Old Summer Time." Ve
got no more George Evans, ve got no more old summer time.

De fog it vould drive you nuts. Fred Nible [Niblo], de monologue vid class, vid jokes, vid humor.

Now vot ve got Christian comedians? Not a soul. Some guy
come out vit de hair hanging down, say, "All I know is vot I read
in de papers . . . " Fooey, vot he read in de papers, ve can read
de papers, same as him, maybe better.

And de black faces in de ancient days. Ah vot black faces we
had in dem days. You should see it a black face, called Frank
Tinney, vot a comedian, no jokes, no nothing, just a comedian,
and a little boy in de Gus Edwards act, a little skinny Jew, vas
he funny, vas he pop eyed? He black 'em up de face and he jump
around so fast de audience couldn't hit him. He could sing, like
de bird, dance, make jokes, vot jokes he made. If he couldn't
hear one he would make one.

He vas a fine little boy. He vas good to his grandmother
who had raised him. He vas good to his sweetheart who he
didn't have de money to marry. Everybody liked him, even the
Christians.

I don't see him so soon, but I reads it his name in de papers,
and von day I save it up money, and I go to de Beeg Ziegfeld
Follies, and dere is my little friend, de little skinny Jew, and
I clap de hands, and he is still de little Jew but de big hit. And
I come out of de big theatre and I feel so happy for my little
Jewish friend is famous. And I read where he marry de little
Shiksa, and he have lots of little shiksas, and you know it for, it
is a shiksa, it's a goil.

And I see him in de big fine pictures, vot fun, and I hear him
over de radio, and ven he sing, "One Hour Vit You," and finish,
I turn off the radio and I am happy, and I feel so happy. It's my
little Jewish friend.

W. C. Fields has written that he first met Rogers in either South Africa or Australia in 1903 (*W. C. Fields by Himself*, 19–20, 153). Fields was on a worldwide vaudeville tour and Will was in those countries at this time. It is therefore quite possible that the two did meet well before they worked together in the *Follies*. When Rogers joined the *Follies* in 1916, Fields was already a headliner in the Ziegfeld production.

They remained good friends after their years in the *Follies*, although Rogers was never as close to Fields as he was to Cantor. What Rogers and Fields shared were long, grueling apprenticeships in vaudeville before becoming stars. Both knew the determination and hard work it took to get to the top. Rogers respected Fields' marvelous sense of timing and classic comedy films. Fields likewise admired Will's humor, although the public adoration of Rogers at times irked him.

Legend has it that Will once visited Fields in a sanatorium. Learning that Fields could not receive visitors, Rogers managed to sneak into the comic's room. A nurse, who had witnessed the meeting of the two former Ziegfeld stars, said to Fields after Rogers left: "Isn't he a *wonderful* man? I just love that voice!" "The son of a bitch is a fake," Fields replied. "I'll bet a hundred dollars he talks just like anybody else when he gets home" (Robert Lewis Taylor, *W.C. Fields: His Follies and Fortunes* [Garden City, N.Y.: Doubleday, 1949], 105).

Fields sent the following telegrams to Rogers; the first when he was recuperating from a gall bladder operation, and the other when he was starring in the musical *Three Cheers*.

HOLLYWOOD, CALIFORNIA
JULY 3, 1927

SORRY YOU HAD TO LET GO OF THOSE TANNEN BIRTH STONES LOVE
AND A GOOD OLD FASHIONED HUG

BILL FIELDS

NEW YORK NY
OCT 31, 1928

DEAR BILL AFTER CAREFULLY ANALYZING AND QUIETLY RUMINAT-
ING I STILL CONTEND THAT YOU ARE GIVING THE BEST COMIC
PERFORMANCE AND THE MOST ENTERTAINING I HAVE SEEN IN MY
TIME   MISS STONE WAS ALSO WONDERFUL AND ANDY TOMBES IS
GIVING A GREAT PERFORMANCE   GOD HOW WE ENJOYED IT ALL
MAY WE NEVER MEET IN COMBAT AS ALWAYS

BILL FIELDS

TG, OkClaW.

Fields was saddened by the news of Rogers' sudden death in
an airplane accident and wrote the following tribute to his
Follies colleague.

THE NEAREST THING TO LINCOLN
THAT I HAVE EVER KNOWN

IT makes me laugh when I read of some of the "junk" written
about my dear friend, Bill Rogers. They try to make him out to
be an altogether different person than he really was. Rogers was
a very human being and were he alive today, he wouldn't stand
for all this saccharine pap that is being written about him.

Rogers loved to tell the story of how he went to South America to teach the gauchos to lasso cattle. How the gauchos a
hundred yards behind him threw their lariats over his head and
caught the cattle, whereas Bill missed his steer. How he cried
and cut up his rope and accepted a position as chambermaid for
a parcel of mules being sent to Durban, Natal, South Eastern
Africa to the British for the Boer War. How he later went to

W.C. Fields by Himself: His Intended Autobiography, commentary by Ronald J. Fields
(Englewood Cliffs, N.J.: Prentice Hall, Inc., 1973), 152–154.

Australia in 1903, where I first met Rogers when he was doing a roping act with Fitzgerald Brothers Circuit [Wirth Brothers Circus].

Rogers returned to America and did a stage act with a horse and a sheriff from his home state. Rogers later toured Europe where we met in Berlin and London. He came back to New York and I met him on Broadway. . . . He asked me if I would speak to Ziegfeld on his behalf. He would go to Atlantic City for the opening of the Follies of that year and did not want any salary and he would pay his own fare and would go on in case there was a stage wait. If there wasn't a stage wait—which there usually was in the small Savoy Theatre in Atlantic City—he would not disturb the show and would not ask to be permitted to go on the stage.

I went to Ziegfeld and explained the whole situation but Ziegfeld couldn't see it. He told me he had $75,000 invested in the show and couldn't take the chance so consequently Rogers didn't go to Atlantic City.

Later, I think it was the same season, Rogers joined a Schubert [Shubert] musical [*Hands Up*]. For the finish of his act, he would jump through a rope. This was before Rogers became a raconteur—he was practically doing a "dumb" act at this time. The rope constantly became entangled in his feet and the trick could not be accomplished. After many tries, Jake Schubert ran down the aisle, through the box yelling, "Drop the curtain." They were ringing the curtain down on Bill Rogers but he was such a lovable character that the audience resented Jake's hastiness and nervousness and applauded so vociferously that the show was unable to proceed. They demanded Rogers. Rogers returned crying and after three more tries accomplished the feat and I don't believe that anyone ever heard an audience go into such ecstasies. After Roger performed the trick, more than 50% of the audience walked out of the theatre and the show was a fiasco.

Rogers then went to a short engagement on the Century Roof and that was also a flop. Gene Buck, a Ziegfeld scout, saw Rogers on the Century Roof and suggested that Ziegfeld engage him for the Amsterdam Roof.

Rogers played the Amsterdam Roof with considerable success. It was practically the same audience night after night.

Rogers did a set routine but he discovered that the people wouldn't laugh at the same gags every night and what was known as a "belly" laugh the first few nights became barely a titter after the second or third week.

He talked the situation over with the most wonderful woman I have ever known in my life—his dear wife Betty. He must get new gags and where was he to get them from? Betty's sage counsel was to read the newspapers and talk of the topics of the day. That gave Rogers the impetus to his great fame and success.

I was with him for years in the Follies and he did an entirely different monologue every night, a thing I have never known in my 37 years of trouping.

Rogers was the nearest thing to Lincoln that I have ever known. His death was a terrible blow to me.

In a weekly article imitating a radio bedtime story, Will reminisced about the actor Fred Stone (a close friend), Eddie Cantor, and W. C. Fields.

FAIRY TALES FROM STAGELAND

I don't often talk Theatre to you. Most people in any business talk it all the time. But I have bored you all with Politics lately and shall have to feed you portions daily when the Democrats meet for their Fight; so I would like to take you all on a little jaunt behind the scenes with me, and we will visit the new Stars in this wonderful Fairyland of Make-Believe. (I know this sounds to you by now like one of those Radio Stories that all good children are supposed to go to sleep by.)

Now, all you little ones who can read bad English, sit right

"Radio Fairy Tales of Real Life Behind Scenes," *New York Times*, 22 June 1924, sec. 8, p. 2.

still, and your Uncle Will will tell you a few short Stories for all you good little Theatregoers.

This is a true story, and I want you to put your nose right up against the paper so you can read every word. There's not a rabbit or an old Br'er Fox in it. If your inclination runs to Animals or Insects, why, you had better drop this and reach for the instrument where the static comes out, for we are dealing with real Fairies in a real Fairy story. We must be up and away before Old Sleep-Eyes gets us.

Once upon a time there was a good Father and a wonderful Mother, and they had three little Fairy Daughters [Fred and Allene Stone and their daughters, Dorothy, Paula, and Carol]. And the good Father and the good Mother had to go away from home every night to work to make money to support a nice beautiful home for the three little Fairies. They had to work hard and long, and practice up new and novel things, for these Fairies worked and lived in a Land of Make-Believe. They had to sing funny songs, and learn funny and clever dances, to try to amuse the practical people, who are not in this Make-Believe Land, but still come to it to forget their daily troubles.

So the good Mother and the good Father would tuck their little treasures in bed, and then off to work, and even if one of the little Angels were not feeling well, the good Mama and the good Papa had to go just the same, every night, because they had to make Practical People laugh.

The Practical People thought it was all fun. They didn't know that some times when this old Funny Fairy Clown was making funny faces his heart might be heavy, though his feet were light.

They worked, and saved, and prospered for years, until those Practical People got to learn not only that they were funny and made them laugh but also that they were good, and loved each other, and were a very happy little family in this land of Buffoonery.

Then came a wonderful night in this Enchanted Palace where these two loved ones toiled to make others merry. It was the opening night, when they were to show their new tricks and make new merriment.

Now Old Mr. Practical Audience didn't know that in addition to all else they had done, they had been teaching the Eldest of the Fairy daughters all this Magic of make-believe. For this good Father and good Mother had decided that if this land of Mimicry was good enough for them and had made them live happily, why, it was good enough for their Fairy daughter.

So the Mother cared for the other little ones while the Father taught his Daughter his accumulation of Dances of a lifetime, and when she appeared and did these wonderful things those old Practical People made it the night of a lifetime, long to be remembered in the hearts of the People of Make-Believe land. And today the Fairy daughter reigns as absolute Queen over the biggest City of all the Western World and she don't even know or realize it.

She only knows she wants to please and amuse. That should be the Moral of this little Story. "No matter in what field, you may do something to be acclaimed." For be it make-believe, or be it practical, remember the lesson of this little Creature who doesn't know how wonderful she is and will always be that way, even though she is the newest and biggest Star today of all Theatreland.

Some day it will be all five, in this little enchanted old merry-making House where people come to be amused, for the two little Sister Fairies are playing make-believe and following in the steps of their wonderful Sister. They will have much hard work, and will have to cut out some of the play. But, won't it be worth it! Instead of being put to bed every night they can go to this old merrily haunted House and play jokes on the Old Father, and make the Practical Ones laugh because he won't be nimble enough to catch them.

That will be all for tonight, children. What? One or two of you are not asleep yet? What's the matter with you? Want to hear another one? All right.

Once upon a time there was a little Poor Boy [Eddie Cantor]. Oh, he was awfully poor, and he lived in a great crowded City, and his old Grandmother couldn't make enough to support them, so he had to sell Papers on the street. He learned to sing a Song, and he used to sing in little cheap Theatres on Amateur nights. He was just one of a million of the same race but with not half the chance of most of them. Yet he kept trying, and bringing the pennies home to his old Grandmother, and he learned all he could about this wonderful land of Make-Believe.

He kept working up and up, with none of the advantages that

the little Fairy Girl had. He didn't have a good Father as a wonderful teacher to show him. He had to learn just as the little
Fairy Girl's good Father had learned, by what these old practical
people call Hard Knocks.

He wasn't much to look at. He didn't have the little Fairy
Girl's beautiful face, and he was little and skinny. But he
wouldn't be discouraged. He would put black soot all over his
face because it was cheaper than makeup, and he became
known by that. He was ambitious, and he studied what the Practical People wanted, and he tried his best to supply it, till one
day a big (what Make-Believe call) Manager [Ziegfeld] come
along and put him in a wonderful fine show, and last year he
was heralded as one of the Kings in the mighty realm of fun
making.

What became of the old Grandmother who raised him, do I
hear one of you wideawake say? One night when our little Hero
was climbing this ladder of success, he had come to this old
Funny Factory [*Follies*] where he was to make people merry
later in the night. He was huddled over in his dressing room,
not as you Practical Ones think, laughing at something funny
he was preparing. No, he was crying when another Old Merry-
maker [Rogers] entered the room they were sharing.

On Inquiry the sudden Old Intruder learned that the crying
was over the thought that the poor old Grandmother had not
lived to hear and share in his success at this time when he could
give her every luxury.

"Oh, but wait a minute, Uncle William, how do you know all
this? You are only telling us this to make us go to sleep, maybe."

Now listen, children, does Uncle William have to tell you
everything? The story is all you need to know. You don't need
to know who it was that Uncle William shared his dressing
room with.

Now, here, it is getting late and I'm going to tell you only a
short one. Once upon a time there was another little Boy in
another Big City [W. C. Fields]. He worked on a Huckster's
Wagon, selling Vegetables. When he couldn't sell them he would
juggle them. The people got so interested in his wonderful feats
in Juggling that they would forget to buy any, so he always had
plenty left to practice with. If they had bought him out he

would still be on that Wagon, because he would not have had anything to practice with.

His feats, of course, led him into this queer assortment of Souls in this Make-the-World-Merry Band. He never spoke a word. He got to be recognized as the king of Pantomime Stage Comedy. He traveled the world over many times. He reached the top in his chosen profession. But it was not the one his ambition inclined to, so one day a good fairy in the shape of a Manager [Ziegfeld] put him in a show and made him talk, and the Practical People went to hear this mere juggler make them merry without juggling, and today he is a crowned king among Merrymakers.

One day on his climb up the ladder he was surprised in his dressing room by an intruder (who was assisting him in trying to chase the gloom away from the Practical People). Well, this Juggler, who even then had gotten so high in the make-believe world that you would hardly think he would associate with a Carrot or a Potato, was fondling an old Picture of a Horse-drawn Wagon overladen with an array of Vegetables. The vegetables looked as if they had all the peelings worn off them where they had been captured from the air in every conceivable manner. Respect and sentiment were written on every line of his face as he gazed at this picture.

"But, Uncle William who told you the story? The intruder?" Never mind who told me the story. Haven't I seen Pictures of Horses and Wagons, and People looking at them? Now, that's enough. You will get no more Stories tonight.

"But Uncle William, why did you just pick out those three?"

Say, now, you go to sleep. Suppose three of your little Boy and Girl friends all had some wonderful good Fairy visit them in the same year, and you knew about them and liked them. Wouldn't you tell your children friends of their good fortune? Sure you would.

SCENE 8

WILL AND THE BOSS

When Rogers left the *Follies* in 1919 for a film career in Hollywood, Ziegfeld gave the Oklahoman a watch engraved "To Will Rogers, in appreciation of a great fellow, whose word is his bond." The gift signified the respect Ziegfeld held for Rogers and the comedian's importance to the producer's successful productions.

Over the years a rare bond had developed between the two—a close relationship that Ziegfeld lacked with most of his other stars. The producer greatly admired Rogers as a person and the values he represented. Several examples illustrate their friendship. Ziegfeld permitted Rogers to take two horses with him when the show travelled. "Will was up early in the morning in the riding arena, practicing fancy rope catches each day with his horses," his wife remembered.

Will was also one of the few people who could kid Ziegfeld. During rehearsals the producer was known to yell, "Stop it! Stop it!" at the orchestra whenever he disliked an act. Several times Rogers would sneak into the orchestra and imitate Ziegfeld so perfectly that the performers believed it was the producer himself. Apparently, Ziegfeld even enjoyed the joke. Over the years they exchanged many gifts. Rogers gave Ziegfeld and Billie Burke's daughter, Patricia, a saddle, and Ziegfeld surprised Rogers once by installing a huge picture window in his ranch home.

Rogers knew that the *Follies* was his big break in show business. Although Ziegfeld worried that he could be sued because of Rogers' political jokes, he always gave Will complete artistic freedom. "I would never have been as lucky again, for no other manager in the world would have let me go my own way and do as I saw fit," Rogers said. "He never bothered me as to what to do or say, never suggested or never cut out." The *Follies* was Rogers' springboard to fame and he remained indebted to Ziegfeld all his life (Betty Rogers, *Will Rogers*, 137, 139, 141).

Will Rogers arrives in New York for a new *Follies* production and is welcomed by Florenz Ziegfeld and *Follies* Girls, 20 May 1924.
(UPI/Bettmann)

In 1918, Rogers wrote Ziegfeld suggesting ideas for his own show entitled "A Mess of Junk." A news story once announced that Ziegfeld had signed a contract with Rogers to produce a new musical comedy, but the impresario never produced a show featuring the humorist (Rennold Wolf, "Ziegfeld to Star Will Rogers in a New Musical Comedy," clipping [1917–18?] in scrapbook, CPpR). An interesting sidelight is that the lariat tricks Rogers mentions in the following letter were later incorporated in his short film *The Ropin' Fool* (1922).

Chicago
February 13, 1918

Mr. Ziegfeld,
Dear Boss:

As I didn't get to see you, I thought it might do no harm to write you out as well as I can a few ideas of a show.

Now, in the fist place, I have an idea of a title that I know is unique and different and, especially, if it is a piece with no connected story; it is "A Mess of Junk." Now, you think that over and see if you don't think its good.

The scene where we use horses, I think should be early and be my first appearance on the stage as it will be a surprise as they do not know that I have kept up on that kind of work and, if it makes a good impression, it will help me in what I do later. Its a big, full stage set of Western scenery and a moving picture company are at work. They set up the camera, a big, loud talking director (we could use [Ned] Wayburn); now, he explains "I have found a guy to do these stunts, but I don't think he's any good; he looks like a 'nut' to me and I don't think he can throw a rope in the creek, but we will have to try him. All right, come on out here; I will think of the tricks and you do them." He names some trick he wants done and all I say is "Well, I don't know but I'll take a crack at it." He criticises the costume, says "You don't look like a moving picture cowboy" and everything with him is all wrong; even when you do a trick right, its wrong to him. Then he'll announce another trick and I say— "I'll take a crack at it." He says— "You won't do, you don't look at the camera and smile like [Douglas] Fairbanks, and you don't look mean enough for W. S. Hart." Now, its my idea that he can have all the talk with other people standing on the stage, but I never say a word; just do as he says and he keeps bawling me out, telling me how bad I am.

Now, during this scene, I have a lot of good tricks on horses that have never been done before; you see by him asking me that announces the trick and lets the audience understand what I am going to do, but other people on the stage have all the talk and comedy; all I do is the work. Now, here are a few of the tricks—I can rope all the horses in one throw that you can get on the stage; I think about five, maybe six.

I do part of the catches while I am sitting on one horse and catch the other horse as he goes by. Now, here are a few of the original tricks that I have been practicing on all this time. I rope a horse by the neck, the rope crossing in a perfect figure 8 on his chest and catching his front feet; I rope a horse by the neck, the rope crossing in a figure 8 and catching the rider with the upper part of the loop; throwing three ropes at once and catching the horse by the feet and by the neck and the rider.

Here is one no one has ever tried; throwing four ropes at once, the fourth with my foot; all catching different places. Standing down over the footlights on a horse with a rope about 90 feet long, spinning it clear out over the audience.

Now, for a comedy finish, he keeps hollering at me what to do; he gets over by the camera and operator; I am on my horse. I throw a big loop over him, camera, operator and all; I have it tied to my saddle and drag him off the stage.

Now, I have an idea of a sensation, dangerous looking stunt; just as the curtain comes down on this full stage scene, run around into one, and have a horse standing there ready; this horse dashes across the stage in one right over the footlights at a dead run with me hanging down on his side by one leg and one leg over the saddle horn; and pick up a handkerchief backwards and out at the small entrance in one on the other side. It looks like he is going to scrape me off as he goes out; you see its so quick, I think it would be a good stunt and it would be easy.

Now, I have an idea of a way to do a lot of my newspaper stuff. Its a country Post Office; got an old stove and three or four fellows around talking; I am the old Rube that reads all the papers and knows about everything they ask me and all the time I am moving around and doing something; for instance, they say "I see by the papers that so-and-so, has happened"; all I do is "Yes, so-and-so-etc." You see, they are doing the straight for me and it will make a gag go better than if I had to repeat it all myself. Not one of those musical comedy Rubes, but a legitimate character like you really see. I will have all the gags necessary for it.

Now, I am practicing on a new dance to do with a girl in a rope; a fast Texas-Tommy, where we do all those fast spins; that would go good in a show, following some other dances.

Now, the blackface idea: I am made up as Bert Williams, the colored chauffeur; come on to a scene where it is one of those gasoline filling stations and I come on; this mule of mine—its not a donkey, its a big mule and its white and black and blue and every color; the funniest looking thing you ever saw; looks like Urban had painted it. Now, he is made up like an automobile. I steer him with a wheel; the saddle is all made up like the seat of a car, different brakes, and levers, mud guards and a bumper. Now, some other comedian is running this filling station. We take the hose and put them in the mule's mouth and he starts pumping. Could get a lot of comedy out of "How much does the tank hold" and talk about the car. The end of this hose is sweetened and the mule chews on it. I unscrew a cap from the top of the mule's head, like the radiator cap on a car, and have smoke in there that comes out as if it was a hot radiator; then pour in water. Now, he backs and turns just like a car; as I am on him and leaving, I arrange an explosion or shot in the opposite side of the mule from the audience and it is supposed to be a blowout and I have no extra tubes. I and the other fellow are looking at the mule's front foot; I tie a handkerchief around his leg in such a way that when I get back on him and start off, he limps off on three legs; also showing as he exits a red tail light and a license tag fastened on his tail. Now, I come right back on and, regardless of that roof thing, I can sing a Bert Williams song; I kid about it and the leader says "Why don't you sing a song?" I say "I'll take a crack at it" and make that a catch line that runs through the show.

Now, I have the song all ready; a black faced comedian used it in vaudeville and it is sure fire for he has a lot of good extra choruses; I would use a lot of local topics in each chorus and do his dance at the finish; I know I can do this as out home at the minstrel shows we used to sing coon songs. Put a sure fire gag in each chorus and it is sure to go.

Now, for my specialty in one, most of the talk would be on the show, kidding myself, but doing a lot of new tricks with the rope all the time. I have an idea of a dressing room scene on the stage where a lot of the male principals and I dress and we could talk on the show and how it was going and name people who really were out front and what really had happened that night, with all the acts kidding me about being the star and wouldn't I like to be back with The Follies and see an audience? Each act tells how good they have gone; there is a wonderful scope to a scene lack this. It would be my idea to have it closing the show, instead of closing the show with a number. I come off just ahead of it from my specialty in one and right into the dressing room with all of them asking me how I did and we talk and discuss things and gags and how they have gone that night and who we saw out front. You see, you cover the [Raymond] Hitchcock idea only in a different way.

Now, the people, one by one, dress and leave saying "goodnight." Some are to meet the girls; some say they are going out to hit you for more money; well I am the last one and I am not satisfied with the way I have done and feel disappointed. Someone impersonating you comes in and says "Oh, cheer up, you didn't do so bad," or something to that effect. You go out and I am alone; watchman comes in and says "all out" and I leave with either some little pathetic touch—"Well I guess that act was right; this thing is too fast for me; back to The Follies and just be one of the mob," or some comedy line after this little pathetic scene as I went out and the curtain came down.

Now, what do you think of that for a novelty ending to a musical show? You see, they have never had a men's dressing room with performers talking about what really happened. There is your intimacy without getting fresh with the audience and they are being let in on something.

Now, get some novelty opening to the show with the stage hands making the set in full view of the audience, which would be a novel opening and save a scene and number. Now, there is any amount of comedy to be gotten out of this dressing room as all your principals are there and, besides, the pathetic touch, there would be any amount of things to discuss and get laughs.

All these things I have explained mean a third of your show; you don't need a story; the other third is taken up with numbers and other third with sure-fire vaudeville specialties. What I think would be one of the best acts in the world for a show would be the Avon Comedy Four; they are the surest fire act in the show business; the best singing Quartette; can do a full stage scene; all lead numbers and you would get all the Jewish audiences in America to come see them as they are big favorites.

Now, I won't tell you what I want for all this as I want your wife to take the body back to New York alive; I want some real money next year, but if some man gives me the chance I will work my head off to show him I am worth it. I wouldn't do any one of these things next year unless it was in my own show and do them all at once. I figure it would be the surprise of doing them all that would help me.

Now, just to kind of sum up; the horse thing with good roping I know will go and develop into a good comedy number. The Rube, with sure, up-to-date sure fire laughs should go; the mule idea I think is funny and, with the big Jew of the Avon Comedy Four to do it with me, it would be good. The Bert Williams song I simply talk off; I have the dialect and, if the song is good and good extra choruses on up-to-date topics, it should go. A dance with a girl is sure, especially as we have never done it before theatre audiences, and this new one is faster and better than the old one. My specialty in one I have enough new rope tricks for it; besides up to then you have not done any talking in my own character, so you see this is the first time they really see you as you are. I don't think you want a great big show; get good people and we might put it over. Now, you don't have to have a story with this; that title covers it all—"A Mess of Junk."

I may be all wrong on this, but I think a show framed up this way would be the easiest to get together and the cheapest; I can put on everything I explained to you here with four weeks' work; if you would let me leave this show about three weeks before it closed and send on an act in one from the Roof, like Savoy and Brennan, of [or] Van & Skenk, we could put it on out of town in at least six weeks and would not interfere with rehearsals of The Follies; then, if it was no good, take whatever scenes in it that did go and put them in the follies. Lets try it and get it off our chest. There is sure to be something in the show to be fit to go in the Follies.

If I left the show about four or five weeks before it closed, then we would have plenty of time to see what we had before The Follies rehearse. I would want to play the Roof while rehearsing as I have to work to keep myself up to date.

Now, you and Mr. [Abe] Erlanger put this on and don't spend a lot of money on it and maybe you can make some money out of it.

How about coming to Chicago for a Summer run if it proved any good? Wire me on receipt of this what you think of it all.

Well, after writing these few lines, I'll stop. Tell Mrs. Ziegfeld I have two sure-fire gags about her for the new show.

Regards to both, Yours truly,

TL (carbon copy), OkClaW.

After suffering a financial loss producing his own movies, Rogers returned to the *Follies* in 1922. When he left a year later to do a series of silent movies produced by Hal Roach, Ziegfeld wrote him the following letter. At the end of the typewritten letter Ziegfeld added in ink "A Real Man"—an expression of friendship from the producer.

New York
June 2, 1923

My dear Will:

It is with sincere regret that the time has come where you are leaving The Ziegfeld Follies, after one solid year in New York City. I want you to know that I appreciate the fact that your word is good for anything on this earth, and to have you say you will do a thing is the same as if it was done. I knew when you gave me your word you would stay for the run of the play in New York City you were under the impression The Follies would run in New York until the last of September, as it usually does. But we are all surprised that we are still at the old stand where we started last June, and my great regret is that you are not going to continue with us.

I have never had anyone appear in any of my attractions that was a greater joy to be associated with than you, and I trust when the time comes for you to return to the stage you will know I am always ready to let you do whatever you want to do behind the footlights.

If there is a possibility of my getting to California before you come back, I will certainly look you up. In the meantime, give my love to your family, and it is with regret that I must say au revoir to my friend. A REAL MAN. Very sincerely yours,

Ziegfeld

TLS, OkClaW.

Rogers' departure for Hollywood greatly disturbed the producer. Many stars (Fields, Cantor, Fanny Brice, Marion Davies, and others) left Ziegfeld for a more financially rewarding film career. Ziegfeld sent Rogers this telegram attempting to lure him back to the *Follies*.

NEW YORK, NY
AUGUST 29, 1923

WILL ROGERS

ITS TIME YOU WERE BACK   YOU MAY NOT REALIZE IT NOW BUT EVERYONE AGREES WITH ME THAT ITS A SHAME TO BURY YOURSELF AT A TIME YOUR NAME WAS GETTING A HOUSEHOLD WORD AS AMERICAS GREATEST HUMORIST AND EVERY NEWSPAPER WAS MAKING YOU AS SUCH   IF I HAD HELD YOU TO OUR ORIGINAL AGREEMENT YOU WOULD STILL BE PLAYING IN THE PRESENT FOLLIES AS WE DONT LEAVE NEW YORK UNTIL SEPTEMBER FIFTEENTH   I AM PUTTING ON AN ENTIRELY NEW FOLLIES TO OPEN AMSTERDAM THEATRE OCTOBER EIGHT   I FEEL THAT YOU CAN TAKE ALL THE MOVING PICTURES YOU WANT AROUND NEW YORK AT THE SAME TIME KEEPING YOUR ENVIABLE POSITION IN THE HEARTS OF THE THEATRE GOING PUBLIC   PLEASE WIRE ME IMMEDIATELY AFTER TALKING TO YOUR BOSS MRS ROGERS YOUR DECISION AS IT WOULD BE NECESSARY TO MATERIALLY CHANGE THE NEW FOLLIES WITH YOU IN IT AS I WOULD ENDEAVOR TO GET TWO GREAT SCENES FOR YOU IN ADDITION TO YOUR SPECIALTY AS WE WOULD ALL CONCENTRATE ON YOUR MATERIAL PRACTICALLY MAKING YOU THE STAR OF

Florenz Ziegfeld in his office with Lew Brown and Ray Henderson, authors
of *Rio Rita*, a Ziegfeld musical.
(Gift of Patricia Ziegfeld Stephenson, Will Rogers Memorial)

THE ORGANIZATION   IN THE FOLLIES THAT I HAVE IN MIND WITH
YOU IN IT I MUST OPEN OCTOBER EIGHT SO THERE IS NO TIME TO
LOSE AND I HOPE YOU REALIZE THAT YOUR PICTURES SHOULD
COME SECOND TO YOUR PUBLIC APPEARANCE   I HAVE JUST SEEN
[LEON] ERROL   I WANT YOU TO COME WITHOUT FAIL   BILL AN-
SWER QUICK

ZIEGFELD

TG, OkClaW.

Will rejoined the *Follies of 1924* as its featured star, and as this letter indicates, Ziegfeld often granted him special favors to keep him in the show.

New York
August 22, 1924

My dear Bill:

I tried everywhere to get you on the phone today before leaving for Easthampton, but it was impossible to find you.

Gene Buck tells me he had a long talk with you and we are to see the new skit Tuesday at 3 P.M.

Gene also told me you insisted on being away three matinees during the Polo Games—that your heart and soul are set upon seeing these games. You know Bill, there isn't anything I would not do for you, but you must realize we have an enormous organization, enormous expense, and with the productions necessary now with The Follies it takes a year to get our production back. To give matinees without you in them *would be absolutely impossible.*

There is only one thing to do. Of course it is going to entail a great loss, because unquestionably our matinees will be greatly hurt. There is only one solution—give the matinee on Friday instead of Saturday, and on Monday instead of Wednesday. Mr. Holzman will see you about this, and I think we can get a good story through the dramatic column so we will be able to have them, owing to your desire to see the Games I agreed to this, so you know what high esteem I hold you.

What the result will be Bill we will only have to wait to determine, but I want to please you in every way I possibly can. I would like to talk with you, so if you can call me at 115 M Easthampton when you get this I will be glad to talk with you.

Very sincerely yours,
Flo

TLS, OkClaW.

Will left the *Follies* for the last time in the fall of 1925 to go on a lecture tour around the country. For the next several years, Ziegfeld sent Rogers many telegrams pleading with him to return to the *Follies*. The showman, who habitually wired his friends and associates, supposedly had a special arrangement with Western Union which allowed him to send three million words each year at a reduced rate (Gerald Boardman, *Jerome Kern: His Life and Music* [New York: Oxford University Press, 1980], 203). At one time Will received so many telegrams from Ziegfeld that he wired the producer collect: "Keep this up. Am on my way to buy more Western Union stock" (Michel Mok, "The Cowboy Ambassador," n.d., clipping in scrapbook, CPpR).

NEW YORK NY
OCTOBER 21, 1925

WILL ROGERS
CARE FONTENELLE HOTEL
OMAHA NEBR

DEAR BILL I READ WITH INTEREST IN THE WORLD THAT YOU HELD ME UP FOR YEARS   WELL BILL I AM WILLING TO BE HELD UP SOME MORE   WHEN WILL YOU START AGAIN   AM SURE YOU ARE MEETING WITH GREAT SUCCESS REGARDS

ZIEGFELD

TG, OkClaW.

NEW YORK
OCT. 26, 1925

WILL ROGERS
PARK THEATRE
YOUNGSTOWN OHIO

MY DEAR BILL GLAD TO GET YOUR WIRE AND DELIGHTED BEYOND WORDS OF YOUR GREAT SUCCESS   AT SAME TIME AM DISAPPOINTED YOU ARE NOT READY TO COME BACK   WE OPEN CHI-

CAGO DECEMBER TWENTIETH   YOU WILL HAVE SO MUCH MONEY
BY THAT TIME YOU WILL WANT TO WORK FOR ME FOR NOTHING
BECAUSE YOU KNOW I SHOULD HAVE BEEN ON THAT TOUR   I AM
OPENING A PLAY LIKE MIDNIGHT FROLIC IN A NEWLY CON-
STRUCTED BUILDING BY [JOSEPH] URBAN ESPECIALLY DESIGNED
FOR PURPOSE   HAVE HICKMANS BAND FROM LOS ANGELES AND
OPEN JANUARY 14TH FOR TEN WEEKS   IF YOU DONT WANT TO
PLAY THE TEN WEEKS PLAY PART OF IT   YOU HAVE ALWAYS
WANTED TO GO TO FLORIDA AND YOU CAN MAKE UP YOUR SALARY
BY TEN MILLION DOLLARS IN REAL ESTATE DOWN THERE   I HAVE
PARIS SINGER INTERESTED WITH ME IN THEATRE DOWN THERE
AND HE HAS INSIDE TRACK ALL REAL ESTATE THERE   JUST PUT
THAT THINKING CAP OF YOURS ON AND FIGURE OUT BEST WAY FOR
YOURSELF   OF COURSE I WOULD LOVE TO HAVE YOU WITH FOLLIES
IN CHICAGO   BILL FIELDS FOUND OUT CONTRACT BREAKING NOT
SO EASY   HE WALKED OUT IN BOSTON AFTER THIRD WEEK BUT IS
PREPARED TO WALK BACK AGAIN IN PHILADELPHIA TONIGHT   IT IS
FUNNY IN THIS WORLD EVERYBODY HAS IT COMING TO THEM GOOD
OR BAD   HOPING TO HEAR FINALLY YOU WILL COME TO FLORIDA
AND MUST KNOW WELL IN ADVANCE AND HOPE YOU WILL   WITH
SINCERE REGARDS

FLO

TG, OkClaW.

PALM BEACH FLORIDA
APRIL 2, 1926

WILL ROGERS
GOLDSBORO NORTH CAROLINA

HAD GENE [BUCK] ON PHONE IN NEW YORK LAST NIGHT   TOLD ME
HE HEARD FROM YOU   ARE BOTH ANXIOUS TO HAVE YOU IN FOL-
LIES   AS YOU KNOW GREAT HANDICAP IS HAVING YOU IN NEW
YORK AND THEN LOSING YOU FOR OTHER TOWNS FOR SEVENTEEN
YEARS   I ALWAYS GAVE THEM ORIGINAL NEW YORK CAST IN LAST
FOUR YEARS FOLLIES SHOW   LOSS OF HALF MILLION DOLLARS
THEY RESENT NOT HAVING NEW YORK CAST   IS THERE NO WAY
YOU CAN GIVE ME ONE YEAR WITH FOLLIES   WE OPEN FIRST WEEK

IN JUNE AT GLOBE THEATRE WHICH HAS LESS CAPACITY THAN AM-
STERDAM BUT IS A GOOD HOUSE   [J. P.] MCEVOY HAS WRITTEN
FOUR SKETCHES AND I THINK ALL OF THEM BETTER THAN FIELDS
HAD LAST YEAR   GENE BUCK SUGGESTED SKETCH DONE AT LAMBS
CLUB IDEAL FOR YOU   MCEVOY SKETCHES YOU WOULD DELIGHT
IN   PLEASE GIVE MATTER REAL THOUGHT AND DECIDE TO POST-
PONE VISIT TO EUROPE   ROTTEN OVER THERE ANYWAY   YOU WILL
PROBABLY HEAR FROM GENE TOMORROW   I DO NOT THINK YOU
FULLY REALIZE WHAT IT MEANS IF YOU COULD SHAPE YOU PLANS
TO PLAY ENTIRE FOLLIES TOUR   WE COULD GET WONDERFUL PUB-
LICITY AND I COULD MAKE THE TWENTIETH FOLLIES AND PROB-
ABLY THE LAST THE GREATEST OF THEM ALL   OF COURSE IF YOU
HAVE ALREADY OBLIGATED YOURSELF TO [CHARLES L.] WAGNER
PERHAPS YOU CAN POSTPONE IT UNTIL FIRST FEBRUARY WHICH
WOULD ENABLE YOU TO TAKE IN PRINCIPAL CITIES   PHONE ME AT
ONE NINE TWO FOUR PALM BEACH OR WIRE ME   THE QUICKER YOU
DECIDE THE BETTER FOR ALL CONCERNED AS WITH YOU IN FOL-
LIES MANY CHANGES NECESSARY   ADVISE YOUR CALLING GENE AT
GREATNECK ONE FIVE FIVE   DO NOT FAIL TO CALL ME OR ANSWER
REGARDS

ZIEGFELD

TG, OkClaW.

ZIEGFELD BUILDS A NEW THEATRE

Ziegfeld built his own theater in 1926, hiring Joseph Urban
to design a magnificent auditorium. The theater opened on
2 February 1927 with the musical *Rio Rita*.

THE cornerstone of the new Ziegfeld Theatre, Sixth Avenue and
Fifty-fourth Street, which will be opened in January, was laid

New York Times, 10 December 1926, col. 2, p. 30 (copyright © 1926 by The New York
Times Company, reprinted by permission).

yesterday afternoon. Will Rogers was master of ceremonies and Vincent Lopez and his orchestra provided music. The cornerstone was cemented in place by Patricia Burke Ziegfeld, the theatrical manager's young daughter.

"Mr. Ziegfeld chose this corner because of the absence of saloons," said Mr. Rogers. "Since the saloons have disappeared there have been many more theatres, and this accounts for the fact that the entertainment is not as good as it was." Apropos of the placing of copies of yesterday's newspapers in the cornerstone, Mr. Rogers added: "Now I've discovered what they do with old papers."

NEW YORK
JAN. 31, 1927

FLO ZIEGFELD
ZIEGFELDS OWN THEATRE
ON THE RAGGED EDGE OF PARK AVENUE
NEW YORK

I SURE AM GLAD YOU ARE GOING TO HAVE YOUR OWN THEATRE. I DONT THINK ANY MAN CAN DO GOOD WORK IN SOME ONE ELSES THEATRE. I KNOW HOW IT WAS WITH YOU, YOU COULDENT PUT ON AS GOOD SHOWS AS YOU WOULD HAVE LIKED TO FOR IF YOU HAD IT WOULD HAVE ONLY MEANT THAT THEY WOULD HAVE MADE MORE MONEY. AND WHY MAKE MORE MONEY WHEN YOU KNEW THAT THROUGH YOUR ARTISTIC EXPOSURE, CHARLEY [DILLING-HAM] AND ABE [ERLANGER] WOULD GET THEIR CUT OUT OF IT. THE MINUTE YOUR MIND IS OFF RENT YOU CAN SETTLE DOWN AND DO SOMETHING WORTH WHILE. JUST THINK WHAT YOU WILL ACCOMPLISH WHEN THERE IS NO ARGUMENT OVER PERCENTAGE WITH ERLANGER. WHY YOU WILL FEEL LOST. I FEEL THAT THIS IS JUST THE STARTING FOR YOU OF A CHAIN. JUST THINK WHAT SHU-BERT AND SCHULTE AND LOEW AND NEDICK AND THE OWL AND CHILDS, ALL DID WITH ONE IDEA. WHY FLO I FEEL THAT YOU ARE JUST IN YOUR INFANCY IN THEATRE OW[N]ING, YOU ARE JUST LIKE

TG (typewritten draft on Western Union form), OkClaW.

Patricia Ziegfeld Stephenson (*at left*), Will Rogers, and Billie Burke (Mrs. Ziegfeld), joining in Florenz Ziegfeld's radio show at Los Angeles radio station KHJ, 4 April 1932. (Bettmann Archive)

POOR ANNE NICHOLS WHEN SHE HAD ONLY ONE ABIE. RESERVING YOU BEST CORNER LOTS IN BOTH CLAREMORE AND BEVERLY HILLS AT SMALL INCREASE, PROMOTE LOCAL CAPITAL, THATS WHAT THEY ALL DO, YOU DONT FURNISH ANYTHING BUT NAME AND GIRLS. I HOPE YOU NEVER HAVE TO PUT IN MOVIE SCREEN. YOUR OLD HIRED HAND.

WILL

Ziegfeld sent the following telegrams when he learned about Will's gallbladder operation.

NEW YORK NY
JUNE 15, 1927

WILL ROGERS
BEVERLY HILLS CALIF

I READ IN THE PAPERS YOU ARE SICK I ALWAYS WAS WORRIED ABOUT THE TERRIBLE LIFE YOU WERE LIVING IN DUMPS AND ON RAILROAD TRAINS NO HUMAN BEING CAN STAND THIS LIFE I HOPE HOWEVER IT IS NOTHING SERIOUS ALL WE HAVE THAT IS WORTH WHILE IS OUR HEALTH AND I HOPE YOU WILL REALIZE IT IN TIME AND GIVE UP BARNSTORMING AND COME TO NEW YORK GO IN THE FOLLIES AUGUST FIRST AND GET YOURSELF A NICE COUNTRY PLACE WITH A POLO FIELD AND REST FOR AT LEAST THREE OR FOUR MONTHS YOU CAN ALWAYS TAKE THAT PICTURE OF SAM RORK AND DO IT HERE NOW MAKE ME VERY HAPPY AND SEND ME A WIRE THAT YOU WILL OPEN WITH THE FOLLIES AUGUST FIRST I KNOW YOU REMEMBER THE DAY YOU TOLD ME THAT IF YOU EVER GOT FOUR HUNDRED DOLLARS A WEEK YOU WOULD BE SATISFIED BECAUSE YOU PROMISED YOURSELF WHEN YOU LEFT OKLAHOMA THAT SOME DAY YOU WOULD BE GETTING FOUR HUNDRED A WEEK NOW LOOK AT THE DARN SALARY I NEED SOME OF THE ROGERS LUCK IN THE NEXT FOLLIES AND YOU HAVE TO GIVE IT TO ME IF ONLY FOR A MINUTE SORRY YOU ARE NOT HERE TONIGHT TO HELP ME WITH THE LINDBERGH RECEPTION AT THE ZIEGFELD THEATRE LOVE

FLO

TG, OkClaW.

NEW YORK NY
JUNE 20, 1927

WILL ROGERS
BEVERLY HILLS CALIF

MY DEAR WILL I AM DELIGHTED TO READ IN THE PAPERS THAT
YOUR CONDITION IS WONDERFUL AFTER YOUR OPERATION I HOPE
YOU WILL SOON BE YOURSELF AGAIN I THINK YOU SHOULD TAKE
A VERY MUCH NEEDED REST AND SHOULD APPEAR IN THE FOLLIES
AUGUST IF ONLY FOR A SHORT TIME TO CONVALESCE YOU KNOW
THAT IS THE SHOW THAT BRINGS YOU THE LUCK LET ME KNOW
HOW YOU ARE GETTING ON LOVE

FLO

TG, OkClaW.

YONKERS NY
JULY 4, 1927

MAYOR WM R ROGERS
BEVERLY HILLS, CALIF

MY DEAR BILL DELIGHTED TO READ YOURE HOME AGAIN WHERE
I KNOW YOU WILL GET THE BEST OF CARE LET ME KNOW HOW
YOU REALLY ARE WE ALL SEND LOVE WERE REHEARSING THE
FOLLIES AND EDDIE CANTOR AND THE REST OF US MISS YOU
TERRIBLY

ZIEGFELD

TG, OkClaW.

Will Rogers
New Amsterdam Theatre
New York
[Ca. 1927]

My Dear Mr Ziegfeld,

I knew you were away and I understood for I know you to well to think you dident think of me in my trouble. I had such a lovely letter from your Wife and got your wire when you heard of my misfortune. I was very sorry to be out of the show but I couldent help it. I am so glad I went. Thank you Boss, you are a good Boss.

Yours as ever
Will

ALS, OkClaW

Ziegfeld sent a congratulatory telegram to Rogers when he substituted for Fred Stone in the Broadway musical *Three Cheers*. Stone had broken his leg in an airplane accident.

CHICAGO ILL
[OCTOBER 1928]

WILL ROGERS
GLOBE THEATRE

THREE CHEERS TO YOU BILL   THERE IS STILL SOME SENTIMENT LEFT IN THE THEATRE   WE ARE NOT ALL GOVERNED AND CONTROLLED YET YOU ARE DOING A NICE THING TONIGHT FOR OUR DEAR FRIEND FRED [STONE] WHO COULD ALWAYS BE DEPENDED UPON AND I KNOW DOROTHY [STONE] WILL APPRECIATE WHAT YOU ARE DOING   BUT REMEMBER YOU ARE ONLY PINCH HITTING   YOU STILL BELONG TO ME   SORRY I CANNOT BE THERE TONIGHT BUT I AM SENDING THE BOSS BILLIE LOVE

FLO

TG, OkClaW.

SCENE 9

THE CURTAIN FALLS

A notorious spendthrift, Ziegfeld spent lavish sums of money not only in his productions but in his personal life as well. He dressed in expensive hand-tailored clothes and imported lavender shirts. On the large estate at Hastings-on-the-Hudson, Burkely Crest, owned by his wife, the actress Billie Burke, he kept a menagerie of animals including buffalos and pet baby elephants. He also frequented the gambling tables, having made and lost a fortune at Monte Carlo.

Ziegfeld invested enormous sums of money on Wall Street in the twenties, buying mostly on margin, and he was reported to have lost more than a million dollars in the 1929 stock market crash. Billie Burke remembered her husband coming home late one evening and sitting on the bed, crying. "I'm through," he said. "Nothing can save me" (Billie Burke, *With a Feather on My Nose*, 222). Bankrupt and unable to pay his bills, Ziegfeld was pursued by creditors and inundated with lawsuits. He borrowed money from friends and relatives and mortgaged Burkely Crest.

But Ziegfeld, always the visionary, tried to stage a comeback. He produced the Broadway musical *Smiles* (1930), starring Fred and Adele Astaire and Marilyn Miller; but this production flopped, as did *Hot Cha* (1932). Hoping to recapture the golden age of the *Follies*, he produced the last edition in 1931, starring Ruth Etting, Helen Morgan, Jack Pearl, and Harry Richman. Criticized by reviewers as old-fashioned, the *Follies of 1931* was not a box-office success.

Clearly, the glory days of the *Follies* had passed. Ziegfeld's extravaganzas perfectly matched the fun-loving mood of the Jazz Age, but were out of sync with the somber mood of the Great Depression.

Adding to Ziegfeld's problems was his declining health. During the production of *Hot Cha* in March 1932, he fell ill with pneumonia. He complained about memory loss and painful headaches, and in the summer of 1932 he developed pleurisy. Billie Burke, who was shooting a movie in Los Angeles, decided that her husband should recover in California. On the long train ride west Ziegfeld became delirious and started hallucinating about his past life. Yet his health seemed to recover while living in his wife's home in Santa Monica.

During this time Rogers was an important companion and often visited Ziegfeld. But Will sensed these were his friend's last days. Ziegfeld suffered a relapse and was rushed to Cedars of Lebanon Hospital, where he died on 22 July 1932. Will was at the hospital the day The Great Glorifier passed away.

A year before he died Rogers wrote the following remembrance of his "Old Master."

LONG LIVE THE OLD MASTER

WELL Sir every man that has ever done anything out of the ordinary is a character, and I would call Flo Ziegfeld a man that had done something out of the ordinary, plum out of the ordinary. He had given to the American Public for Lord knows how many years, an entertainment that must have given them more pleasure and happiness than any other, for they have paid more to see it than to any other man in the World.

A Circus with all its tremendous aggregation of assorted animals from the four corners of the earths. Yet Mr. Florenz Ziegfeld can take just one breed, in fact just one-half the breed, the she of the specie, and can assemble such a round up of beauty that combined with the best there is to offer at that time in the amusement line, and he can concoct an evenings entertainment that you remember it till the next year.

A funny thing about the "Follies" all the years I was with it, in hearing people speak of the show that year, they never spoke of it in comparison to any other show. It was always "Its better than last year's, or its not so good as last years." It always stood alone for there was no other show that they could remember for a year.

His hardest opposition has been himself. If he had been new every year, and that particular show was his first, why each one would have been heralded as a masterpiece. But naturally they had to compete with each other. But its not of his shows, or his hundred and one other things that anyone could write on by the hour about that he has accomplished in the theatrical world, its just of him that I want to tell you something.

"Will Rogers Tells One on Mr. Ziegfeld," *Los Angeles Examiner*, 25 October 1931, sec. 5, p. 4.

The reason is its fresh in my mind. He was out on the coast a few weeks ago to visit his charming wife who was playing out there in one of the Coast's most successful shows, and as myself and my family are tremendously fond of him and his family why he was up to our Igloo some one evening for dinner. We got him started in on old times, and we had a great evening. Here was the peer of all Revue Producers of all time telling about his barnstorming about the country in his early career. His real start was with [Eugene] Sandow the strong man, I guess the first strong man. That is the first strong man that was strong enough to make people pay to see how strong he was. Well Mr. Ziegfeld dug him up over in Europe, and brought him over here. But let him tell it.

"I remember the first time I was out here on the coast. It was on Sandow's first trip. We had a kind of vaudeville show built around him sorter like Harry Lauder carried, only a better show. One time in Frisco we had him billed to fight a Lion. Just barehanded. It created a lot of excitement and we had a packed house. We were bringing Rome to Frisco. It was not a part of our program, it was a special stunt that was arranged there. It wasent framed either.

"This fellow Sandow really thought he was better than a Lion, so we got him a big old Lion. He entered the temporary Coliseum with more bravo than any Christian in the early days ever faced one. The Women kinder half hid their eyes, appearing like they dident want it to be seen that they were looking at such a sight, but secretly hoping something would happen. Instead of the Lion making for him, he had to make for the Lion. Well the old Lion took to outer edges. Sandow had to follow him, in fact chase him.

"The Lion dident pay any more attention to him than a house cat would. Well there wasent much fight. Everybody hollered that the Lion was doped, but he wasent. I wouldent even think of such a thing. I love Lions, especially after I counted up the house. Well Sandow kept at him, at least he kept at him till I could get the money from the Box Office to a fast moving conveyance. It was a terrible shock to me to hear the Lion was not the King of Beasts for I had read it all my life.

"Sandow dressed for his performance in a Tiger skin, in fact he brought that style of raiment over here. He was years ahead of Elinor Glyn, who used it as a mattress. Well Sandow left the Arena De Lions not ahead of the Lions but ahead of the populace. He wore his tiger skin for pajamas during the rest of that night ride. He was as downhearted about the Lion as I was. I never went to Frisco till the year of their big fair out there, when I took the Follies out. I thought the Odor of the Lion had vanished, but some of the newspapers had a memory and said, 'The man that arranged for a man to whip a Lion one time is in our midst again. We will watch him this time. If his Follies are doped then give us some of the dope!'

"Did I tell you what happened when we were on our way to the Coast? Well the train broke down and a wheel come off a car. When they got a new one fixed I got about 10 men to carry the old broken one into our stateroom. When we arrived at Oakland the Press Boys met us and I had them come in. They saw the wheel in the drawing room. 'What in the world is this?' 'Oh, that's a wheel we broke off and the Professor just picked it up and brought it in here.' They photographed it, and it made a great story, when as a matter of fact Sandow couldent even have rolled it downhill.

"He was a great fellow, this Sandow, a very high class man, a fine man, and perhaps the strongest of any of them, the most beautiful body. The Women fell for him hard. An imitator was right ahead of us claiming that he was the real Sandow. We finally had him brought to court, and as the case was progressing and all was argument as to who was which and what, I suggested to our Lawyer to tell the Judge to test them and see which was the real one. I had Sandow's big Iron Dumb Bell brought in, and the Judge asked the other fellow to lift it. He pulled a Kidney loose and couldent even get it out of the box. Sandow reached down, picked it up with one hand and was ready to make a forward pass with it out of the back window. We won the case. I wish I had some way of testing all my imitators."

He has had a great experience has Mr. Ziegfeld. He looks and is just the same as the days I went with him on his Midnight Frolic Roof (the first show) in 1914 [1915]. A many one of us got our start, our real start with him. Those were great old days those Folly days, packed houses, wonderful audiences, never bothered me as to what I was to do or say, never suggested or never cut out. And to think after 30 years of giving them the best in town he still has the best show in New York. That shows it wasent the performers that made Ziegfeld shows (for hundreds have come and gone). It was just Ziegfeld. I think he holds the record for being Champion. He knew colors, and he knew beauty. He knew how to keep nudeness from being vulgar. His was a gift, and not an accomplishment. Long live the old Master.

〰〰〰〰〰〰〰〰〰〰〰〰〰〰〰〰〰〰〰〰〰〰〰〰〰〰〰〰〰〰〰〰

Rogers took charge of making the arrangements for Ziegfeld's funeral which was held at the Pierce Brothers Mortuary in Los Angeles. It was a small private funeral attended by about one hundred close friends, including Will and many other *Follies* stars. Billie Burke and her daughter lived at Will's ranch for a time after the funeral. After Ziegfeld's death, they remained close friends of the family.

BILLIE BURKE

I think that Will loved Flo almost as much as Flo loved him. I know when Mr. Ziegfeld was so ill and he came out here we didn't know what to do about getting a place for him to rest. He said "I don't want to do anything until Will gets here." Will was out on a sort of tour and hadn't got back. And I wanted to get him to a ranch someplace. But he wouldn't budge until Will got here. And then of course when the end came why they were the first to be my side.

Billie Burke interview, 15 August 1966, tape, OkClaW.

Patricia Ziegfeld Stephenson, the daughter of Billie Burke and Florenz Ziegfeld, on her pony Sally. The saddle was given to her by Will Rogers. (Gift of Patricia Ziegfeld Stephenson, Will Rogers Memorial)

PATRICIA ZIEGFELD STEPHENSON: THE FAMILY NEXT DOOR

MY father and Will had a warm, comfortable rare relationship. They could ask anything of one another and it was as good as

Patricia Ziegfeld Stephenson, interview by editor, Los Angeles, 25 April 1991.

done. They had a rapport with one another and could talk about things they couldn't talk about with other people. They appreciated the same things. My father and Will were outdoor people and my father enjoyed riding with Will at his ranch in Santa Monica.

In a way we were like the family next door. I remember when we were in Los Angeles during the summer of 1929. My father had come out to discuss the movie version of *Whoopee* with Sam Goldwyn. Will and Aunt Betty did everything they could to make us feel at home. We visited the ranch frequently. He let me have my own pony to ride whenever I felt so inclined—and that was about every day. He would visit us at the beach house we were renting and swim in the pool. He knew how to do all sorts of crazy dives.

Will was also very helpful when my father was ill in Los Angeles in 1932. He came to the hospital the night my father died and took mother and me back to the ranch where we stayed for about a week. Mother was so grief stricken that Will took the situation in hand. He helped arrange the funeral services and perhaps even took care of some of the hospital bills. He helped so many people during rough times and always did it very quietly and unobtrusively. He would never talk about it. After Will's death, mother and I remained very close friends with Aunt Betty and her children Will Jr., Mary and Jim. They were always like the family next door.

BETTY ROGERS: PARTNERS IN THEATRICAL HISTORY

WILL had great admiration and respect for Mr. Ziegfeld. Many of the actors in the *Follies* called him "Ziggy" or "Flo," but to Will he was "Mr. Ziegfeld" in speaking to or about him. The close friendship between the two men did not develop until years later, when Will left the stage for good.

I had never met Mrs. Ziegfeld—Billie Burke—until she came out to California to live. She took a house not far away from the

Betty Rogers, *Will Rogers*, 141–142.

ranch and her daughter, Patricia, use to ride with our children. When Mr. Ziegfeld came West on visits, he and Will often rode together.

We saw a great deal of Mr. Ziegfeld during his last illness. Miss Burke brought him to California when his health failed. His death was a great shock to us all. Will and I had seen him that afternoon, and Miss Burke and Patricia had had dinner with him in his room in the hospital. They stayed quite late, until after eight o'clock. He seemed much improved and Miss Burke left him to go to one of the studios where she was working that night on a picture. At ten o'clock our telephone rang. Mr. Ziegfeld had suffered a sudden relapse. He died before any of us could get to him.

I like to remember Mr. Ziegfeld and Will as they looked on one of their many horseback rides together. Mr. Ziegfeld was mounted on one of Will's spirited polo ponies, Sundown, a beautiful dapple gray. He was a well-set-up rider and there was great style about everything he did. I watched the two men as they rode along side by side—Mr. Ziegfeld in a handsome pair of light-colored, winged chaps, sitting straight and erect, his gray hair sleek and glistening in the sun; Will carelessly sprawled in his saddle on his old speckled roping pony, Soapsuds, wearing his faded blue overalls, his shaggy hair blowing awry in the wind.

There they were, the greatest producer of all time, and the vaudevillian with his rope who had pulled the *Follies* out of many a tight place. So different they were and yet with so much in common. Each was grateful to the other. Once they had been partners in making theatrical history and now they were even closer, they were friends.

EDDIE CANTOR

EARLY next morning my phone rang, announcing that Ziegfeld had passed away. It was such a shock that I sat stupefied at the telephone and cried as bitterly as if I had lost my own father.

Eddie Cantor and David Freedman, *Ziegfeld: The Great Glorifier* (New York: Alfred H. King, 1934), 163–166.

Later in the day, Mrs. Rogers called me up and asked me to
help Will make the funeral arrangements. Rogers and I went
to a local minister and I'll never forget how Will tried to explain to the minister what he should say at the services. The
great humorist's eyes were filled with tears and he kept floun-
dering for words like a bewildered child. He said, "You see,
you don't know Zieggy like we do. He was great, he was wonderful, he wasn't just a producer. You see, he made all of us—we
would be nothing without him. I tell you he was great, he was
wonderful."

Later on I arranged for John Boles, my neighbor, to sing at
the services. All of Zieggy's stars who were in Hollywood packed
the little chapel in Los Angeles—many of his most beautiful
girls, too. It was a new kind of setting for Ziegfeld beauties—
there in black sat Marion Davies, Lilyan Tashman, Billie Dove,
Dorothy Mackaill, Lina Basquette—and when Boles sang *Going
Home*, they all bowed their heads and wept. Many celebrities
who never worked for Flo came to pay him a last tribute—
Winfield Sheehan, Irving Thalberg, Norma Shearer, George M.
Cohan, William Randolph Hearst, and all the picture stars and
executives who knew him. The entire ceremony was extremely
simple. Will Rogers saw to that. He allowed no announcement
of the event in the papers. He wanted no public demonstration
and no curiosity seekers. This was not the funeral of a theatrical
potentate, but the passing of a man, loved by his friends.

After the services, Jobyna Howland, who played opposite me
in *Kid Boots*, threw her arms around me and sobbed, "He's
gone, Eddie, he's gone."

"The King is Dead—Long Live the ———" —but not in our
time. There will be no one to take the throne.

Ziegfeld was unique. The touch of beauty and artistry that he
bequeathed to the American theatre and American womanhood
has become the common heritage of the land.

The sadly ironic part of the last services rendered this internationally famous genius was the fact that the local minister,
who eulogized Ziegfeld, repeatedly mispronounced his name.
He kept saying, "Ziegfield," and every time he made the mistake, it struck every one of us a blow to the heart, for we felt
how little strangers knew or understood this man who had been
largely responsible for spreading whatever little happiness there

was still left. But it didn't matter—he could tell us nothing that we did not know about Zieggy.

Aside from Billie Burke and Patricia, I know of nobody who was more affected by Zieggy's passing than Will Rogers. Will was as inconsolable as a child. He had lost some one whom he loved, a man whom he worshiped and, for weeks, he could not overcome the tragedy of the blow.

A few days after Ziegfeld's death, Will wrote the following "Daily Telegram," which was published in hundreds of newspapers.

BEVERLY HILLS, July 24. [To the Editor of the Times:] Our world of "make believe" is sad. Scores of comedians are not funny, hundreds of "America's most beautiful girls" are not gay. Our benefactor has passed away. He picked us from all walks of life. He led us into what little fame we achieved. He remained our friend regardless of our usefulness to him as an entertainer. He brought beauty into the entertainment world. The profession of acting must be necessary, for it exists in every race, and every language, and to have been the master amusement provider of your generation, surely a life's work was accomplished.

And he left something on earth that hundreds of us will treasure till our curtain falls, and that was a "badge," a badge of which we were proud, and never ashamed of, and wanted the world to read the lettering on it, "I worked for Ziegfeld."

So good-bye, Flo, save a spot for me, for you will put on a show up there some day that will knock their eyes out. Yours,

Will Rogers

Los Angeles Times, 25 July 1932, p. 1.

Will's final tribute was a eulogy he wrote for Ziegfeld. Since newspaper reports never mention he spoke at the funeral, Rogers probably never delivered his remarks.

THIS is the first time that I have ever appeared as a witness before the court of the Lord. I have no credentials, I am not an accredited witness, I am just an ex-hired hand that wants to speak a few words for our "boss."

Our religious beliefs among us here are many, but one is universal, and that is there is a divine being higher than earthly.

Our profession of acting must be honorable and it must be necessary for it exists in every language and every race. It's as old as life itself. Amusement must be necessary, for it's given to babes and children to laugh and to play.

In our life the curtain plays a great part, the curtain either rises or falls. The curtain has fallen for our boss, our master.

"Notes for Tribute at Florenz Ziegfeld's Private Funeral Service," TMs, Original Speech #006–63, OkClaW.

WHO'S WHO IN THE CAST

Adler, Felix (1891–1963). A gag and screen writer, Adler wrote stories and titles for many silent films.

Allen, Henry Justin (1868–1950). A newspaper editor, Allen served as governor of Kansas (1919–1923) and U.S. senator (1929–1930).

Astor, Nancy L. (1879–1964). A native of Virginia, Lady Astor (Nancy Witcher Langhorne) was the first woman member of the House of Commons (1920–1945), a supporter of Prohibition, and the wife of Lord Waldorf Astor.

Avon Comedy Four. A turn-of-the-century vaudeville act featuring Joe Smith, Charlie Dale, Will Lester, and Jack Coleman, known for a hilarious school sketch.

Babson, Roger W. (1875–1967). An educator, economist, and author, Babson was well known for his business statistical organization, which supplied information on securities, and for his business forecasting reports.

Baker, Newton Diehl (1871–1937). An influential politician and diplomat, Baker served as U.S. secretary of war (1916–1921) and avidly supported the League of Nations.

Balfour, Arthur James (1848–1930). A British statesman and philosopher, Balfour served as prime minister of England (1902–1905) and as British minister of foreign affairs during World War I. He initiated the Balfour Declaration (1917) supporting a Jewish national homeland in Palestine.

Barrymore, John (1882–1942). Barrymore was a distinguished Shakespearean actor, film star, and radio performer.

Baruch, Bernard Mannes (1870–1965). A financier and statesman, Baruch was chairman of the War Industries Board
(1918–1919) and attended the 1919 Versailles Peace
Conference as a member of the economic drafting
committee.

Basquette, Lina (1909—). A child screen star, Basquette was
the leading dancer in the *Follies of 1923*. She later left
the *Follies* for a career in the movies.

Belasco, David (1853–1931). An American theatrical producer
and playwright whose productions were noted for many
stage innovations, including creative lighting and real-
istic sets.

Blasco-Ibáñez, Vicente (1867–1928). A popular Spanish author,
Blasco-Ibáñez was best known for the novels *Blood and
Sand* (1906) and *The Four Horsemen of the Apocalypse*
(1916).

Bliss, Tasker Howard (1853–1930). A West Point graduate,
General Bliss was chief of staff in 1917 and one of the
five U.S. delegates to the Versailles Peace Conference.

Boles, John (1896–1969). An actor and singer, Boles performed
on Broadway and in films, playing leads in musicals, dra-
mas, and romantic comedies.

Borah, William Edgar (1865–1940). A Republican senator from
Idaho (1907–1940), Borah opposed the League of Na-
tions and helped initiate the Washington Disarmament
Conference (1921–1922).

Brady, James Buchanan (1865–1917). An American financier,
railroad magnate, and philanthropist, Diamond Jim
Brady became known for the lavish collection of dia-
monds that adorned his clothes.

Brice, Fanny (1891–1951) A famous singer and comedian,
Brice starred in many editions of the *Follies* and later
became a film and radio star playing Baby Snooks.

Brisbane, Arthur (1864–1936). A newspaper journalist and editor of William Randolph Hearst's New York *Journal*,

Brisbane was known for his syndicated column, "Today," and as an advocate of the yellow journalism that helped incite public opinion against the Spanish in the war of 1898.

Bryan, William Jennings (1860–1925). Three-time Democratic nominee for president and a flamboyant orator, Bryan served as secretary of state (1913–1915) and as prosecuting attorney for Tennessee in the Scopes trial (1925), supporting the state's antievolution law.

Buck, Gene (1885–1957). An American song writer, Buck helped organize Ziegfeld's *Midnight Frolic*, wrote many lyrics for the *Follies*, and later served as president of the American Society of Composers, Authors, and Publishers.

Burbank, Luther (1849–1926). A California horticulturist who experimented with new types of fruits and plants, he developed the Burbank potato and many varieties of flowers.

Burke, Billie (1886–1970). Billie Burke was a famous theater and motion-picture star and the wife of Florenz Ziegfeld.

Burleson, Albert Sidney (1863–1937). Postmaster general from 1913 to 1926, Burleson was later chairman of the United States Telegraph and Telephone Administration.

Busch, Adolphus (1839–1913). A Gilded Age entrepreneur, Busch built the Anheuser-Busch brewery in St. Louis, Missouri, and developed it into America's leading beer producer.

Bush, Frank (?–1927). A vaudeville monologist, Bush played in several circuits around the country.

Cantor, Eddie (1893–1964). A star of the *Ziegfeld Follies* and other Broadway productions, Cantor went on to fame as a top-flight radio and screen entertainer.

Carmen, Sybil (?–1929). A *Follies* show girl, Carmen performed in several Ziegfeld productions with Rogers.

Caruso, Enrico (1873–1921). The famous Italian operatic tenor made his debut at the Metropolitan Opera House in 1903 and during his life sang over 600 times at the Metropolitan.

Castle, Irene (1893–1969). Irene Castle and her husband, Vernon, revolutionized ballroom dancing and were the most popular dance team in America before pre–World War I.

Castle, Vernon Blythe (1887–1918). A famous dancer with his wife, Irene, Vernon Castle popularized the Castle walk, the tango, the turkey trot, and the one-step. He died tragically in an air crash while serving in the British Royal Flying Corps.

Chaplin, Charlie (1889–1977). Born in England, Chaplin is considered the world's greatest silent-film comedy star for his portrayal of the loveable "little tramp."

Cherry Sisters. The five Cherry Sisters (Effie, Jessie, Ella, Lizzie, and Addie) gained fame as the worst act in vaudeville, and the audience enjoyed throwing rotten eggs at them.

Clemenceau, Georges (1841–1929). Premier of France (1906–1909, 1917) and World War I leader, Clemenceau represented French security interests at the Versailles Peace Conference.

Cohan, George Michael (1878–1942). American songwriter, actor, and dance man, Cohan became famous for his patriotic tunes "You're a Grand Old Flag," "I'm a Yankee Doodle Dandy," and "Give My Regards to Broadway."

Collier, William (1866–1944). An American comedic actor and playwright, Collier also appeared in many popular plays, including *On the Quiet* and *Never Say Die*.

Coogan, Jackie (1914–1984). Coogan began his film career as a child star appearing in *The Kid* and became a leading screen actor.

Coolidge, Calvin (1872–1933). As the thirtieth president of the United States (1923–1929), Coolidge supported business expansion and tax reductions, but his administration was noted for its lackluster legislation.

Coué, Émile (1857–1926). The pioneer of autosuggestion, the French psychotherapist Coué developed the idea of optimistic behavior through the repetition of verbal formulas.

Creel, George (1876–1953). As chairman of the Committee on Public Information (1917–1919), Creel, a journalist, helped mold public opinion in support of America's involvement in World War I.

Croker, Bula Benton Edmondson. Wife of New York Tammany Hall boss Richard C. Croker, Croker was sued by her sons for Croker's wealth when he died in 1922.

Curtis, Charles (1860–1936). A Kansas Republican, Curtis served as U.S. senator and as vice president of the United States (1929–1933).

Daniels, Josephus (1862–1941). A statesman and journalist, Daniels was secretary of the navy under Woodrow Wilson (1913–1921) and later U.S. ambassador to Mexico (1933–1941).

Davies, Marion (1897–1961). A *Ziegfeld Follies* show girl, Davies later became a leading motion-picture comedien.

Dawes, Charles Gates (1865–1951). A financier, statesman, and vice president of the United States (1925–1929), Dawes proposed the Dawes Plan (1924) to regulate World War I German reparations payments.

Depew, Chauncey Mitchell (1834–1928). A lawyer and politician, Depew was a railroad attorney, a U.S. senator, and a well-known after-dinner speaker.

Dillingham, Charles (1868–1934). A prominent theatrical manager, Dillingham was one of Broadway's most active producers, staging over 200 productions.

Dolores (Kathleen Rose). A model and Ziegfeld Girl, Dolores became famous for her elaborate gowns in Ziegfeld productions.

Dove, Billie (1900–). Dove was a featured performer in the *Ziegfeld Follies* and became a famous silent-movie star billed as "The American Beauty."

Duff-Gordon, Lady Lucile (1864?–1935). A famous English dressmaker who designed many elegant fashions for the *Follies*.

Edison, Thomas Alva (1847–1931). America's most ingenious inventor, Edison invented the phonograph, the incandescent electric lamp, the carbon telephone transmitter, the quadruplex telegraph, the motion-picture projector, the stock ticker, and many other important devices.

Edwards, Gus (1879–1945). A composer and impresario, Edwards produced schoolboy vaudeville acts and cabaret entertainments. He discovered many talents, including Eddie Cantor and George Jessel.

Ellis, Melville (1876?–1917). A pianist in revues and vaudeville, Ellis also worked as a stage producer and costume designer.

Erlanger, Abraham Lincoln (1860–1930). Erlanger was a powerful producer and theater owner. His theatrical syndicate, Marc Klaw and Erlanger, controlled many Broadway show places and was a major investor in the *Ziegfeld Follies*.

Errol, Leon (1881–1951). A vaudeville comedian, *Follies* star, and film actor, Errol was known for his funny "rubber legs" walk on stage and his portrayal of a comic drunk.

Evans, George (1870–1915). "Honey Boy" Evans was a black-face comic and singer on the vaudeville circuit. Supposedly he helped write the song "In the Good Old Summer Time."

Fairbanks, Douglas, Sr. (1883–1939). Fairbanks was a popular film actor famous for his swashbuckling roles in adventure films and cofounder of the United Artists studios with his wife, Mary Pickford, Charlie Chaplin, and D. W. Griffith.

Fields W. C. (1880–1946). A vaudeville comic juggler and *Ziegfeld Follies* star, Fields increased his fame in films in which he portrayed a humorous, cantankerous character, such as *The Bank Dick* (1940) and *Never Give a Sucker an Even Break* (1941).

Firpo, Luis Angel (1895–1960). An Argentine boxer, Firpo was called the "Wild Bull of the Pampas" and in 1923 lost to Jack Dempsey in a heavyweight title fight.

Ford, Henry (1863–1947). The famous automobile manufacturer established the Ford Motor Company in 1903. He pioneered assembly-line methods and affordable mass-produced cars, including the Model T, for the average American.

Gallagher (?—1929) **and Shean** (1868–1949). A hit song-and-comedy team in vaudeville and the *Follies*, Ed Gallagher and Al Shean became known for their catchy song "Absolutely, Mr. Gallagher? Positively, Mr. Shean."

Garfield, Harry Augustus (1863–1942). Chief fuel administrator during the critical time of World War I (1917–1919), Garfield improved coal production and rationed fuel by instituting heatless days and gasless Sundays and reduced fuel for industries not vital to the war effort.

Garibaldi, Giuseppe (1807–1882). An Italian general and fervent patriot, Garibaldi helped unify Italy through guerilla campaigns against Austria and victories with his famous Redshirt volunteer army.

Gary, Elbert Henry (1846–1927). A lawyer and industrialist, Gary helped organize the U.S. Steel Corporation and served as its chairman (1901–1927).

George V (1865–1936). George, who became King of England in 1910, was a popular monarch during World War I, when he rallied British forces against Germany.

Glass, Carter (1858–1946). A Virginia statesman, Glass served in the U.S. House of Representatives (1902–1919) and Senate and as secretary of the treasury under Woodrow Wilson (1918–1920).

Glyn, Elinor (1864–1943). An English writer, Glyn wrote the popular novel *Three Weeks* (1907), a love story, and scripts for the movies, including Clara Bow's *It* (1927).

Goldwyn, Samuel (1882–1974). A leading motion picture producer, Goldwyn organized Goldwyn Pictures Corporation in 1916. Will Rogers acted in Goldwyn films from 1919 to 1921.

Gordon, Cliff (1878?–1913). A successful vaudeville comedian, Gordon was known for his German dialect routines.

Grauman, Sid (1879–1950). Impresario and theater owner, Grauman built the Chinese Theater on Hollywood Boulevard and other exotic cinemas.

Grayson, Cary Travers (1878–1938). A navy admiral, Grayson was Woodrow Wilson's physician and became widely known when the president became ill at the Versailles Conference.

Greeley, Horace (1811–1872). A journalist and politician, Greeley founded the influential New York *Tribune* (1841), ran unsuccessfully for president in 1872, and became famous for his slogan "Go West, Young Man."

Haggin, James Ben Ali (1882–1951). Haggin was a *Ziegfeld Follies* artist known for his tableaux, or living-picture settings, featuring poses of paintings, historical subjects, and other scenes.

Haig, Douglas (1861–1928). A British field marshal and commander in World War I, Haig led the assault on the German army in 1918.

Harding, Warren G. (1865–1923). The twenty-ninth president of the United States (1921–1923). Harding's administration was rife with scandals and corruption and was a favorite target of Rogers' jokes.

Harrison, Byron Patton (1881–1941). A Mississippi politician, Harrison served as a U.S. representative (1911–1919), and senator (1919–1941), and as the temporary chairman of the 1924 Democratic Convention.

Hart, Max (1874–1950). As a theatrical agent Hart had many vaudeville stars among his clients, including Will Rogers, Eddie Cantor, W. C. Fields, and other *Follies* headliners. He may have been the person who convinced Rogers to drop his vaudeville horse act and do a solo monologue.

Hart, William Surrey (1864–1946). A stage actor and film star, Hart was a pioneer filmmaker in the genre of silent westerns. The melodramatic *Hell's Hinges* (1916) is considered one of his finest films.

Harvey, George Brinton McClellan (1864–1928). A journalist and diplomat, Harvey edited the *North American Review* (1899–1926) and was appointed U.S. ambassador to Great Britain.

Hearst, William Randolph (1863–1951). Hearst's newspaper empire included the San Francisco *Examiner*, the New York *Journal-American*, and many other papers known for sensational "yellow journalism." He also served in the U.S. House of Representatives.

Hickman, Art (1886–1930). Hickman, an orchestra leader, directed the California Band which entertained in the *Follies* and was popular in the 1920s.

Hitchcock, Raymond (1870–1929). The American singer and comedian "Hitchy" was featured in many hit musicals and revues on the Broadway stage, including the *Follies of 1921*.

Holzman, Benjamin F. (1891–1963). A newspaper editor, Holzman became head of Ziegfeld's publicity department in 1924 and later was an agent with the William Morris Agency.

Hoover, Herbert Clark (1887–1954). Before becoming the thirty-first U.S. president (1929–1933), Hoover, a mining engineer, served as food administrator (1917–1919) and secretary of commerce (1921–1928).

House, Edward Mendell (1858–1938). "Colonel" House was a close advisor of Woodrow Wilson, the president's personal representative in Europe (1914–1916), and a member of the U.S. Peace Commission at the Versailles Conference (1919).

Houston, David Franklin (1866–1940). An influential Texas Democrat politician, Houston served as secretary of agriculture (1913–1920) and secretary of the treasury (1920–1921).

Howland, Jobyna (1880–1936). A screen and theater star, Howland was featured in the Broadway shows *The Texas Nightingale* (1922) and *Kid Boots* (1923).

Hughes, Charles Evans (1862–1948). A New York Republican statesman and jurist, Hughes held many important positions, including governor of New York (1907–1910), U.S. secretary of state (1921–1925), and chief justice of the U.S. Supreme Court (1930–1941).

Johns, Brooke. An American singer and musician, Johns starred in the Broadway show *Jack and Jill* in 1923.

Johnson, Hiram Warren (1866–1945). A California lawyer and political reformer, Johnson served as governor of California (1911–1917) and U.S. senator. An isolationist, he opposed ratification of the Versailles Treaty (1919–1920).

Kellermann, Annette (1887–1975). Called "The Divine Venus," Kellermann was an Australian swimmer who gained attention by being the first woman to wear a one-piece bathing suit (1907) and for her diving and swimming act and water ballets in vaudeville revues.

Kelly, Harry. A *Ziegfeld Follies* comedian, Kelly appeared in many skits with Rogers, W. C. Fields, and others.

Kelly, Lew (1879–1944). A burlesque stage comedian who also appeared in supporting roles in many Hollywood comedies of the 1930s, including Laurel and Hardy's *Pack Up Your Troubles*.

King, Allyn (1901–1930). A *Follies* show girl and stage and screen actress, King was a big hit in many Broadway revues and silent films.

La Follette, Robert Marion (1855–1925). A leading Wisconsin politician and progressive, La Follette served as reform governor of Wisconsin (1900–1906) and U.S. senator (1906–1925). He fought against the League of Nations.

Lansing, Robert (1864–1928). A lawyer and diplomat, Lansing served as secretary of state (1915–1920) in the Woodrow Wilson administration.

Laurell, Kay (1890–1927). A *Follies* show girl called "The American Venus," Laurell created a sensation by appearing nude as "September Morn" and in tableaux scenes.

Lewis, James Hamilton (1863–1939). Known for his expensive clothes and political cleverness, "Ham" Lewis served as U.S. senator from Illinois (1913–1919, 1931–1939) and as majority whip.

Lindbergh, Charles Augustus (1902–1974). A hero of the 1920s, Lindbergh made the first transatlantic solo flight in 1927 and was closely associated with Rogers, who supported commercial aviation.

Lipton, Thomas Johnstone (1850–1931). A Scottish tea manufacturer, Lipton formed Lipton Limited with large land holdings worldwide. He was an avid yachtsman, known for his unsuccessful competition for America's Cup.

Lloyd, Harold Clayton (1894–1971). One of the great comedians of the silent screen, Lloyd became famous for portraying naïve young men perpetually in trouble in such films as *Safety Last* (1923) and *The Kid Brother* (1927).

Lloyd George, David (1863–1945). A Welsh statesman and prime minister of Great Britain (1916–1922), George was a great leader of the English people during World War I and headed the British delegation to the Versailles Peace Conference. (1919).

Lodge, Henry Cabot (1850–1924). A Republican statesman from Massachusetts, Lodge was a U.S. senator (1893–1924). He led the opposition to U.S. membership in the League of Nations.

Loew, Marcus (1870–1927). Loew owned many vaudeville and motion-picture theaters and was a leading distributor of films.

Longworth, Alice Roosevelt (1884–1980). The daughter of Theodore Roosevelt and the wife of Congressman Nicholas Longworth, she was known for her elaborate Washington parties and behind-the-scenes political influence. Longworth was an acquaintance of Rogers.

Lopez, Vincent (1898–1975). A popular orchestra leader, radio performer, and screen actor, Lopez appeared in the movie *The Big Broadcast* in 1932.

Lorraine, Lillian (1892–1955). A famous *Follies* star and talented singer with large expressive eyes, Lorraine gained fame for her elaborate costumes and jewelry and lavish life-style, which several times led to bankruptcy and failed marriages.

Lowell, Abbott Lawrence (1856–1943). Educator, professor of government, and president of Harvard University, Lowell wrote several books on political science.

McAdoo, William Gibbs (1863–1941). A Democrat political leader, McAdoo was secretary of the treasury (1913–1918) in the Wilson administration, chairman of the Federal Reserve Board, and senator from California.

McEvoy, Joseph Patrick (1894–1958). A newspaperman, novelist, and playwright, McEvoy wrote the book for many *Follies* shows and other Broadway revues.

McGuffey, William Holmes (1800–1873). A well-known educator, McGuffey became famous for his *Eclectic Readers* (1836, 1837), elementary school textbooks that were widely used in the nineteenth century.

Mackaill, Dorothy (1906–1977). A Follies chorine and British movie star, the blue-eyed blonde performed in siren and flapper roles on the silent screen.

Marshall, Thomas Riley (1854–1925). Marshall served as governor of Indiana and vice president under Woodrow Wilson (1913–1921).

Meyer, Eugene (1875–1959). A banker, government official, and newspaper executive, Meyer served as chairman of the War Finance Corporation (1918–1927), governor of the Federal Reserve Bank (1930–1933), and publisher of the *Washington Post* (1933–1946).

Miller, Marilyn (1898–1936). One of Ziegfeld's most famous and beautiful stars, she drew rave reviews in the *Follies of 1918*, starred in Ziegfeld's show *Sally* (1920), and later became a successful movie actress.

Minter, Mary Miles (1902–1984). A silent screen star, Minter received considerable publicity when her lover, the director William Desmond Taylor, was killed in a still-unsolved murder.

Mitchel, John Purroy (1879–1918). An attorney and politician, Mitchel served as mayor of New York City from 1914 to 1917 and introduced reforms including tax relief and a zoning plan.

Mussolini, Benito (1883–1945). The premier and dictator of Italy (1924–1945), Mussolini founded Fascism and, in alliance with Hitler, declared war on the Allies in 1940. He was killed by partisans in 1943.

Newberry, Truman Handy (1864–1945). A Republican politician from Michigan, the naval officer and financier Newberry served as secretary of the navy (1908–1909) and U.S. senator (1919–1922).

Niblo, Fred, Sr. (1872–1948). A vaudeville and screen actor, Niblo directed many famous silent movies, including *Ben Hur* and *The Mark of Zorro*.

Nicholas II (1868–1918). As the last czar of Russia (1894–1917), Nicholas's conservative policies, misgovernment, and vacillation helped precipitate the Russian Revolution in 1917.

Nichols, Anne (1891–1966). An actress, screenwriter, and playwright, Nichols was best known for her comedy play *Abie's Irish Rose* (1922), which she also produced.

Omar Khayyam (1048?–1123). A Persian poet, mathematician, and astronomer whose popular poem *The Rubaiyat of Omar Khayyam* has been translated into many languages.

Orlando, Vittorio Emanuele (1860–1952). The Italian statesman Orlando led the Italian delegation to the Versailles Peace Conference (1919), where he demanded territorial concessions for his nation.

Otis, Charles A (1868–1953). Ohio Republican politician and financier who founded the securities firm of Otis and Company.

Pennington, Ann (1893–1971). A *Follies* star, Pennington was a talented dancer known for her dimpled knees. She performed with Rogers in the Ziegfeld shows.

Pershing, John Joseph (1860–1948). U.S. General "Black Jack" Pershing led the attack against Pancho Villa in Mexico (1916) and served as commander of the American Expeditionary Force in Europe during World War I and U.S. chief of staff (1921–1924).

Post, Wiley (1898–1935). An American flying ace, Post broke the record for a solo flight around the world in 1933 in the *Winnie Mae*. He experimented with substratospheric flights and was killed with Rogers when their plane malfunctioned near Point Barrow, Alaska.

Ralston, Samuel M. (1875–1925). A Democratic politician, Ralston served as governor of Indiana (1913–1917), U.S. senator (1923–1925), and was a dark-horse candidate who withdrew his name for the presidential nomination at the 1924 Democratic Convention, which eventually led to the nomination of John W. Davis.

Rickenbacker, Edward Vernon (1890–1973). An American pilot in World War I, Rickenbacker shot down twenty-six aircraft and was awarded the Congressional Medal of Honor. Afterwards he became an automotive and airline executive.

Ring, Blanche (1876–1961). A popular vaudeville and musical comedy singer who sang in an Irish brogue, Ring introduced audience participation singing and became famous for her theme song, "I've Got Rings on My Fingers." Rogers appeared with her in *The Wall Street Girl* (1912).

Ritchie, Albert Cabell (1867–1936). A Democrat political figure, Ritchie served as a four-term governor of Maryland from 1920 to 1935 and was nominated unsuccessfully for president at the 1924 Democratic Convention.

Rockefeller, John Davison, Sr. (1839–1937). An oil magnate, entrepreneur, and philanthropist, Rockefeller organized the Standard Oil Company (1870) and the Standard Oil Trust (1882), the original modern-day conglomerate that virtually controlled the petroleum industry through a vast production and distribution network.

Rockne, Knut Kenneth (1888–1931). A famous football coach known for his daring offensive tactics, Rockne coached at Notre Dame University (1918–1931) and developed the team into a football powerhouse with a record of 105 victories.

Roosevelt, Theodore (1858–1919). A flamboyant political Progressive as well as a devotee of the Old West, Roosevelt resided on a Dakota ranch in the 1880s, led the Rough Riders in the Spanish-American War (1898), was elected a reform governor of New York (1899–1900), succeeded to the presidency on the death of William McKinley in 1901, and was reelected in 1904.

Root, Elihu (1845–1937). An author, lawyer, diplomat, and internationalist, Root, a Republican, served as U.S. secretary of war, reorganizing the army (1899–1904), and as secretary of state in the Theodore Roosevelt administration (1905–1909). He later was elected senator from New York (1909–1914).

Ruth, George Herman (1895–1948). An immortal New York Yankee baseball player, Babe Ruth established a record of sixty home runs in 1927 and a lifetime batting average of .342.

Sandow, Eugene (1867–1925). Ziegfeld managed this famous German strong man on the vaudeville stage and made him into an overnight sensation through well-organized publicity stunts that included posing virtually in the nude.

Savoy (1888?–1923) **and Brennan** (?–1961). A popular two-man vaudeville act featuring Bert Savoy as a female impersonator and Jay Brennan as the straight man.

Schenck, Joseph T. (1891–1930). A screen and stage actor, Schenck teamed with Gus Van in a comic two-man vaudeville act.

Schwab, Charles Michael (1862–1939). A steel magnate known for his efficient business methods, Schwab was president of the Carnegie Steel Company (1897–1901), the U.S. Steel Company (1901–1903), and owner and president of Bethlehem Steel (1903–1939).

Shearer, Norma (1904–1983). A popular screen actress, Shearer appeared in many movies in the 1930s and won an Oscar for best actress in *The Divorcee* (1930).

Sheehan, Winfield (1883–1945). An American film director and producer, "Winnie" Sheehan was vice president of Fox Film Corporation and produced several of Rogers' films, including *State Fair* (1933), *David Harum* (1934), and *Stand Up and Cheer* (1934).

Sheppard, Morris (1875–1941). An ardent prohibitionist, as U.S. senator (1913–1941) Sheppard supported a constitutional amendment prohibiting the manufacture, importation, and sale of liquor.

Shubert, Jacob J. (1880–1963). Jake Shubert was a theatrical producer who with his brother Lee owned and managed many theaters in New York as well as other major cities, and also produced plays and operettas.

Smith, Alfred Emanuel (1873–1944). A powerful and colorful Democratic political figure, Al Smith served four terms as a reform governor of New York (1919–1920, 1923–1928) and was defeated for the presidency in 1928 largely because of opposition to his Catholicism and his support of Prohibition.

Stone, Dorothy (1905–1974). Daughter of Fred Stone, the stage actress appeared with her father in *Stepping Stones* (1923) and played with Will Rogers in *Three Cheers* (1928).

Stone, Fred Andrew (1873–1959). A prominent stage and screen actor and a close friend of Rogers, Stone did a song-and-dance act with David Montgomery in vaudeville and performed in many Broadway shows.

Sumner, John Saxton (1876–1971). A moral crusader, Sumner headed the New York Society for the Suppression of Vice.

Sunday, William Ashley (1862–1935). A former professional baseball player, Billy Sunday was a flamboyant evangelist and avid supporter of Prohibition whose revival sermons in the 1920s attracted large crowds.

Swope, Herbert Bayard (1882–1958). A well-known journalist, Swope was editor and feature writer for the New York *World* and won the Pulitzer Prize (1917) for his writing.

Taft, William Howard (1857–1930). A lawyer, jurist, and Republican politician, Taft served as civil governor of the Philippines (1901–1904) and U.S. secretary of war (1904–1908), and was elected twenty-seventh president of the United States (1909–1913).

Tashman, Lilyan (1899–1934). One of Ziegfeld's most stunning show girls, Tashman was a big hit in the *Follies* and went on to star in other Broadway shows and the movies, where she played sophisticated women and became known as "The Best-Dressed Woman in Hollywood."

Thalberg, Irving (1899–1936). The American film producer Thalberg became chief producer at Metro-Goldwyn-Mayer in 1927 in charge of all productions.

Tiller Girls. A precision dancing act from England popular in the *Follies* and other revues.

Tinney, Frank (1878–1940). A blackface comic, Tinney was a well-known vaudeville and *Follies* comedian and appeared in other Broadway shows such as *The Century Girl* (1916).

Tombes, Andrew (1889–1961). Stage and screen star Andy Tombes appeared with Will Rogers in *Three Cheers* (1928) and performed in many films in the 1930s and 1940s.

Tumulty, Joseph (1879–1954). A close friend of Woodrow Wilson, Tumulty acted as his assistant while Wilson was president of the United States.

Turpin, Ben (1869–1940). A stage and screen comic actor known for his large mustache and crossed eyes, Turpin starred in vaudeville, burlesque, and films.

Tynan, Brandon (1879–1967). Born in Ireland, Tynan was a versatile stage and screen actor and a talented impersonator who appeared in the *Follies of 1922*.

Ulric, Leonore (1894–1970). A stage and screen actress, Ulric was a star in many Broadway productions and films, including *Camille* (1936) and *Temptations* (1946).

Underwood, Oscar W. (1862–1929). A lawyer and a powerful politician, Underwood served in the U.S. House of Representatives (1895–1915) and Senate (1915–1927).

Urban, Joseph (1872–1933). A leading set designer, the Austrian Urban created the scenery for the *Midnight Frolic* and *Follies* productions, using dazzling colors that awed audiences.

Valentino, Rudolph (1895–1926). Born in Italy, Valentino portrayed glamorous and courageous romantic Latin heros in such films as *The Sheik* (1921) and *The Young Rajah* (1922).

Van (1888–1968) **and Schenck** (1891–1930). The comic vaudeville team of Gus Van and Joseph Schenck performed dialect songs in the *Midnight Frolic* (1918) and several editions of the *Follies* from 1919 to 1921.

Victor Emmanuel II (1869–1947). The king of Italy from 1900 to 1946, but largely a figurehead after Mussolini became premier.

Villa, Pancho (1877–1923). A Mexican revolutionist, Villa opposed the government of Venustiano Carranza. When his forces crossed into New Mexico, Wilson ordered General Pershing to pursue him into Mexico.

Viviani, René Raphael (1863–1925). A French statesman and Socialist, Viviani served in the Chamber of Deputies (1893) and as minister of labor and premier (1914–1915).

Wadsworth, James Wolcott, Jr. (1877–1952). Republican politician Wadsworth served as senator from New York (1915–1927) and in the House of Representatives (1933–1951).

Wagner, Charles L. (?–1956). A producer and theatrical agent, Wagner managed Rogers' national lecture tour beginning in 1925.

Wales, Prince of (1894–1972). Edward, Prince of Wales, became king of England (Edward VIII) in January 1936. He frequently visited the United States. Rogers, who played polo with him, often made him the subject of jokes. Edward VIII abdicated the throne in December 1936 to marry Wallis Simpson, a divorcee.

Watterson, Henry (1840–1921). A Pulitzer Prize–winning journalist, Watterson was editor of the *Louisville Courier-Journal* (1868–1918) and staunchly opposed Prohibition and the League of Nations.

Wayburn, Ned (1874–1942). Wayburn directed many of the *Ziegfeld Follies* and *Midnight Frolic* productions and was largely responsible for the shows' success through his exhaustive auditions and rehearsals.

Welch, Joe (1869?–1918). A vaudeville dialect comic, Welch portrayed unfortunate Jewish and Italian characters on stage.

White, Henry (1850–1927). A career diplomat, White was the only Republican member on the U.S. Peace Commission to the Versailles Conference (1919).

Wilhelm II, Kaiser (1859–1941). Ruler of Germany from 1888 to 1918, Kaiser Wilhelm was exiled to Holland after Germany's defeat in World War I.

Willard, Jess (1883–1968). Heavyweight champion of the world, Willard won the title by defeating Jack Johnson in 1915.

Williams, Bert (1874–1922). The talented black performer Williams was a popular pantomimist and vaudeville comic and singer. He starred in many editions of the *Follies* from 1910 to 1919 and also was famous for his rendition of the song "Nobody."

Wills, Nat (1873–1917). Wills played "The Happy Tramp" on the vaudeville stage, making audiences laugh with his droll monologue.

Wilson, Imogene (1902–1948). A *Follies* chorine, Wilson became well known when she was assaulted by her lover, Frank Tinney (1924). Later she became a film star using the name Mary Nolan.

Wilson, Woodrow (1865–1924). After being president of Princeton University (1902–1910) and governor of New Jersey (1911–1913), Wilson served as president of the United States from 1913 to 1921. During his terms considerable progressive reform legislation was passed, and during World War I he formulated his Fourteen Points peace plan.

Wrigley, William, Jr. (1861–1932). A Chicago entrepreneur who organized the Wrigley Company to produce chewing gum. He had a summer home on California's Santa Catalina island, which he owned.

Ziegfeld, Florenz, Jr. (1867–1932). A flamboyant and creative impresario, Ziegfeld forged new directions in the American musical theater through his *Follies* productions and other Broadway musicals such as *Show Boat* (1927).

BIBLIOGRAPHICAL ESSAY

The Will Rogers Memorial in Claremore, Oklahoma, is the major repository of Will Rogers' papers. The Memorial, which is dedicated to preserving the Will Rogers heritage, holds an enormous amount of primary source material, including published and unpublished manuscripts. Particularly important for this study were Rogers' gag book, notes pertaining to the *Follies*, scrapbook clippings, and correspondence between Rogers and Ziegfeld.

There are innumerable published works about Rogers. A useful resource for research is Peter C. Rollins, *Will Rogers: A Bio-Bibliography* (Westport, Conn.: Greenwood Press, 1984). Betty Rogers' biography, *Will Rogers: His Wife's Story* (1941; Norman: University of Oklahoma Press, 1979), is also a good introduction to her husband's life and career.

Other biographies important to understanding Rogers include Joseph H. Carter, *Never Met a Man I Didn't Like: The Life and Writings of Will Rogers* (New York: Avon Books, 1991); Richard M. Ketchum, *Will Rogers: His Life and Times* (New York: American Heritage Publishing Company, 1973); Homer Croy, *Our Will Rogers* (New York: Duell, Sloan and Pearce, 1953); Donald Day, *Will Rogers: A Biography* (New York: David McKay Company, 1962); David Randolph Milsten, *Will Rogers: The Cherokee Kid* (Chicago: Glenheath Publishers, 1987); and E. Paul Alworth, *Will Rogers* (New York: Twayne Publishers, 1974). Will Rogers' family background and early life in Indian Territory are covered in Ellsworth Collings, *The Old Home Ranch: The Birthplace of Will Rogers* (Claremore: Will Rogers Heritage Press, 1986).

Studies dealing with particular aspects of Will Rogers' career include Bryan B. Sterling and Frances N. Sterling, *Will Rogers in Hollywood: An Illustrated History of the Film Career of America's Favorite Humorist* (New York: Crown Publishers, 1984). Rogers' involvement in radio is discussed in Arthur Frank Wertheim, *Radio Comedy* (New York: Oxford University Press, 1979). A study analyzing Rogers' humor and place in American history is William Richard

Brown, *Imagemaker: Will Rogers and the American Dream* (Colum-
bia: University of Missouri Press, 1970). Two works which discuss
Rogers in the context of American humor are Walter Blair and Hamlin
Hill, *America's Humor: From Poor Richard to Doonesbury* (New York:
Oxford University Press, 1978), and Norris Yates, *The American Hu-
morist* (Ames: Iowa State University Press, 1964).

There are many compilations of Will Rogers' writings. Anthologies
include *The Autobiography of Will Rogers,* edited by Donald Day (Boston: Houghton Mifflin, 1949) and Paula M. Love, *The Will Rogers
Book* (Waco, Texas: Texian Press, 1972). Bryan B. Sterling has com-
piled *The Will Rogers Scrapbook* (New York: Grosset and Dunlap,
1976); *The Best of Will Rogers* (New York: Crown Publishers, 1979);
and with Frances N. Sterling, *A Will Rogers Treasury* (New York: Bo-
nanza Books, 1982) and *Will Rogers' World* (New York: M. Evans and
Company, 1989).

There is no major archival collection containing the papers of Florenz Ziegfeld; however, the Theatre Collection of the Library for the
Performing Arts, New York Public Library, Lincoln Center, does have
large clipping files pertaining to the *Ziegfeld Follies*. The Department
of Special Collections in the Doheny Library at the University of
Southern California contains some programs and scripts in the Ned
Wayburn Collection.

The literature about the *Ziegfeld Follies* is substantial. Three vol-
umes dealing in detail with this subject are Randolph Carter, *The
World of Flo Ziegfeld* (New York: Praeger, 1974); Marjorie Farnsworth,
The Ziegfeld Follies (New York: G. P. Putnam's Sons, 1956); and
Charles Higham, *Ziegfeld* (Chicago: Henry Regnery, 1972). Consider-
able information concerning the show can also be found in Robert
Baral, *Revue: The Great Broadway Period* (New York: Fleet Press
Corp., 1962); Robert C. Toll, *On With the Show: The First Century of
Show Business in America* (New York: Oxford University Press, 1976);
and Gerald Boardman, *American Musical Revue: From the Passing
Show to Sugar Babies* (New York: Oxford University Press, 1985).

Lewis A. Erenberg's *Steppin' Out: New York Nightlife and the Transformation of American Culture, 1890–1930* (Westport, Conn.: Greenwood Press, 1981) discusses the significance of the *Midnight Frolic* in
the context of Manhattan night clubs. The history of the New Amsterdam Theatre can be found in the *Theatre Historical Society Annual*
5 (1978). Florenz Ziegfeld writes about the *Follies* Girls in "Picking
Out Pretty Girls for the Stage," *American Magazine* 88 (December
1919): 119.

The recollections of Ziegfeld's family and associates are also important for understanding the impresario and the phenomenon of the

Follies. These include Billie Burke's autobiography, *With a Feather on My Nose* (New York: Appleton-Century-Crofts, 1949) and Patricia Ziegfeld's *The Ziegfelds' Girl: Confessions of an Abnormally Happy Childhood* (Boston: Little, Brown, 1964). Anna Held writes about her relationship with Ziegfeld in *Memories* (Paris: La Nef de Paris, 1954); the English translation has been published as Liane Carrera, *Anna Held and Flo Ziegfeld* (Hicksville, N.Y.: Exposition Press, 1979). Bernard Sobel, Ziegfeld's publicist, recalls his career with the producer in *Broadway Heartbeat: Memoirs of a Press Agent* (New York: Hermitage House, 1953).

Eddie Cantor has written about Will Rogers and the *Follies* in several books. Among them are *Take My Life* (Garden City, N.Y.: Doubleday, 1957); *As I Remember Them* (New York: Duell, Sloan and Pearce, 1963); *My Life Is in Your Hands* (New York: Harper and Brothers, 1928); and *Ziegfeld the Great Glorifier* (New York: Alfred H. King, 1934). W. C. Fields comments about Rogers and Ziegfeld in *W. C. Fields by Himself: His Intended Autobiography*, commentary by Ronald J. Fields (Englewood Cliffs, N.J.: Prentice Hall, 1973).

INDEX